You Shall Not Bow Down and Serve Them

You Shall Not Bow Down and Serve Them

—— *The Political Economic Projects of Jesus and Paul* ——

Richard A. Horsley

CASCADE *Books* • Eugene, Oregon

YOU SHALL NOT BOW DOWN AND SERVE THEM
The Political Economic Projects of Jesus and Paul

Copyright © 2021 Richard A. Horsley. All rights reserved. Except for brief quotations in critical publications or reviews, no part of this book may be reproduced in any manner without prior written permission from the publisher. Write: Permissions, Wipf and Stock Publishers, 199 W. 8th Ave., Suite 3, Eugene, OR 97401.

Cascade Books
An Imprint of Wipf and Stock Publishers
199 W. 8th Ave., Suite 3
Eugene, OR 97401

www.wipfandstock.com

PAPERBACK ISBN: 978-1-6667-2706-7
HARDCOVER ISBN: 978-1-6667-2061-7
EBOOK ISBN: 978-1-6667-2062-4

Cataloguing-in-Publication data:

Names: Horsley, Richard A., author.

Title: You shall not bow down and serve them : the political economic projects of Jesus and Paul / Richard A. Horsley.

Description: Eugene, OR: Cascade Books, 2021. | Includes bibliographical references and index.

Identifiers: ISBN 978-1-6667-2706-7 (paperback). | ISBN 978-1-6667-2061-7 (hardcover). | ISBN 978-1-6667-2062-4 (ebook).

Subjects: LCSH: Bible. | Sociology, Biblical. | Palestine—Social life and customs—To 70 A.D. | Bible. Gospels—Criticism, interpretation, etc. | Bible. Epistles of Paul—Criticism, interpretation, etc. | Jesus Christ. | Paul, the Apostle, Saint.

Classification: BT205 H57 2021 (print). | BT205 (ebook).

11/15/21

Contents

Acknowledgments | vii
Abbreviations | viii

Introduction: What Texts Included in the Bible Were About | 1

Part 1: **Economic Justice in the Bible**
1. The Dominant Insistence on Justice in the Bible | 21

Part 2: **The Political Economic Project of Jesus vs. the Roman Imperial Order**
2. Gospel Stories and Political Economy | 41
3. Historical Development of the Complex Context of Jesus' Mission | 51
4. The Political Economic Project of Jesus' Mission and Movement(s) | 68
5. Prophetic Condemnation of the Rulers' Control and Extraction | 83

Part 3: **Paul and Political Economy: An Alternative Society of Local Communities among Peoples Subject to Rome**
6. Political Economy in the Early Roman Empire | 99
7. The Economic Base of the Movement that Led to Paul's Mission | 111
8. Paul's Agenda for the Assemblies of an Inter-People Alternative Society | 128

Part 4: **The Bible and the New Form of Empire**
9. Biblical Studies and the New Form of Empire | 155
10. (Proto-) Hebrew Bible Texts and Global Capitalism | 173
11. (Proto-) New Testament Texts and Global Capitalism | 190

Bibliography | 221
Subject Index | 231

Acknowledgments

The author and publisher are grateful to the journal *Interpretation: A Journal of Bible and Theology* for permission to reprint an adapted version of "You Shall Not Bow Down and Serve Them: Economic Justice in the Bible," in *Interpretation* 69 (2015) 415–31.

Let me express appreciation to Bruce Worthington, Neil Elliott, Roland Boer, Christina Petterson, Robert Myles, Ryan Hansen, and others for the stimulating essays to which I responded in Bruce Worthington, ed. *Reading the Bible in an Age of Crisis: Political Exegesis for a New Day*, (Minneapolis: Fortress, 2015).

Finally, I am deeply appreciative in particular for the generous encouragement, advice, and assistance that K. C. Hanson has given throughout the process of revision of these chapters and the steps toward publication of this book.

Abbreviations

Ancient

1QS	Community Rule from Qumran Cave 1
4QFlor	Florilegium from Qumran Cave 4 (4Q174)
Ant.	Josephus, *Antiquities of the Judeans*
b.	Babylonian Talmud (Babli)
CD	Damascus Document
Legat.	Philo, *Legatio ad Gaium* (Embassy to Gaius)
m.	Mishnah
War	Josephus, *The Judean–Roman War*

Modern

BJS	Brown Judaic Studies
BPCS	Biblical Performance Criticism Series
CBQ	*Catholic Biblical Quarterly*
HTR	*Harvard Theological Review*
HTS	Harvard Theological Studies
JBL	*Journal of Biblical Literature*
JJS	*Journal of Jewish Studies*
JSJ	*Journal for the Study of Judaism*
JSNT	*Journal for the Study of the New Testament*
LAI	Library of Ancient Israel
NTS	New Testament Studies
WUNT	Wissenschaftliche Untersuchungen zum Neuen Testament

Introduction

What Texts Included in the Bible Were About

The Bible is thought to be a compendium of religious texts, in the field of biblical studies as well as in contemporary culture generally. The Hebrew Bible is the sacred scripture of the religion of Judaism and the New Testament the sacred scripture of Christianity, which took its start within Judaism but quickly split off into a separate religion.

Biblical studies, a division of the broader field of theology, developed with the assumption that biblical texts are, virtually by definition, religious. Biblical studies was the product of western European bourgeois societies in which religion, politics, and economics had already become split into largely separate spheres and institutions. In the aftermath of the French Revolution, in which the leaders aspired to "strangle the last king in the entrails of the last priest," a tacit agreement emerged that the church/religion and the state/politics would not interfere with the other's affairs. Already it was agreed that neither the church (religion) nor the state would interfere with business (industry), although states eagerly chartered, aided, and defended businesses based in their own countries. Biblical studies and reading of the Bible in general then projected this assumption that religion and politics and economics are separate spheres of life and institutions back onto biblical texts and the contexts they address.

Biblical texts themselves, however, tell a different story. It does not take long when browsing through the written text of the Bible or consulting one's memory of particular episodes or passages to realize that Jesus and earlier the prophets were addressing economic matters. In the Lord's Prayer, Jesus "teaches" his followers that the kingdom of God is about having enough food for subsistence and cancellation of one's debts. Jesus' command to "love your enemies" means to make survival loans from one's own meager resources to aid the desperately needy, as is clear from the subsequent lines in the so-called "Sermon on the Plain." The summarizing "punch-line" is "love your enemy, *do good*, and *lend*." The prophet Micah condemned wealthy rulers for scheming to seize people's land:

> ... because it is in their power,
> they covet fields and seize them;
> houses and take them away;
> they oppress householder and household,
> people and their inheritance. (Mic 3:1–2)

Similarly the prophet Isaiah pronounced God's condemnation of wealthy rulers because they "join household to household" and "add field to field," so that it is no longer possible for people to eke out a living (Isa 5:8–9).

If we avoid projecting modern assumptions, then several interrelated features of "biblical" texts become evident.

1. The texts that were included in the Hebrew Bible and the Christian New Testament, commonly referred to with the metaphor of "books," were/are about *economics*; more precisely, about concrete economic realities such as people having enough food to eat.

2. More comprehensively the texts were/are about *all aspects of life* that were inseparable historically, in contrast with modern Western societies in which they have become separate. That is, the texts were about *concrete political-economic-religious realities* of ancient societies in which there was a *division and conflict* between the vast majority of people who lived at subsistence level and a tiny minority of rulers who gained their wealth and power by expropriating a portion of the people's produce.

3. The texts included in the Bible were/are about political-economic-religious *action*.

4. The texts included in the Bible were/are about *collective action*, often *movements* that aimed to establish (associations of) communities that were semi-independent of wealthy and powerful rulers—and sometimes succeeded, at least for a time.

A few examples from several of the texts can illustrate these observations.

The Texts Were/Are about *Economics*

In Genesis, the story of Cain and Abel indicates that people lived from farming and herding, that the economy was agrarian. A famine in which Jacob/Israel, his twelve sons, and their people were desperately hungry led them to emigrate to Egypt where they thought food would be available. In Exodus and Deuteronomy, the people are commanded not to steal from one another, to leave some of their crops in the fields for the needy to glean, and to make loans (at no interest) to needy neighbors. In First Kings, the prophet Elijah aids a hungry widow and her son in a time of drought and famine. In several texts, such as the Psalms, God is particularly concerned about impoverished widows and orphans and residents from elsewhere. Early in Acts the disciples and others forming a new community in Jerusalem share their goods in order to have sufficient food for all.

The Texts Were/Are about All Aspects of Life

The texts were about all aspects of life, more specifically, about the *concrete political-economic-religious realities* of ancient societies in which there was a *division and conflict* between the people and the wealthy powerful rulers.

The brief tower of Babel story in Genesis and the more elaborate narratives of the Hebrew people's hard bondage under Pharaoh in Egypt are both about how the glorious, elaborate palaces and temples and monuments in the ancient "civilizations" of Mesopotamia and Egypt were built on the backs of the people who were forced to labor as well as yield up their crops to powerful regimes in command of military forces. In Exodus, when the people liberated by Yhwh from hard bondage under Pharaoh make a covenant, they are commanded not to "bow down and serve" the gods of those imperial civilizations. In First Samuel, when the people want a king to help lead them in resistance to the raids on their crops by the Philistine armies, the prophet Samuel warns them what a king would do in consolidation of royal power to exploit them: take a tenth of your grain and vineyards and cattle to feed his army with which he will force further servitude of the regime. Sure enough, in the extensive subsequent narratives in Second Samuel and First and Second Kings, this is what the kings do. The highpoint comes under the legendary building program and wealth of Solomon based on taxation and the forced labor of the people. The books of the prophets include an array of indictments and condemnations of kings and their officers for economic exploitation of the people.

Such narratives continue in the Gospels. In Luke, the story of Jesus' birth among the shepherds who were the poorest and humblest of subsistence agrarians begins with the decree of Caesar Augustus that the people must pay tribute. In the Matthean birth narratives, the Roman client-king Herod sends out death-squads to head off any potential leadership of a revolt by his tax-base (which he taxed heavily to fund his army as well as his extensive building programs, including his massive rebuilding of the Jerusalem temple). In the Gospel of Mark, Jesus condemns the scribes and Pharisees for scheming to divert support of the Jerusalem temple resources that families need to feed their no-longer productive parents. The climax of the Gospel stories include several prophecies by Jesus of God's condemnation of the temple and high priesthood for exploitation of people. And in a crafty circumlocution Jesus declares that the people do not owe tribute to Caesar.

The Texts Were/Are about Political-Economic-Religious *Action*

The texts are not philosophical treatises that speculate about the nature of God. Rather they portray Yhwh as acting: "I am Yhwh who brought you out of Egypt." And Yhwh acts only through action by people. For the exodus to happen, the people must flee. The covenant commandments expect the people to obey: they are to act and interact according to the principles articulated in the commandments. Jesus insists that people not just hear but *do* his words (commandments). They are to *practice* justice according to the commandments and time-honored customs. In his performative speeches, Jesus makes things happen, such as the renewal of the (Mosaic) covenant and the sending of envoys to expand the movement of renewal. Jesus confronts the high priestly rulers in the temple. Paul travels to the sites of his mission with co-workers where they catalyze new communities. The Apocalypse insists that the members of the assemblies refuse to participate in the ubiquitous ceremonial honors to the divine emperor in imperial temples in their cities.

The Texts Were/Are about *Collective Action*, often *Movements*

In Exodus, the people flee from their bondage in Egypt and then make a covenant that will hopefully enable them to maintain non-exploitative political-economic-religious relations among themselves in independence of human and divine rulers. Joshua and Judges include a series of collective actions to resist attacks and domination by human rulers and to maintain their independence. In Second Samuel and First and Second Kings, the people mount revolts against exploitation and forced labor imposed by their kings. In the Gospels, the people, in response to Jesus' action of healing and performative speech, have formed communities that then tell stories about Jesus' and their own collective political-economic-religious action. The people addressed in Paul's letters and the Apocalypse have come together to form new communities explicitly loyal to a new Lord and Savior different from the imperial Lord and Savior who was the major Force/Power that controlled the cities in which they resided.

The Self-Limitation of Biblical Studies

The field of biblical studies has been slow to recognize these interrelated features of "biblical" texts. Why? This has been determined by several interrelated modern developments.

Given the separation of religion, politics, and economics, the Bible was by definition religious. The purpose of biblical studies was to interpret biblical texts. In the further development of higher learning in the late nineteenth and early twentieth centuries, academic disciplines proliferated and divided institutionally, each with its own controlling discourse and paradigm of questions to be posed and solutions that were acceptable. The separate disciplines and fields, each with its own discourse, became distinctive "silos" of knowledge and analysis that had little interaction with one another. Biblical studies—in the United States carried out mostly in theological schools institutionally separate from universities and in Europe in university departments that have little or no interaction with others—often seems to be off in its own ghettoized discourse in separation from historical analysis and knowledge.

Insofar as biblical texts were by definition religious, biblical studies imposed the modern separation of religion from political-economic realities, not only onto the texts, but also onto the ancient world that the texts were about. Texts later included in the Hebrew Bible were thus understood as about and expressions of the religion of ancient Judaism. Texts later included in the New Testament were about and expressions of early Christianity. In the Christian theological scheme of Christian origins that became prominent and still persists in the field, guided by the unique revealer Jesus and organized by the most important apostle, the new religion of Christianity became more universal as it became more "Gentile" and broke off from the more parochial religion of Judaism. The temple was the central religious institution of Judaism, the high priests its "religious leaders," the "books" of the Law and the Prophets were already the Scriptures widely available so that all or most Jews had read them. Assuming the separation of "church and state," Jesus' demonstration in the temple was merely a "cleansing" to purify it in preparation for the advent of the kingdom of God.

Another operating assumption in modern western European culture was individualism. Only as individuals did people live and operate in the separate spheres of religion, politics, and economics. Insofar as biblical texts were (only) religious, belonging to the sphere of religion now reduced basically to individual faith, they pertained mainly to the individual's relation to God: salvation, piety, character-development, discipleship, personal values. Insofar as the individual also lived and operated in the separate spheres of economics and politics that operated according to their own rules, norms, criteria, and values, scriptural texts might be relevant but only indirectly as individuals carried personal values based on Scripture into the other arenas.

But since Jesus and Paul were assumed not to have been involved in politics or economics, nothing they said or did in scriptural texts could possibly pertain to individuals' involvement in politics or economics. Assuming the separation of "church and state" in antiquity, Jesus' response to the Pharisees about the tribute to Caesar was interpreted as his injunction to render taxes due to the state, in the political sphere, and to render the worship due to God, in the religious sphere. At several points in the Gospels, Jesus evidently addressed economic matters, such as "wealth" and "poverty." But since Jesus was speaking in the religious sphere about matters belonging to the economic sphere, these cannot be commands for people's action in the economic sphere. Rather they must be understood as suggestions for attitudes or values.

Paul was understood as the hero of (Christian) faith. In his own personal struggles as a faithful Jew to gain the feeling of acceptance by God by obsessively keeping the law, he had a breakthrough of feeling "justified by (his faith in God's) grace," he broke with the (supposed) excessive legalism of Judaism. So long as biblical texts were about religion and interpretation was uninformed by historical studies based on a wider array of textual and other evidence, there was no place for the possibility that they might also be about economics and politics.

The invention of the printing press made possible the inexpensive availability of the Bible in vernacular translations so that modern individual silent readers could read and study their sacred Scriptures. Coincidentally or not, the formatting of the printed Bibles matched the individualism of the individual silent reader. In the formatting of printed Bibles, texts were fragmented into separate verses coded by chapter and verse. Individual verses were then taken out of context as proof-texts for particular doctrines or homiletical points in sermons or parental admonition of children or simply for the pious meditation of individuals. This focus on separate verses was the same among biblical scholars as among ordinary readers, and became formalized in handbooks such as concordances, theological dictionaries, and commentaries. This reading habit of focusing on individual verses persists in much of the field, most striking perhaps in studies of the historical Jesus. This reading habit also expresses and reinforces the assumption that the text(fragment)s are intended for consumption by religious believers today. By abstracting the text-fragments from their literary context, biblical scholars forego the possibility that the literary context might open onto the historical context, in which the religious dimension was inseparable from political-economic matters.

Those are interrelated reasons why the field of biblical studies has not recognized that biblical texts are concerned with all aspects of life, political-economic-religious divisions and conflicts, and collective anti-establishment actions in movements.

Opening Up

Particularly in the last fifty years, some biblical scholars have broadened their interests and begun to recognize that biblical texts are also about politics and economics. This tiny minority have been reticent, however, about stepping outside of their assigned field as interpreters of religion and religious texts. Biblical studies had been placed on the defensive by scientific definition of the acceptability of knowledge in the university and timidly stuck to its assigned area and role in the disciplinary academic division of labor. Those interested in broadening the field's concerns also had the problem of not seeming "too far out" of the field. Sociology, a mere academic field, and not a separate sphere of reality, seemed acceptable in a way that politics and economics were not. But, of course, the historical realists did not want to appear to have left religion or the overall field of theology behind. So a magisterial historical study of the origins of the people of Israel that drew on many other disciplines took the subtitle, "The Sociology of the Religion of Israel."[1] Studies that were concerned with social-economic-political liberation of *campesinos* in Latin America and African-Americans and women in the global North took the general titles of "theologies of liberation." Only after successful anti-colonial movements had forced Western academics to recognize the realities of European and

---

1. The subtitle of Norman Gottwald's massive, magisterial investigation of the history of early Israel in 1979, *The Tribes of Yahweh*.

North American colonialism did it seem safe as well as appropriate to characterize the subjugation of Judeans and Galileans and other peoples to the Roman Empire as a "colonial situation."[2]

Another approach was to investigate the historical context of political-economic-religious division and conflicts and the many popular movements and revolts in late "second temple" Judea and early Roman Palestine, as evidenced in contemporary (non-biblical) sources. Such critical historical investigation could avoid the synthetic constructs of (early) Judaism and (early) Christianity that had been effectively blocking recognition of these historical realia.[3]

Only in the late 1990s were a few biblical scholars prepared to argue explicitly that Roman imperial conquest and domination was the context of most all historical developments and texts in the eastern Mediterranean world in the first century BCE and first century CE. It helped that Western historians of the Roman Empire had become much more candid about the brutality of Roman conquest, for example, in the utter destruction of Carthage or the "classical" city of Corinth and its terrorizing wars of conquest of peoples from Palestine to Britain.[4] This led to arguments that Jesus and Paul and the movements they catalyzed were opposed not to Judaism and the Jews but to the Roman imperial order in Palestine and the Greek cities, respectively.[5] Others researched and explained that the Persian Empire was the context and, to a degree, the determining power of history and texts in the formation of the temple-state in the tiny territory of Yehud. Once it was recognized that the priestly aristocracy in charge of the Jerusalem temple-state were appointed and maintained in power by a succession of imperial regimes, perhaps it seemed only appropriate to recognize and investigate politics as inseparable from religion.

---

2. As in my *Jesus and the Spiral of Violence* in 1987.

3. This is the approach I took in many articles and books, such as *Bandits, Prophets, and Messiahs* (1985), *Jesus and the Spiral of Violence* (1987), and *Galilee: History, Politics, People* (1995).

4. For example, Mattern, *Rome and the Enemy*.

5. Unavoidable current "geopolitical" events also opened the way to wider critical historical recognition. Shortly after a few of us had drawn attention to the Roman imperial context of the missions of Jesus and Paul or the Gospel of Matthew, the second Bush administration mounted the massive second invasion of Iraq in 2003. The "Paul and Politics" Section sponsored further critical discussion of the Roman imperial context of Paul's mission in the Annual Meeting of the Society of Biblical Literature. Within the next few years, as the disaster of the invasion became unavoidably evident, many program units of the SBL were sponsoring sessions at the Annual Meetings on the imperial contexts of "biblical" and related texts. Interest waned, however, as news of the United States' war-making and misadministration receded from the news media.

By around 2010, it was finally time to open up recognition and discussion of biblical texts' concern with economic matters that were inseparable from politics and religion. Because economic concerns had not been included in the field, however, biblical scholars are woefully unprepared to investigate economics in historical societies different from the modern capitalist West. In the rare instances where biblical scholars had discussed economic structures and issues in "biblical" texts, they had projected the patterns they were familiar with from nascent capitalism in early modern Europe. Historians and historical economists were of little help since they had either been projecting early modern political economic forms onto antiquity or assuming that, just as economics is a separate modern academic field, so the economy and economic matters were separate and independent of other aspects of historical reality. Unfortunately, little help is available from the field of economics since most professional economists, like their predecessors who developed the field, assume (and advocate) that "the economy" is separate from other aspects of society.

Critical investigation of the historical contexts of "biblical" texts, however, quickly finds that economic matters were not separate but embedded with other aspects of society. Historical political-economic-religious structures and dynamics were significantly different not only from early modern Western European capitalist societies but dramatically different from the highly complex transnational global capitalist system that has emerged in the last generation. By maintaining critical awareness of these differences, "biblical" scholars will have to learn as we go. It is particularly important to discern the broader political-economic-religious structures and dynamics of particular historical situations that determined the life-circumstances of people, prophets, scribal circles, and the possibilities of protest and resistance. Also important is to consider the overall contours of particular texts, the process or stages in which they were developed, their social-economic-religious location and perspective, and the ways they have drawn on Israelite tradition. Analysis by the previous generations of biblical scholars, prior to the "literary turn" in biblical studies, may be helpful in these regards.

Challenges to the Print-Cultural Assumptions from New Lines of Research

Biblical studies is also relatively unprepared to investigate economic matters in "biblical" texts insofar as the field has been projecting modern Western print-cultural assumptions and concepts onto the texts. Biblical studies developed in modern Western society in which it was assumed that texts were "written" by "authors" and were "widely available" and "read" by people. The books of the Torah and the Prophets were assumed to have been scriptures known by all or most Jews already in second temple times. The Gospels were assumed to have been "written" by individual "authors" (referred to, following tradition, by their canonical names) and available for individual "readers." Biblical studies diversified considerably so that biblical scholars developed particular specializations on a particular book or figure and/or in a particular kind of "criticism." Yet in all its diversity, the field has retained its print-cultural assumptions.

Just in the last twenty or thirty years, however, scholars pursued new lines of research, the results and implications of which are now undermining and challenging the basic assumptions and trusted generalizations in the field about its texts. These lines of research are forcing us to rethink what the texts are, how they originated and functioned in their historical contexts, and what they may be sources for. A brief summary of the results of these lines of research and their implications must suffice here:[6]

- *Communication in antiquity was predominantly oral.* Literacy was extremely limited, perhaps 10% in Greek cities and as low as 3% in early Roman Palestine, where it was limited mainly to scribal circles who were serving in (or had dissented from) the Jerusalem temple-state. Ordinary people could not have read written texts.[7]
- Even texts composed by literate elite were performed in groups of people and they were performed orally even after they had become written on scrolls.[8]
- The manuscripts of books later included in the Hebrew Bible that were found among the Dead Sea Scrolls, as closely examined by leading text-critics, indicate that there was no standard "text" of any of these books. Rather these books existed in multiple versions that were still developing in continuing scribal cultivation.[9]
- Scribes, who had received specialized training, including reading and writing, nevertheless learned the texts important for service in the Jerusalem temple-state by hearing them recited orally. The texts thus

---

6. For an overview of these lines of recent research and their interrelationship, see Kelber, *Imprints*; Horsley, "Oral Communication, Oral Performance"; and Horsley, "Can Study of the Historical Jesus Escape."

7. Harris, *Ancient Literacy*; Hezser, *Jewish Literacy*.

8. Small, *Wax Tablets*.

9. Ulrich, *Dead Sea Scrolls*.

became "written on the tablet of their heart," that is, "inscribed" in their memory as well as on unwieldy scrolls.[10]

- Scribes composed new texts on the basis of previous texts while drawing on a rich reservoir of orally cultivated cultural materials.

- The texts these scribes composed/produced and inscribed on scrolls were not necessarily intended to be "read" or "consulted." Some were what might be called monumental and/or constitutional texts, laid up in the temple and/or kept in scribal circles.[11]

- Corresponding to the oral-written cultural repertoire of learned scribal circles was *popular Israelite/Judean tradition orally cultivated in village communities: legends, stories, customs, etc.* that paralleled some or much of what was included in the scribal written texts.[12] The scribes who produced books such as Genesis or Deuteronomy or Joshua or Judges or First Kings adapted these into their broader narratives and collections of laws/customs. But they continued to be cultivated orally by non-literate ordinary people.

- Early manuscripts, fragments, and quotations of the Gospels and Epistles exhibit great variation, according to leading New Testament text-critics. There were evidently numerous versions, for example, of Gospel texts until at least the fourth century. Putting texts in writing evidently did not provide any more stability than oral tradition or repeated recitation.[13]

- Recordings of multiple oral performances of (unwritten) epic poems or sagas and study of those in other fields finds that the particular lines and stanzas change while the main story or plot remains consistent from performance to performance. This analogy suggests that the basic story in a Gospel or in a visionary history in Daniel or overall narrative in a "biblical" book was likely more stable than particular lines/fragments/episodes.[14]

- Even more clearly than scribes (who were literate), ordinary people (who were not trained to read) learned texts from hearing oral recitation/performance.

10. Carr, *Tablet of the Heart*; Horsley, *Scribes, Visionaries*.

11. Niditch, *Oral World*; Horsley, *Scribes, Visionaries*, chaps. 5–6.

12. Horsley, *Text and Tradition*, chap. 5; Horsley, "Can Study of the Historical Jesus Escape Its Typological Captivity?"

13. Epp, "Multivalence"; Parker, *Living Text*.

14. Horsley, "Can Study of the Historical Jesus Escape."

- Just as texts produced in scribal circles developed in further stages of composition before they assumed the contours in which we have them in manuscripts, so the Gospel texts produced in groups of ordinary people must have undergone development before they reached the contours in which we have them in manuscripts.[15]

The implications of these closely related lines of recent research are evident. Reading "biblical" texts concerned with all aspects of life in historical contexts is thus a more complex matter than previously understood in a field based on the assumptions of print-culture. The results of the related lines of recent research reinforce earlier critical analysis that discerned that these texts developed/were composed in stages in somewhat different historical contexts and were composites that included earlier traditions. The scribally-produced texts later included in the Hebrew Bible are composites of overall narratives composed by scribes in the interest of the temple-state or earlier monarchy *and* stories, legends, songs, customs, and prophecies many of which were adapted from Israelite popular tradition.

They are thus sources for at least two "levels" of culture and social-political practice, and possibly a third. They are direct sources for the culture, interests, and political-economic-religious practice of the Judean rulers and scribal circles serving in the temple-state. Insofar as they adapted stories and customs of Israelite popular tradition, they are indirect sources for the people subject to (the monarchy and) the temple-state. This is important for historical investigation because, with the exception of the Gospels, the people themselves (being non-literate) did not produce written texts that articulated their own interests, practices, and collective actions. The historical contexts of the scribal texts at different stages in their development can often be discerned from the texts themselves (a particularly clear case is the book of Isaiah).

At least some Judean scribal texts articulate yet a third level of interests. Although the principal function of Judean scribal texts was evidently to support and legitimate the Jerusalem temple-state (or the earlier monarchy), some of these texts also expressed criticism of their worst abuses of power. Scribes had a sense of their own authority independent of that of their patrons in the ruling aristocracy. Scribes collectively were the guardians of established Judean traditions of torah, prophecies, and wisdom of different kinds. When their high priestly patrons collaborated too closely with the dominant imperial regime, some scribal circles mounted protests and even resistance, as evident in the book of Daniel (and in some of the texts included in *1 Enoch*).

15. Wire, *Mark Composed in Performance*; Horsley, "Mark's Story Composed."

The Gospels are stories of the ongoing conflict between the people of Judea and Galilee and their Jerusalem and imperial rulers as it came to a crisis in the first century under the Roman Empire. Ongoing investigation of the historical context indicates that the Gospel stories, in broad terms, fit that context, which included several movements of renewal and resistance led by popular prophets and kings. The Gospels are by no means mere collections of the separate sayings of Jesus and pronouncement stories about him.[16] They are rather sustained stories about Jesus, as a prophet like Moses and Elijah, generating a movement of the renewal of (the people of) Israel in the villages of Galilee and beyond. The Gospels, that we have as "oral-derived texts," were evidently orally-memorially developed (collectively "composed") in branches of the movement that Jesus and his disciples catalyzed in Galilee and Judea in mid-first century Roman Palestine. They are unique texts insofar as they are sources for the origin/development and practices of the only popular movement of renewal of Israel and resistance to the local and imperial rulers for which we have more than brief accounts in the histories of the Judean historian Josephus—a movement that spread rapidly in the eastern Mediterranean into world-historical significance.

The letters of Paul are less complex to deal with as sources. They provide evidence for the spread of one branch of the movement of renewal resulting from the mission of Jesus and mainly for the agenda of the principal organizer of that branch. Given the diversity in the communities and the differences in their immediate historical situation, the communities he and his co-workers catalyzed responded somewhat differently.

The Foci and Agenda of These Chapters

This study focuses on what appear to be the respective political-economic-religious projects in their respective historical contexts of the two figures and their movements that receive the most attention in texts of the New Testament. In investigating how Jesus and the Gospels deal with economic matters, it became evident to me, as never before, that both Jesus and the Gospels were *acting* and insisting on *collective practice of covenantal social-economic relations in village communities* as the center of his project of renewal of the people of Israel. Similarly, Paul was pushing concrete economic practice and actions on the communities of the movement he was expanding, although there was far less common basis in the communities

---

16. If Jesus had only uttered pithy aphorisms and criticized the Pharisees, nothing of historical significance would have happened. Rather, he generated a movement of renewal in village communities.

that he was catalyzing anew for how they would respond to his vision of an alternative to the Roman imperial order.

Part 2 is devoted to an investigation of the political-economic-religious project of Jesus in the historical context of a political-economic-religious crisis for the people of Israel. As portrayed in the Gospels, Jesus was not just teaching about certain issues. He was not urging certain attitudes toward "wealth" and "possessions." He was not trying to inculcate or revive certain "values." In his healing and teaching in the village communities of Galilee and beyond, he was generating a movement of the renewal of the people of Israel. The principal social-economic-political form of the people of Israel was those village communities. The collective identity of the people in those communities was identification with Israelite stories of resistance to and liberation from oppressive rulers. Life in the village communities that was as independent as possible in its semi-self-governance had traditionally been guided by the Mosaic covenant and related customs. Economic subsistence had become far more difficult and village communities had begun to disintegrate under the impact of Roman imperial conquest and subjection of tribute to Caesar and the predatory practices of the high priestly and Herodian client rulers imposed by Rome.

Drawing heavily on the Israelite popular tradition in which he and the people were deeply rooted, Jesus carried out a campaign of healing and exorcism in village communities. Most prominent in the Gospel accounts, in addition to the healing of the illnesses and possessions suffered by the people under imperial rule, is Jesus' renewal—indeed reenactment of—the Mosaic covenant. In his covenant renewal speeches, delivered in performative speech, he assured the people of renewal under the direct rule of God and demanded that the people revive the collective cooperation and mutual aid that was at the center of the covenant. In his performance of the role of a prophet of renewal in line with the deep Israelite tradition of prophets, moreover, Jesus then also confronted the Jerusalem rulers, pronouncing God's condemnation of their exploitation of the people and, it seems, condemnation of the ruling institutions of the temple and high priesthood.

Chapter 2 deals with problems of conceptualizing economics and the political-economic-religious structure and dynamics in ancient Palestine. The historical context in which Jesus worked and the Gospel tradition developed had become very complex in several ways that biblical studies as a field has been relatively unaware of, partly because the structural conflict and diversity of movements has been effectively blocked by the synthetic construct of Judaism. It seems that the most appropriate way of opening up the complexity of the context is to trace how it developed historically, from the establishment of the temple-state to the devastating Roman conquest and imperial rule, in chapter 3.

Chapter 4 lays out how Jesus and the Gospels framed and collectively renewed the covenantal community life in opposition to the pressures of the Roman imperial order in Galilee and Judea. The Gospels themselves are evidence that the political-economic-religious movement of practicing covenantal communities that Jesus generated in Galilee and beyond expanded fairly rapidly among other peoples subject to Roman imperial rule. Chapter 5 examines the Gospels' portrayal of how Jesus, continuing in the traditional role of an Israelite prophet leading a movement, took concrete "direct action" in confrontation with the (Rome-appointed) Jerusalem rulers, demonstrating and pronouncing God condemnation for their economic exploitation of the people.

Part 3 explores how Paul attempted to expand the renewal movement that Jesus and the disciples had generated into a network of social-economic communities that embodied an alternative to the Roman imperial order in the cities of the eastern Roman empire. Chapter 6 attempts to move beyond problematic constructions of "the Roman . . . economy" to a more precise sense of the political-economic-religious structure in those cities in the first century CE, some of which had been Roman colonies. As ground-breaking research by some Roman historians have found, the "emperor cult" that was earlier dismissed as merely a superficial religious facade of imperial politics turns out to have been the pervasive political-religious institution in which the elite of the cities in Greece controlled the local and regional economy as well. Unlike the context in Roman Palestine, slavery loomed large as an extensive economic reality that affected all social relations in the broader empire.

Chapter 7 attempts to fill what is usually a lacuna in analysis of how a branch of the movement of renewal of Israel begun by Jesus expanded toward the mission of Paul and his coworkers that included other peoples subjected by Rome. It expanded fairly quickly, step by step among Judean diaspora communities in cities of Syria and Asia Minor, one of the distinctive interstices in an otherwise powerful and pervasive Roman order and one that provided an economic base for the expansion.

Chapter 8 examines closely Paul's ad hoc communications with the assemblies he and his coworkers catalyzed and finds a considerable number of indications that he and to varying degrees the assemblies were attempting to live economically as well as ideologically independent of the local Roman political order. Not only did they refuse to participate in the ideologically and economically controlling "emperor cult," but they attempted to become self-sufficient communities that did not participate in the local imperial order generally. More broadly the collection for the poor among the saints in Jerusalem gave striking embodiment to the sharing among the far-flung communities of the movement that was not a new religion but (in Paul's mind at least) an alternative social order in the midst of the Roman imperial order. In contrast to predominantly conservative readings of Paul, he appears rather to have advocated the emancipation of slaves in the communities. Indicative of how the "Pauline" communities went in various directions, however, some reverted to the dominant social-economic form of a slave-holding patriarchal (kyriarchal) family, while others evidently continued to practice the emancipation of slaves, using a common fund for buying their freedom along with other purposes.

Part 1 serves as a brief overview and introduction to the more extensive historical investigations in Parts 2 and 3. Chapter 1 (a reworking of an invited article in a 2015 issue of *Interpretation*) begins with an overview of "biblical" texts according to whether they insisted on economic justice for the people or offered divine blessings to institutionalized injustice or attempted to mitigate and reform the worst of the rulers' exploitation of the people. The chapter then offers a brief sketch of the institutionalized injustice of the Roman imperial order in Judea and the people's opposition in revolts and renewal movements, the historical context of the Gospel stories of the mission of Jesus. Addressed to this context, the Gospels portray Jesus as condemning the Roman and Jerusalem rulers' intensifying economic exploitation of the people in Palestine and insisting that the people practice economic justice in their village communities by renewing the Mosaic covenantal cooperation and mutual sharing at the center of Israelite popular tradition.

Part 4 considers whether "biblical" texts understood in their historical contexts have any pertinence to the current situation of biblical studies in the new form of Empire, that of global capitalism.

Chapter 9 attempts to expose the current dilemma of the field of biblical studies by juxtaposing brief surveys of two developments. With virtually no acknowledgment from biblical scholars that their political-economic circumstances had changed during the late twentieth century, global capitalism had come to control most aspects of contemporary life; it had become the new form of Empire. Meanwhile, despite its considerable diversification, biblical studies retained its long-standard controlling constructs and distinctive discourse. Indeed the field seemed only somewhat aware that the Bible had become the imperial Bible and biblical studies had often served as the handmaid of empire in the historical steps in which global capitalism had developed.

This juxtaposition poses challenges to the field that chapters 10 and 11 attempt to address, however inadequately, by focusing on certain texts or episodes in texts later included in the Hebrew Bible and New Testament respectively. The texts that were included in the Bible exhibit and address unstable agrarian political-economic-religious systems very different from the unstable globalized capitalist system in which we live. It seems naive to imagine that "biblical" stories, statements, or laws could provide models or injunctions for action in resistance to the far more complex and pervasive imperial domination of global capitalism. Once it is recognized that biblical texts portray collective action to resist domination and exploitation under a sequence of historical empires, then it seems more appropriate to consider critically what course of action might be taken to resist the more complex and pervasive domination and exploitation under the empire of global capitalism. Certain biblical texts about historical or legendary resistance, of course, might inform or inspire collective action in the more complex imperial system today. Perhaps precisely because they derive from different historical contexts, some "biblical" texts may be suggestive of unfulfilled possibilities because of developments in subsequent history. These texts—understood and appreciated in their historical contexts—could help challenge the universality of the categories of capitalism and offer concrete examples of how to think and act collectively in non-capitalist terms.

Part 1
Economic Justice in the Bible

1

The Dominant Insistence on Justice in the Bible

Introduction

Modern Western culture often separates "religion" from "real life" and reduces religion to individual faith. This narrowing of religion to the confines of individual faith has enabled a burgeoning capitalist economy that weakens social relations and responsibilities, hampers political regulations, and marginalizes religion to other motivations and concerns. The economic crash of 2008 has led many people to discern how global capitalism has become the new form of empire, with one percent of the population becoming ever richer and the remaining ninety-nine percent ever poorer, while millions of people are displaced and destitute.

This is the context in which many biblical interpreters are recognizing that the books of the Bible are about *all* of life, and that biblical teachings contain more about politics and economics than about "religion" in the narrow, modern understanding of this term. This essay seeks to demonstrate that in much of the Bible God's concern is about economic justice for the people, and that God opposes those who would exploit and oppress the people. God's radical concern for economic justice is articulated by the teaching (*torah*) of Moses, the pronouncements of the prophets, and the good news proclaimed by Jesus. To appreciate just how fundamental the concern for economic justice is in biblical texts, it is necessary to wriggle out from under some certain assumptions to discern the different "voices" or "layers" in the texts, and to appreciate the collective social forms and commitments in which biblical economic life was embedded.

Economic Justice, Institutional Injustice, and Reform in the Hebrew Bible

The narrative that became paradigmatic for much of the rest of the Hebrew Bible is the portrayal of the Hebrews subjected to hard labor in Pharaoh's Egypt (Exod 1:8–14; 5:1–21). The origin of Israel as a people began with Yhwh's effecting justice for—or liberating (Heb. *šapaṭ*)—the people in leading their escape in the exodus. Yhwh then gave the Israelites the covenant on Mount Sinai, with the commandments as guidelines for maintaining justice among the newly liberated people (Exod 20:1–17). For some time we have recognized that in the Mosaic covenant, Yhwh acts as the king of Israel who demands the people's exclusive political and religious loyalty. When the people later invite Gideon to become their king, he refuses; Yhwh is their king, and they should have no human ruler (Judg 8:22–23). What we are only beginning to discern is that most of the covenantal commandments pertain to the people's social-*economic* interaction.

Early Israel was an agrarian society in which multiple families or households lived in village communities. The survival of the community as a whole depended on the viability of the component households, which were the basic units of subsistence production and consumption. That the commandments focus on economic interaction can be seen most obviously in the prohibitions against coveting (scheming to take control of) in Exod 20:17 and stealing their fellow Israelites' means of livelihood and household members (as sources of labor) in 20:15. The commandment against swearing falsely (20:16) governs interaction between households, such as borrowing. The prohibition of adultery (20:14) protects the core relationship in the family, the basic unit of production. The commandment against murder (20:13) protects the lives of individuals, but also the labor that each member of the household contributes to the household's livelihood. Even the command to honor parents (20:12) has an economic aspect: to continue to provide for them when they can no longer contribute agricultural labor. Obedience to all of these commandments or principles of social-economic interaction, each of which protects people's rights in certain respects, would prevent someone from exploiting others to gain political-economic power over the rest (and become king).

If we read the full text of the second commandment prohibiting the making and worshiping of idols (20:45), it becomes evident that it, too, is at least partially concerned with economic justice. "Idols" were representations of the gods of ancient Near Eastern kingdoms and empires, the natural-civilizational forces that determined the productivity of the land, hence people's lives, such as "Lord Storm" (Ba'al). The Israelites were commanded not to "bow down and serve" these forces with their labor and produce (as they had been forced to do in Egypt), thus not to render tribute, tithes, and offerings to the kings and priests who claimed to be their regents. The economic justice that the covenant aimed to protect—and the economic injustice that it aimed to prevent—thus had two foci: maintaining non-exploitative economic relations among Israelites in their village communities and avoiding political-economic subjection to human rulers and ruling institutions that claimed divine authority.

The Mosaic covenant and its commandments were the ideal principles of economic interaction that early Israel attempted to observe, according to the stories in the first half of the book of Judges or perhaps "Liberators" (šôpeṭîm, such as Deborah and Gideon). After the establishment of the monarchy, the commandments were the criteria in prophecies that condemned exploitation by rulers, and they also became the criteria for judgment on particular kings in the books of First and Second Kings. The legal collections (Covenant Code, Holiness Code, and most of Deuteronomy) in the books of the Torah/Pentateuch, moreover, are covenantal customs, laws, and measures to guide social-economic life in Israelite society.

With the covenantal commandments as the basic criteria, the books of the Hebrew Bible include three different stances toward economic justice/injustice that move from (1) a radical insistence on economic justice, with God's condemnation of oppression of the poor by the wealthy and powerful to (2) an acceptance of the monarchic or temple-state system of economic exploitation with concerns for "reform" that mitigate the injustice, and finally to (3) divine legitimation of economic power and oppression.

Radical Insistence on Economic Justice

Radical insistence on economic justice appears mainly in legal collections in the Pentateuch and in the earliest layers of prophecies in several prophetic books. Scholars have discerned earlier (covenantal) customs in the legal collections that in their current form supported the centralization of political-economic-religious power in the monarchy and/or the temple-state, such as the book of Deuteronomy and the Holiness Code (Lev 17–26).[1] The precise form of the (earlier) village customs cannot easily be determined. But legal collections include laws and mechanisms such as prohibition of interest on loans, cancellation of debts after seven years, and release of debt-slaves seized as labor to pay off loans (Exod 22:25–27; Lev 25:35–37; Deut 15:1–2, 12–15). Such customs appear to be measures that would protect the

1. See esp. the careful analysis by Knight, *Law, Power, and Justice*.

economic viability of each component family/household in a village community (even if not economic equality). They suggest that economic rights to a basic livelihood were recognized. Other measures, such as allowing the needy to glean and leaving the land fallow every seven years, suggest that village communities took collective responsibility to aid needy families and treat the land responsibly so as not to overuse it (Lev 19:9–10; 23:22; Deut 24:19–22; Exod 23:10–11).[2] These covenantal customs and measures that encouraged economic justice are all the more interesting in comparison with similar customs and measures that historians and anthropologists have found operative in many other agrarian societies, which James C. Scott calls "the moral economy of the peasant."[3]

These very practical measures to ensure economic justice and the economic rights protected by the Mosaic covenantal principles (commandments), are then clearly the criteria for Yhwh's condemnation of exploitation and oppression of villagers by kings and their officers in the earliest layer of several prophetic books (Amos, Micah, Isaiah).[4] These prophets indict rulers for manipulating villagers into debt in order then to take control of their land (and/or labor), the basis of their livelihood, in violation of the commandments against coveting and stealing.

> Woe to those who devise wickedness,
> and evil deeds on their beds!
> ... because it is in their power.
> They covet fields, and seize them,
> houses, and take them away;
> they oppress householder and house,
> people and their inheritance.
> (Mic 2:1–2; cf. Amos 5:11; 8:4–6; Isa 5:8)

Micah, Isaiah, and Amos insist that the fields and households that had been parceled out among villagers as the basis of their economic livelihood were their unalienable inheritance. Although this was not "private property," in the way moderns understand it, because it was embedded in community cooperation and collective responsibility, the prophets insisted that people had economic rights. These prophecies went to the root of the covenantal

---

2. Overview in Horsley, *Covenant Economics*, 1–32.

3. Scott, *The Moral Economy of the Peasant*.

4. On these prophets and the situations they addressed, see esp. Coote, *Amos among the Prophets*; Chaney, *Peasants, Poverty, and Political Economy*, 121–46.

demands for economic justice, as evident in the "no ifs, ands, or buts" divine sentences passed on the oppressive rulers.

> Y{sc HWH} enters into judgment
>> with the elders and princes of his people:
> it is you who have devoured the vineyard;
>> the spoil of the poor is in your houses.
>> (Isa 3:14–15; cf. 10:1–4)

> I will tear down . . . the great houses . . .
> Because you trample on the poor
>> and take from them levies of grain.
>> (Amos 3:15; 5:11)

> Hear this, you rulers of the house of Jacob
>> and chiefs of the house of Israel
> who abhor justice and pervert equity,
>> who build Zion with blood
>> and Jerusalem with wrong!
>> (Mic 3:8–12)

Jeremiah pronounced God's judgment against the very institution of the temple for violation of all of the economic commandments, that is, the Mosaic covenant as a whole. Y{sc HWH} was condemning the whole system of injustice (Jeremiah 7; 26; plus condemnation of the Davidic monarchy, 21:11–14; 22:1–9, 11–17).

A Reformist Stance toward Economic Justice

Most of the books or book-layers in the Hebrew Bible take a "reformist" stance toward economic injustice; that is, they accept the system despite its fundamental economic injustice. The books of the Torah, Kings, and the "middle" layer in several prophetic books legitimate or at least accept the centralization of power in the monarchy or temple-state that demands a portion of the people's produce in tithes, offerings, and other taxes, and sometimes expropriates lands and labor.

Despite the prophet Samuel's warning of the injustices that a monarchy would bring, the people nevertheless insist on a having a human ruler (1 Sam 8). The only remaining role for the Mosaic covenant is as a source of criteria for the idealistic "rights and duties" of kings that Samuel promulgates as a feeble compromise (8:6–8; 10:17–25). In the books of Torah and Kings, rulers are thus held to certain ideals (e.g., Deut 17:14–20). With the consolidation of monarchic power, however, people could only tell stories of royal abuse of power, such as the parable of Naboth's Vineyard (1 Kgs 21:1–19). Prophets exhorted rulers to change their ways lest they too be sentenced in the divine court, and sometimes they spoke in severe, sarcastic tones:

> Listen you heads of Jacob,
>> and rulers of the house of Israel!
>
> Should you not know justice?—
>> you who hate the good and love the evil,
>
> who tear the skin off my people,
>> and the flesh off their bones . . .
>
> (Mic 3:1–3)

Some of the historical narratives and legal collections that take the reformist stance toward injustice are what some interpreters would call "ideological." They set up ideals that the rulers are supposed to observe, but they do this by coopting the (Mosaic) covenantal customs and measures of the people in support of the centralization of power in a monarchy or temple-state. The most obvious cases are the book of Deuteronomy and the related historical narrative of the great reform by King Josiah in 2 Kings 22–23, which include references to principles of justice (Mosaic *torah*) in support of centralization. Sometimes, the fundamental covenant criteria are recognized but applied only to blatant oppression, while the text continues to support the imperial system. For example, Nehemiah forced the predatory Judean aristocracy to restore the people's land and family members whom they had seized as debt-slaves (Neh 5:1–13). But he did not relax the Persian imperial demand for tribute that had drawn them into poverty in the first place.

Divine Blessing on Institutionalized Injustice

The third principal stance toward economic (in)justice in the Hebrew Bible is found in texts that legitimate or even provide divine blessings on institutionalized structural injustice. The most obvious cases are the unconditional promise to David's dynasty (2 Sam 7), the "royal" psalms, and the "enthronement" psalms that articulate a divine cosmic foundation for the monarchy (e.g., Pss 2; 24; 29; 89; 97–99; 110). If YHWH empowers the imperial king who is enthroned on the holy hill to smash conquered kings like pottery, what can't the king do to the villagers (Ps 2)? We find out in the extensive narrative that glorifies Solomon's imperial reign (1 Kgs 4–10), in which the king gives lavish banquets based on exploitation of the people's land and labor (peasants cannot afford to eat meat); constructs the temple on the backs of forced labor (reminiscent of bondage in Egypt); rectifies his "balance of trade" for royal edifices and luxury goods by ceding twenty villages, including the villagers, to Hiram of Tyre (Israelite villagers were mere pawns in inter-monarchic trade); and wields military power, again funded by the only economic base, the peasants' produce and labor. Criticism of these practices is only hinted at in the narrative sequel, and the problems are explicitly blamed on Solomon's foreign wives (1 Kgs 11:1–8).

The books of Ezra and Nehemiah portray the rebuilding of the temple and restoration to power of the descendants of the Jerusalem elite (previously deported by the Babylonians) as sponsored by the Persian imperial regime. The Jerusalem temple-state thus became the local representative of Persian rule that maintained order and gathered tribute. The temple-state remained a representative of imperial rule through the ensuing succession of empires.

Some of the prophecies addressed to the restoration of the temple appear to legitimate the institutionalized injustice embodied in the temple-state. The prophet Haggai threatens the people that the productivity of the land is dependent on their rendering up the revenues demanded by the temple-state (Hag 1:7–11). Some late prophetic texts boast that Jerusalem/Zion will be the new imperial city to which other peoples will bring tribute (Isa 60).

The divine blessing on institutionalized injustice, however, is by no means the dominant stance in the books of the Hebrew Bible. The scribal circles that served as the intellectual retainers of the temple-state produced books that helped legitimate the temple and high priesthood. But they included in those books extensive collections of (adapted!) Mosaic covenantal "laws and ordinances" and teaching (*torah*) evidently intended to restrain the abuse of power that would exacerbate economic injustice by reducing peasants to tenants.[5]

---

5. See further discussion in Knight, *Law, Power and Justice*; Horsley, *Scribes, Visionaries*, esp. chaps. 3, 4, and 6.

Insistence on Justice in the Gospels

If some modern Christians perceive that the New Testament seems unconcerned with economic justice issues, this is largely because we modern readers tend to extract the first followers of Jesus from the social-economic structures in which they were embedded. We tend to make historical conflicts disappear by imposing modern theological concepts onto ancient texts. Particularly problematic has been a persistent supersessionist scheme according to which the "new" and "universal" religion of "Christianity" emerged from and broke away from the "old," parochial religion of "Judaism," beginning with the ministry of Jesus. But the separate religions of Christianity and Judaism did not emerge until a century or more after the time of Jesus. The Gospels portray Jesus as a prophet who is engaged in renewal of Israel. The political-economic structure and dynamics in late second temple Judea and Galilee in which the Gospel stories of Jesus' mission originated were similar to those reflected in the Hebrew Bible, except that conflict between rulers and ruled became more complex and intense.[6] The mission of Jesus, situated in the imperial context of the Roman Empire, was deeply rooted in Israelite tradition, particularly the Mosaic covenant, which he adapted creatively in his ministry of renewal of the people.

Structural Injustice of the Imperial Order in Judea and Galilee

The Roman conquest (63 BCE, again in 4 BCE) seriously exacerbated the fundamental divide between rulers and ruled. Roman conquests were brutal. The Romans' destruction of villages, enslavement and slaughter of people, and crucifixion of opposition leaders were intended to terrorize subject people into acquiescence to Roman rule. The Romans laid the people under tribute (25% every second year; Josephus, *Ant.* 14.202–203) and installed client rulers to control the people and collect their tribute, taxes, and tithes for themselves.[7] Out of many factors that escalated the economic oppression of the people, three are particularly pertinent to the Gospel stories of Jesus' mission.

1. Herod the Great taxed his subjects in order to launch extensive building programs of new imperial cities and temples, give lavish gifts to

---

6. Critical analysis of sources and reconstruction of the history of late second temple Judea and Galilee directly relevant to Jesus and the Gospels in Horsley, *Jesus and the Spiral of Violence*; Horsley, *Galilee: History, Politics, People*; Horsley, *Jesus and the Powers*; and Horsley, *Jesus and the Politics of Roman Palestine*.

7. See Udoh, *To Caesar What Is Caesar's*.

other cities, and expand his court. Foremost in his building program, and especially pertinent to the Gospel stories, was his massive reconstruction of the temple on a vastly expanded and raised platform. "Herod's Temple" quickly became known as one of the wonders of the Roman imperial world, with its holy area more than twice as large as the monumental Roman Forum built later by Trajan. The temple functioned as the provincial representative of the imperial order, as priests offered sacrifices for Rome and Caesar and with a golden Roman eagle installed over the main gate to the vast courtyard.[8]

2. After Herod's death in 4 BCE, the Romans suppressed widespread revolts and installed Herod's son Antipas as ruler over Galilee. Just as it had done a century before, the expansionist Hasmonean high priesthood, after conquering Idumea and Samaria, had brought Galilee under Jerusalem rule. Now the Romans ended Jerusalem's direct jurisdiction. With the ruler of Galilee for the first time residing in Galilee, the collection of taxes became more efficient—a situation that helped support the cost of Antipas's construction of two new capital cities in his first twenty years.

3. Ten years after the death of Herod, the Romans installed the priestly aristocracy as rulers over Judea, under the oversight of a Roman governor. They were appointed by and responsible to the Romans and charged with collection of the tribute. While they no longer had direct jurisdiction over Galilee, the high priestly families at the head of the monumentally expanded temple could increase their wealth with little restraint, though they could not control the resulting protests, resistance movements, and general public unrest. The scribes, including the party of the Pharisees, served as the intellectual-legal retainers of the temple and high priesthood.

Reactions to Economic Injustice: Revolts and Protests

As Roman imperial rule exacerbated the structural injustice of the temple-state, village families became increasingly indebted, and village communities began to disintegrate. That the people continually mounted protests and revolts is an indication that they still valued the covenantal justice that had always been the basis of their social-economic life. Widespread popular revolts in 4 BCE (after Herod's death) and again in 66–70 CE framed the

---

8. See further Horsley, *Galilee*, 110–22, 134–35; and Roller, *The Building Program of Herod the Great*.

mission of Jesus and the expansion of the Jesus movements that produced the Gospels. In between those revolts, contemporary with the nascent Jesus movements, were periodic protests, a Galilean peasant strike, and several movements of renewal and resistance led by popular prophets in the role of a new Moses or Joshua.[9]

The accounts of the first-century Judean historian Josephus offer a number of indications that these protests and movements were reactions to economic exploitation. The protesting crowds that gathered in Jerusalem at Herod's death, for example, clamored for a reduction of taxes and the end of other injustices (*War* 2.4–7). In the revolt of 4 BCE, the people attacked Herodian fortresses to "take back" the goods that had been stored there (War 2.55–65; *Ant.* 17.269–285). In the great revolt of 66–70, the crowd in Jerusalem went directly to the archives to set fire to the records of debts (*War* 2.427). The "messianic" movement led by Simon bar Giora gathered strength as he moved through southern Judea proclaiming cancellation of debts and release of debt slaves (*War* 2.427; 4.507–513).

Two even more explicit indications that covenantal forms, commandments, and a sense of justice continued to be very much alive come from dissident scribal circles: the Qumran community and the group identified only as "the Fourth Philosophy." While most scribes, including the Pharisees, continued in service of the temple-state, those who withdrew to Qumran formed an explicitly covenantal community.[10] The Qumran community expanded on the Israelite model of mutual support by holding all things in common (1QS 6:22–26; cf. Josephus, *Ant.* 18.20). When the Romans placed the high priests in power under a Roman governor in 6 CE, the teacher Judas of Gamla and the Pharisee Zadok, leaders of what Josephus calls "the Fourth Philosophy," organized a refusal to render tribute to Caesar on the grounds that the people owed exclusive loyalty to God as their sole (divine) lord and master (*Ant.* 18.3–4, 23–25). That is, they said that paying the tribute to Caesar was a violation of the first and second commandments.[11]

---

9. Fuller account of the various forms of popular resistance in the context of structural injustice in Horsley, *Jesus and the Spiral of Violence*, chaps. 1–4; and Horsley, *Judean Movements and Leadership in First-Century Palestine*.

10. See the Community Rule (1QS) and Damascus Document (CD) from the corpus of the Dead Sea Scrolls.

11. This controversy is evident in the New Testament in texts such as Mark 12:13–17, where the Herodians question Jesus about paying taxes to Caesar.

Getting the Whole (Gospel) Story

The mission of Jesus and the movement(s) he generated, the story of which the Gospels tell, belong among popular movements of renewal and resistance. One of the important recent breakthroughs in New Testament studies is the recognition that the Gospels are not mere collections of sayings and miracle stories but sustained narratives.[12] More recently, we are learning to read the Gospel stories in their historical context.[13] This enables the readers to recognize that the Gospels are stories of conflict between Jesus movements in the villages of Galilee and the rulers (and their representatives) whom Jesus confronts and who finally succeed in arresting him and handing him over to the Roman governor, who crucifies him. The Gospels are stories about villagers that originated among villagers, and they are addressed to movements that understand themselves as the renewal of Israel. Jesus is a new Moses and a new Elijah engaged in wilderness feedings and healings, who appoints the Twelve as representative of the symbolic twelve tribes. He also stands in the tradition of the prophets who pronounced God's judgment on the Jerusalem rulers because of economic injustice and exploitation of the people.

Jesus' Prophetic Condemnation of Structural Injustice and Economic Exploitation

The sharpest challenges and counter-challenges between Jesus and the Pharisees/scribes who "come down from Jerusalem" concern structural economic injustice. The episode in Mark 7:1–13//Matt 15:1–20 illustrates clearly that these conflicts should not be interpreted to mean that Jesus opposed "Judaism" and the Law/Torah, as many Christians mistakenly think. Jesus (not the scribes and Pharisees) is the one who insists on strict observance of the basic commandments of God at the core of the Torah. The Pharisees and scribes set themselves up as foils when they ask why Jesus' disciples do not observe "the traditions of the elders." These "traditions" were not the core of the law (*torah*) but the orally transmitted rulings that went beyond the laws written down in the books of the Torah that they had promulgated as representatives of the high priestly rulers (Josephus, *Ant.* 13.296–297).

---

12. Pioneering treatments, for example, are Rhoads and Michie, *Mark as Story*; and Kingsbury, *Matthew as Story*.

13. For my own efforts, with collaborators, see Horsley, *Hearing the Whole Story*; Horsley with Jonathan Draper, *Whoever Hears You Hears Me*; Horsley and Thatcher, *John, Jesus, and the Renewal of Israel*.

Jesus shifts the focus to basic economic relations. He cites the commandment of God mediated by Moses that would resonate most personally with Israelites—"Honor your father and mother!"—then charges the Pharisees and scribes with violating this basic commandment. How so? As representatives of the temple-state, they were encouraging villagers to "devote" to God and the temple some of the produce from their land and labor. Jesus accuses the Pharisees and scribes of siphoning off produce needed by these hungry families, including elderly parents. Jesus' continuity with the Israelite prophets could not be more clear in how he applies covenantal commandments to condemn the injustice inherent in impoverishing the people for the sake of enhancing the wealth of the ruling class.[14]

Jesus' declarations against economic injustice become more severe when he focuses on the temple and drives the moneychangers and those who were buying and selling from the temple premises (Matt 21:12–17; Mark 11:15–17; Luke 19:45–48; John 2:13–16). Jesus' action in Herod's temple was not merely a "cleansing." It was rather a prophetic demonstration that symbolized God's judgment. That Jesus quotes from Jeremiah's famous prophetic condemnation of the original temple—"Has this house, which is called by my name, become a den of robbers in your sight?" (Jer 7:11a)—suggests that the criteria for judgment are the covenantal commandments of justice that Jeremiah cited (Jer 7:1–11). The comparison of the temple and high-priests to bandits who take refuge in their fortress hideout compounds the prophetic punch. The high priests were stealing the livelihood of the people while thinking they were safe in their sacred fortress. When he overturned their tables and drove them out, Jesus performed an offensive prophetic action of "civil disobedience" in protest against economic injustice perpetrated by the ruling institution. In so doing, he stood in the long Israelite prophetic tradition of such pronouncements.

A few episodes later (Matt 21:33–46; Mark 12:1–9; Luke 20:9–19), Jesus tells the parable of tenants as another prophetic announcement of God's judgment of the high priests who headed the temple-state. The parable draws on the well-known "song of the vineyard" (Isa 5:1–6), a prophecy against the rulers' exploitation of the people. The high priests immediately understand that Jesus tells the parable against them. They are the tenants who were supposed to ensure justice in God's "vineyard," the people of Israel. But as "wicked" tenants, they have been exploiting the vineyard to enhance their own wealth. It is evident from archaeological explorations in Jerusalem and the northwest Judean hill country that high priestly (and perhaps also Herodian)

---

14. On Jesus' condemnation of the Pharisees and scribes, see Horsley, *Hearing the Whole Story*, 149–76.

families built large estates by manipulating peasants into debt in order to take over their land and force them into becoming tenants.[15] By expanding their own wealth through exploitation of peasant families, the ruling class built ever-larger mansions in Jerusalem. Josephus and rabbinic texts confirm these predatory practices by the high priestly families in the first century CE (Josephus, *Ant.* 20.206–207; b. Pesaḥim 57a).[16]

Following his condemnation of institutionalized injustice, Jesus insists on the fundamental covenantal principle of economic justice in opposition to the imperial demand for tribute. In pronouncing God's judgment on the temple and high priests, Jesus is challenging the Roman imperial order in Judea. The Pharisees recognize how they can entrap him (Mark 12:13-17). The Romans demanded tribute to Caesar as the imperial "Lord" and "Savior" and "Son of God," and they viewed refusal to comply as tantamount to insurrection. Jesus opposed Roman imperial rule by preaching the rule of God, who demanded the people's exclusive loyalty (*pistis/fides*). This was a burning issue for the people, as illustrated a few decades earlier by the revolt organized by Judas the scribal teacher and Zadok the Pharisee, in which the people refused to pay the tribute (Josephus, *Ant.* 18.1).

Jesus tricks the Pharisees (and Herodians) into displaying their own loyalty; they happen to have a denarius on which is stamped the image of Caesar. Jesus wriggles out of their entrapment by avoiding a direct answer to the Pharisees' question, "Is it lawful" to pay the tribute? He moves to the principle of economic justice that underlies the first and second commandments: "Give to the emperor the things that are the emperor's and to God the things that are God's" (Mark 12:17). All those listening, including the Pharisees and, more important, the people, knew what he had just declared: since all things are God's, they did not owe anything to Caesar. In fact the basic commandments of God forbade "bowing down and serving" Caesar (or any other lord and master) with their economic resources.

Practicing Economic Justice
in the Covenantal Communities of Israel-in-Renewal

Covenantal demands for justice in community economic life permeate the prophetic teaching of Jesus in the Gospels. We often miss this message because of the modern tendency to separate religion from political-economic

---

15. Herzog explains how the people would have resonated with this parable because of their own experience of exploitation (*Parables as Subversive Speech*, 98–113).

16. Broshi, "The Role of the Temple in the Herodian Economy"; Goodman, "The First Jewish Revolt."

life. Once we have learned to read the *whole* Gospel story, however, it is both possible and imperative that we move beyond that separation and the individualism that keeps us from recognizing: (1) that village communities were the fundamental form of social-economic life; (2) that the Gospels portray Jesus and the disciples as generating a movement of the renewal of Israel in village communities; and (3) that renewal of covenantal community was the core of the renewal of Israel.

The renewal of covenantal community centered in economic justice is evident in the major speeches and dialogues of Jesus. Best known is "the Sermon on the Mount" (Matthew 5–7), paralleled in Luke's "Sermon on the Plain" (Luke 6:20–49).[17] These parallel speeches exhibit the same covenantal structure: they begin with a declaration of deliverance, followed by covenantal demands (that refer explicitly or implicitly to the original covenantal commands and customs), and end with the double parable that sanctions keeping these demands. When modern Christians read "love your enemies," and "turn the other cheek" out of context, they interpret them as counsels of non-retaliation, key proof-texts for pacifism and nonviolent direct action. If we look for the context in the shorter Lukan version (6:20–35), however, we see that they address economic relations in a village community in which hungry people have been borrowing from and lending to one another. In the demands to "love your enemies, do good, and lend, expecting nothing in return" (v. 35), Jesus is instructing the people to stop quarreling and to return to the covenantal customs of cooperation and mutual aid. In circumstances of poverty and hunger, community solidarity is all the more necessary for survival and resistance to outside pressures.

Matthew's longer version is explicitly a renewal of covenantal *justice*. In rereading this speech, however, it is necessary to counter a long-standing traditional understanding and individualistic reading. The speech addresses communities of people, ostensibly "the crowds," using the plural "you" throughout. The theme of "justice" (*dikaiosyne*) dominates the speech with its frequent recurrence. As a sense of collective community receded, however, people began to interpret Jesus' words as something addressed to individuals. Jesus' radical prohibition of anger or lust, moreover, seemed impossible in normal social interaction, so that in order to comply, some people withdrew to monasteries. An individualistic understanding persists in modern readings and in translations (such as the NRSV), in which the word "justice" (*dikaiosyne*) is translated "righteousness."

Jesus explicitly states, however, that his words and mission are the fulfillment of "the law and the prophets" (Matt 5:17). The so-called "antitheses"

---

17. Further discussion in Horsley, *Covenant Economics*, 103–14, 150–56.

("you have heard it said . . . but I say to you") are not, as many Christians think, a "new" law that replaces or counters an "old" law represented by the scribes and the Pharisees. The series of "but I say to you" (plural) are a radicalization of the ancient covenantal commandments from the Torah that motivate interaction. The commands regarding murder/anger, adultery/lust, and false swearing have economic implications, as discussed above. The demands to give to the needy and lend (Matt 5:38-42) explicitly address economic relations in the community. That Jesus contrasts what he says with "the scribes and Pharisees" in an antithetical formulation is mainly rhetorical. The more substantive contrast comes in the exhortation against the individualistic quest for economic security that seeks wealth (serving mammon). The main emphasis is on serving God by seeking the kingdom of God/heaven and its economic justice, that is, seeking covenantal community and trusting in its cooperative mutual aid as security (6:24-33).

Another unmistakable demand for economic justice comes in a sort of covenantal charter for the communities of Jesus-loyalists that Jesus delivers as he completes his mission in Galilean villages and heads up to Jerusalem to confront the rulers at the Passover festival in Mark 10:17-31 (parallels in Matt 19:16-30; Luke 18:18-30).[18] The wealthy man in this scene appears as a foil: he is seeking "eternal life," in stark contrast to the ordinary people, who sought simply to live and would have been wondering about their next meal. Jesus immediately recites the covenantal commandments as the criteria, not for eternal life, but for entering the kingdom of God (Mark 10:23, 25). "Do not covet" is sharpened to "Do not defraud." In Israelite covenantal society (and in other agrarian societies, as well) the way someone became wealthy was frequently through fraud, that is, by manipulating needy people into taking loans at interest in order to take control of (steal) their land and/or labor.

With the wealthy fellow thus set up as a negative example (of what not to do), Jesus pronounces the principle of economic justice: "It is easier for a camel to go through the eye of a needle than for someone who is rich to enter the kingdom of God" (Mark 10:25)—that is, to enter the renewed society of justice under the direct rule of God. The renewal of Israel in community life is the focus in the last step of the dialogue. Entering the kingdom of God includes the concrete renewal of families/households in covenantal community, *now*, with houses and lands and with persecution, even in circumstances of continuing imperial rule (Mark 10:28-31).

---

18. For further discussion, see Horsley, *Hearing the Whole Story*, 186-94; Horsley, *Covenant Economics*, 116-25, 156-58.

It should be clear from this review that Jesus, the Gospels, and the communities of Jesus-loyalists revived the radical insistence on economic justice evident in the Mosaic covenantal tradition and the prophecies of Amos, Isaiah, and Micah. The Gospels portray Jesus and the disciples as catalyzing a renewal of covenant communities that practice economic justice. The Gospels portray Jesus in bold confrontation with the oppressive ruling institutions through his prophetic pronouncements that they stand under God's judgment. Moreover, as dramatically narrated in the Gospels, Jesus carried out these confrontations in a historical situation where the rulers responded with arrest and public execution by slow torture, a practice that was intended to intimidate the people and discourage uprisings.

Taking Cues from Biblical Texts Today

If the centralization of political-economic-religious power in the Davidic monarchy or the Jerusalem temple-state embodied institutionalized injustice in the Bible, how much more does today's global capitalist system? Laws and prophecies reminded kings and high priests that God condemned economic injustices such as lending to the poor at interest and manipulating them into spiraling debt. And yet, capitalism developed in modern Western culture on the basis of lending at interest, manipulation of debts, and low-wage labor. The International Monetary Fund and the World Bank, set up to "stabilize" the world capitalist economy, has manipulated "developing" countries into loans they cannot repay, then forced them to cut back on services that their impoverished people desperately need. Finance capital has created more subtle devices to siphon off the limited resources people have as the basis of their livelihood, with credit cards at high interest rates and subprime mortgages that inevitably lead to foreclosure for many.

Despite the thunderings of Theodore Roosevelt over a century ago that the captains of industry and Wall Street bankers were violating the Ten Commandments, only recently has public discussion in the United States returned to discussion of the injustice embodied in capitalism that has now taken over the world economy. The economic crash in 2008 finally brought wider attention to power that the megabanks held over the people who lost their homes, pensions, jobs, and health care. The crash demonstrated that billionaires and transnational corporations are able to manipulate the most powerful governments in the world to underwrite the expansion of their wealth and power.

There has been too little reflection on how the insistence on economic justice in biblical texts and history might be related to the far more complex injustice that has become institutionalized in global capitalism. Insofar as professional biblical interpreters and clergy are embedded in the capitalist system (e.g., with our salaries and pension funds), it seems likely that we will remain in a comfortable "reformist" stance. It is possible, however, to derive from the radical insistence on economic justice in the legends of early Israel, the early prophets, and the Gospel stories a few general principles that might be applied to today's more complex constellation of power relations that compound economic injustice.

Implicit in the covenantal criteria of economic justice is that *people have a right to an economic livelihood.* In an agrarian society this meant household and fields in a supportive community. Today a basic livelihood is far more complex, including food and shelter, health care, education, transportation, and some sort of support network.

Correspondingly, people (society/cities/states) have a *collective responsibility to ensure that other members of the community have economic justice,* which means a responsibility to cultivate the common good and to aid the needy. Today this would require an end to or perhaps a roll-back of privatization to restore the common good.

The Gospels portray not individual ethics, but *community renewal* centered on *economic justice as part of a broader renewal and resistance movement of subject peoples* against the Roman imperial order. Ordinary people who have drawn upon biblical texts and history have at times taken similar collective action. Peasants in sixteenth-century Germany, for example, organized themselves to insist on their traditional economic rights. Some Catholic churches a century ago in the United States operated parish credit unions. Today, many collective economic initiatives to support economic justice and oppose institutionalized injustice are underway. Collective divestment in transnational mega-corporations and collective investment of resources and energy in ways that restore livelihoods to people can embody effective resistance to the further centralization of power that drains away people's resources.

In the Gospels' portrayal, finally, Jesus and Jesus movements not only engaged in community renewal of economic justice, but also in *bold confrontation of the controlling institutions that embodied and perpetrated economic injustice.* There is a long and deep tradition of confrontation of repressive political power to insist on political rights. The controlling institutions that perpetuate and exacerbate economic injustice, however, are now those of global capitalism. With transnational corporations now having decisive influence on governments and control of mass media, reforms such as "re-regulation" seem unlikely. Yet many governments still allow collective assembly for protest. The Occupy Wall Street movement in 2011 brought into much broader discussion the "crime scene" in those skyscrapers where finance capital manipulates the world economy. In many of the countries (including the United States) where the transnational institutions of global capital are based, moreover, peaceful civil disobedience is a viable mode of confrontation.

Conclusion

Life in the postmodern world, in which economic injustice is now institutionalized, tends to dull the imagination of any challenge or alternative. The Bible offers plenty of illustrations of a reformist stance that seeks mainly to mitigate the worst effects of institutionalized injustice without initiating real change. But if we take seriously the Bible's more radical insistence on economic justice in the covenantal tradition, the pronouncements of the prophets, and the Gospel story of Jesus' mission, we are led to some fundamental principles that necessitate change: (1) that people have a right to an economic livelihood; (2) the community (society) has a collective responsibility to ensure that people have economic justice; and (3) collective local action toward economic justice is part of a broader renewal that takes seriously the Gospel imperatives.

Part 2
The Political Economic Project of Jesus vs. the Roman Imperial Order

2

Gospel Stories and Political Economy

We have long understood the Lord's Prayer as a plea for the kingdom of God, the subject of its opening petition. The next two petitions of the prayer then immediately indicate what the kingdom is about more concretely: sufficient food and cancellation of debts. Although it is usually unrecognized, the focus of the prayer for the kingdom of God is on economic subsistence. The people who pronounced this prayer, moreover, were affirming that, in connection with pleading that their own debts be cancelled, they were cancelling one another's debts. They were collectively *taking action* to deal with their debt, thus strengthening their communities, through mutual aid, against the political-economic pressures that had brought them into hunger and debt. Whatever the communities were doing, however, was evoking repressive action by the rulers. So they also petitioned God to deliver them from "the testing/trial" of being dragged into court (cf. Mark 8:34–38; 13:9; Luke 11:2–4; 12:2–12).

The Gospel stories portray the interactive mission of Jesus as engaged in collective *political-economic action*. Jesus was not teaching about attitudes toward wealth and poverty or attitudes towards other individuals. He was rather delivering commands about concrete social-economic relations and interaction. The command to "love your enemies" was more fully and concretely, "love your enemies, do good, and lend"! He was addressing not individuals but whole communities, on the one hand, and pronouncing God's judgment against the people's rulers, on the other.

Standard interpretation of Jesus and the Gospels has blocked discernment of the political-economic conflict portrayed in the Gospel stories. It has also blocked recognition of how Jesus was generating a movement in the course of his mission in Galilee and beyond. The separation of religion from concrete political-economic life in modern Christianity and modern western culture generally has been projected onto the Gospel texts. This has, for example, reduced Jesus' obstruction of operations in the temple to a mere religious "cleansing" and has domesticated Jesus' declaration "render to Caesar . . . and to God . . ." into an illustration of the modern separation of church and state. Closely related is the projection of modern western individualism onto the Gospels and Jesus and the focus on his individual sayings. Jesus is reduced to an individual "talking head" uttering pithy aphorisms to individuals, while unengaged in the fundamental social-economic forms of village life and the deepening political-economic conflict in Roman Palestine.

Two constructions of Jesus that became particularly prominent over a century ago and emerged again to prominence at the end of the twentieth century both exemplify the reduction of Jesus to an individual figure. The one presented Jesus as a wisdom teacher of an individualistic discipleship of piety and ethics in withdrawal from the world of political-economic affairs.[1] The other presented Jesus as an apocalyptic prophet of the End of the world in cosmic catastrophe.[2] Both of these lines of individualistic interpretation of Jesus are based primarily on individual sayings of Jesus (purposely) isolated from their literary context, thus ignoring our primary guide to the historical political-economic context (the Gospel stories and speeches). Even at the end of the twentieth century, moreover, we can discern underneath both of these diametrically opposed constructions a focus on Jesus as the unique individual revealer whose teaching led to the origin of the new religion of Christianity from the old religion of Judaism. According to this Christian theological scheme, Jesus only attracted individual disciples. Only after Easter did "the Church" begin and expand rapidly, especially among "the Gentiles," in the mission of Paul.

The Gospel Stories of Jesus' Mission and Movement(s)

The Gospels, however, tell a different story. In the last four decades interpreters of the Gospels have been discovering that they are not mere collections of sayings and "miracle stories" but are sustained narratives, with speeches, that are full of social and political conflict—a development largely ignored

---

1. Harnack, *What Is Christianity?* (1901); and Crossan, *Historical Jesus* (1991). Crossan's book, the leading voice of "The Jesus Seminar," became highly influential partly because it was aggressively marketed by the publisher, recently merged into the Murdock publishing empire, which generated controversy by soliciting and marketing competing theological constructions of Jesus.

2. Schweitzer, *Quest* (1906). Schweitzer's construction of Jewish apocalypticism, restated by Bultmann in his *Theology of the New Testament*, had become standard as a controlling concept in New Testament studies. Schweitzer's apocalyptic Jesus was revived by Allison, *Jesus of Nazareth*; and Ehrman, *Apocalyptic Prophet*.

by interpreters of Jesus. While much literary criticism of the Gospels simply applied recent criticism of modern fiction, some interpreters attempted to understand the Gospels as sustained stories in their historical context.[3]

The Gospels, which purport to be historical stories of concrete events, portray a movement developing in response to Jesus' proclamation and healing as he interacts primarily with villagers but also with the scribal representatives of the Jerusalem temple-state and then with the high priestly rulers appointed by the Romans. It is remarkable, moreover, the extent to which the Gospel stories and speeches "fit" the historical context of Roman Palestine in which they are set: the fundamental political-economic conflict between the people of Israelite heritage and their Roman-appointed rulers had become increasingly unstable so as to evoke the rise of movements of renewal and resistance led by popular prophets. The Gospel stories fit into the historical context known from other sources, such as the accounts of the Judean historian Josephus: Roman imperial conquest and reconquests, installation of client rulers, intensified extraction of the people's resources, and increasing popular resistance. The Gospels are stories of a prophet-led renewal of the people combined with prophetic pronouncements of God's condemnation of the rulers for their extraction of resources that the people needed for their own livelihood.[4]

A brief summary of the Markan story and of the additions that the Matthean and Lukan Gospels made to the basic story can provide a sketch of the broader political-economic-religious conflict involved: Jesus was generating a renewal of the people in their village communities in opposition to and by the rulers and ruling institutions.

In the Markan story, after being divinely commissioned and tested in the wilderness (like Elijah), Jesus begins his mission in the villages of Galilee, proclaiming the direct rule of God and manifesting its presence in many exorcisms and healings. Narratives of sea crossings and feedings in the wilderness frame some of the exorcisms and healings, suggesting that Jesus is a prophet like Moses and Elijah, who later appear with him in a vision on a mountain. The people respond with trust (*pistis*), reinforced by the rapid spread of his fame, generating crowds in and from many villages, a growing movement that he extends into the villages of nearby areas subject to other Roman client rulers in cities such as Tyre and Caesarea Philippi. Giving the movement more explicit social-political form, he appoints the

---

3. See, for example, the investigations by Myers, *Binding the Strong Man*; Horsley, *Hearing the Whole Story*; Horsley, *Jesus and the Politics of Roman Palestine*; Horsley and Thatcher, *John, Jesus, and the Renewal of Israel*.

4. See especially Horsley, *Jesus and the Powers*; Horsley, *Jesus and the Politics of Roman Palestine*.

Twelve as representatives of the people of Israel undergoing renewal in his proclamation and healing, and commissions them to extend these works of renewal in village communities (the principal social-economic form in most agrarian societies). Woven into the sequence of episodes, the scribes and Pharisees come down from Jerusalem to confront his apparent challenges to the prerogatives of the temple-state. He responds with prophetic condemnation of them, for example, for violating the basic commandment of God by manipulating the people to devote (*qorban*) to the temple resources needed by their families. As he completes his mission of healing and teaching in Galilee and beyond, he delivers a (Mosaic) covenant renewal in a series of dialogues focused on family, community membership, economic relations in the community, and leadership of the movement.

Jesus then goes up to Jerusalem and the temple where he engages in a sustained confrontation with the high priests: a prophetic demonstration in the temple, a prophetic parable that announces God's condemnation of the high priests (for economic exploitation), and an announcement that the temple (the central political-economic-religious institution) will be destroyed. Finally the high priests have him arrested and hand him over to the Roman governor, who orders him crucified as "the king of the Judeans," that is, a (presumed) leader of insurrection. In the abrupt "open ending" of the Markan story (in 16:1–8), the women at the empty tomb are told to tell the disciples to meet him back in Galilee—where, presumably, they will continue the movement that he had generated. The Markan story thus presents the (hi)story of Jesus' renewal of the people (of Israel) in opposition to and by the high priestly rulers, who were the face of the Roman imperial order in Palestine.

The Matthean and Lukan Gospels tell the same basic story of Jesus' mission in the villages of Galilee and beyond and his confrontation with and then execution by the rulers, with two major additions. First, these Gospels begin with legends of Jesus' birth under Caesar's decree subjecting the people to pay tribute (Luke) or the Roman client king Herod's massacre of children to prevent the deliverance from imperial domination that Jesus is born to lead—that leads to his family's recapitulation of the story of Israel's exodus from repressive rulers (Matthew)—and genealogies that present Jesus' mission as the fulfilment of the history of Israel. Second, the Matthean and Lukan Gospel stories include speeches by Jesus on key issues of the movement of renewal he is generating. These include a long covenant renewal speech (commonly called the Sermon on the Mount/Plain); a commission of his disciples to extend his mission of healing and proclaiming the direct rule of God in village communities; and a series of woes indicting the scribes and Pharisees for exploiting the people.

The narratives and speeches in the Gospels thus portray Jesus' mission and movement as a renewal of the people of Israel in their village communities, in opposition to and by the rulers at the head of the Roman imperial (dis-)order in Palestine. The Gospels are not just stories, but purport to be (political-economic-religious) histories, however embellished, of Jesus' mission and movement based in village communities, his prophetic pronouncement of God's judgment against the rulers, and his martyrdom that energized the further expansion of the movement. The Gospel (hi)stories also reflect the expansion of the movement that Jesus and his disciples generated in the village communities in Galilee to other areas in Syria-Palestine. The movements continued to evoke persecution by the rulers, but without the serious disruption that would have led the rulers to suppress them militarily. The Gospel stories and speeches continued to tell of the origins of the Jesus movements and of the ongoing collective identity and common life of the communities of those movements.

Exploring Economics in "Biblical" Texts and Their Contexts

Since the term "economics" is used in many different ways, it is important to clarify in what sense it may be used intelligibly in connection with the texts that were later included in the Hebrew Bible and New Testament and the historical situations they addressed. Biblical scholars have tended to project the "market economy" that developed in early modern Europe onto the texts they were interpreting.[5] As interest in economic issues has increased in biblical studies—surely partly as a result of disillusionment with neo-liberalism and the 2008 crash of global finance capital—scholars in the related fields of ancient southwest Asia studies and of the Roman Empire as well as biblical scholars are casting about in search of economic theory appropriate to their subject matter.[6] The field of biblical studies now has the widely knowledgeable and deeply critical theoretical work of Roland Boer, *The Sacred Economy*, that offers a solid and appropriate theoretical basis for study of the wider ancient southwest Asian context of the Judean temple-state and

---

5. The New Testament scholars who gave explicit attention to economics tended to be influenced by the works of Rostovtseff, *Social and Economic History of the Hellenistic World*. On the development of the ideology of capitalism and "the market," see now the highly instructive critical survey by Boer and Petterson, *Idols of Nations*.

6. For example, the articles in Morris and Manning, eds., *The Ancient Economy*. Neo-classical economics, however, is alive and well in studies of "the Roman market economy," for example, in Temin, *Roman Market Economy*; and Mayer, *Ancient Middle Classes*.

its villages.[7] This investigation of the historical political-economic context of Jesus' mission and movement(s) as portrayed in the Gospels and its historical background is broadly informed by Boer's work. The focus here, however, is on what is attested and portrayed in Judean and Gospel texts and pertinent archaeological studies.

What we find in texts that were later included in the Hebrew Bible and in the Gospels that were later included in the New Testament are primarily people who were living in villages and producing crops to feed themselves as well as the kings, officers, and priests who extracted a percentage of those crops as taxes and tithes. The economy portrayed in these texts was basically agricultural. The basis of the economy were the many self-sufficient and semi-independent village communities comprised of multiple households linked by kinship who struggled to obtain a subsistence living from often unforgiving conditions. Those who wielded authority and/or power induced or coerced the productive villagers to yield a portion of their produce to support a more comfortable life for the ruling elite and their retainers and servants in cities. "Economics" was thus not something in itself, independent of other aspects of life, but was embedded in social-political-religious life. It thus is more intelligible and appropriate to think in terms of the political-economic-religious structure and its dynamics rather than of economics or "the economy" as if it were a separate sphere of life. It is necessary, moreover, to consider the cultural tradition in which people were embedded that guided their social-economic interaction and collective sense of identity and what was expected and acceptable.[8]

---

7. Boer, *The Sacred Economy*. In the text and notes, Boer includes telling criticism of other theories and how they fit in the history of "economics" and economic theory. I find Boer's analysis and theory of the political-economy of ancient southwest Asia more appropriate to and helpful in understanding Jesus and the Gospels in the context of Roman Palestine than the subsequent Boer and Petterson, *Time of Troubles*, which informs my analysis of the Pauline letters in the context of the Roman Empire in Part 3. *Time of Troubles* is most important for delivering a broad analysis of political-economic structures in the Roman imperial world and the historical movement toward the emergence of the colonate that dominated in late-antiquity as Christianity became the established religion.

8. In the last few decades some biblical scholars have been borrowing (the mainly structural-functional) Western social science of the mid-twentieth century. Such social science tended to understand social-political structures as stable and to downplay political-economic conflict and historical change. Its focus on social status and stratification tends to hide fundamental conflict between the dominant and the subordinated. See the criticism of structural-functional sociology, which was abandoned by most sociologists after 1970, in Horsley, *Sociology and the Jesus Movement*. The texts that became "biblical," however, feature mostly conflicts between the producers and their rulers that sometimes resulted in changes in historical configurations. The legendary narratives of the origins of the people of Israel, for example, tell of the escape (exodus)

Serious investigation of the economic aspect of such texts in their historical contexts will thus require a serious change in focus to a "wide-angle" lens capable of considering texts and contexts more comprehensively. Moreover, our focus can no longer be confined to theological ideas or "values" or "proof-texts" abstracted from the texts, but must be widened to include *the historical political-economic conflict that is being addressed in the text* and *the historical political-economic action that is being taken* and *the political-economic practices being pursued.*

Moving beyond Synthetic Constructs that Block Understanding of Texts and Contexts

Recent critical examination of the origins of the texts and contexts that are taken as "biblical" suggest that some of the key assumptions and concepts of biblical studies in general—and of New Testament studies in particular—block the way to understanding those texts and contexts. The texts now collected in the Hebrew Bible were evidently produced in scribal circles that served the Judean monarchy and temple-state centuries before they were recognized as books of the Bible.[9] It is thus anachronistic to imagine that the political-economic-religious contexts they presuppose and address were "the biblical world."[10] In the ancient world where communication was largely oral and literacy was confined to elite (scribal) circles,[11] even scribes learned and cultivated texts by oral recitation so that they became "inscribed on the tablet of their heart."[12] Written copies of such elite texts were rare, cumbersome, and confined to scribal circles. So it is unlikely that villagers had direct contact with written texts that still existed in different versions in scribal circles. The Gospels were evidently produced in and for communities of ordinary people long before they were canonized in the New Testament by councils of bishops convened by the Roman imperial court.[13]

---

of the "mixed multitude" of Hebrews subject to forced labor under Pharaoh in Egypt. The ensuing narratives that frame covenantal legal collections tell of the people's attempt to organize a society independent of human rulers who extracted produce. The Gospel stories of Jesus' mission and movement are rooted in this Israelite tradition.

9. Horsley, *Scribes, Visionaries,* chap. 6.
10. Ulrich, *The Dead Sea Scrolls,* 89–90.
11. Harris, *Ancient Literacy;* Hezser, *Jewish Literacy in Roman Palestine.*
12. Carr, *Tablet of the Heart;* Horsley, *Scribes, Visionaries.*
13. For a summary of the implications of several separate but interrelated lines of recent research on oral communication and its interface with writing in the ancient world, see Horsley, *Scribes, Visionaries;* and Horsley, "Oral Communication."

It became standard long ago to refer to Judean texts, society, and history of the "second temple" period (from the Persian Empire to the Roman destruction in 70 CE) as expressions of and evidence for "early Judaism" and to refer to the texts of the New Testament as expressions of and evidence for "early Christianity." Indeed, the subfield of New Testament studies both assumes and explores how the new religion of "early Christianity" originated in and then separated from the older religion of "early Judaism." But these are abstract synthetic constructs that lump together and thus obscure the distinctive texts, figures, movements, institutions, and recurrent conflicts that were the political-economic-religious realities of life in early Roman Palestine and beyond. These historical realities have now been researched and delineated far more precisely and comprehensively than in previous generations when the synthetic constructs were standard.[14] It is now possible to refer fairly precisely to the people of particular areas at particular times, including their movements and revolts; to scribal groups, their political-economic-religious position and support or protest of the high priests; and to the Roman client rulers in particular areas and times, all in the context of changing historical circumstances and conflicts in Palestine under Roman rule.

It may also be important to avoid another synthetic modern scholarly construct that continues to skew interpretation of New Testamen texts. In the late nineteenth and early twentieth centuries Western biblical scholars constructed "Jewish apocalypticism" on the basis of text-fragments, figures, and terms extracted from a wide variety of late-second temple Judean texts (usually labeled "apocalyptic"). It became standard in the field to believe that Jews at the time were caught up in the belief in the imminent End of the World that would unfold according to an "apocalyptic scenario" of key events such "the Last Judgment," "the Great Tribulation," "the Resurrection," and, for the early Christians, "the Parousia." More careful, critical readings especially of early Judean "apocalyptic texts" (the historical

---

14. See, for example, Goodman, *The Ruling Class of Judea*; and Schwartz, *Imperialism and Jewish Society*.

Having become concerned over fifty years ago about the discrepancy between the historical diversity and multiple conflicts and complexity, indeed chaos, evident in our textual sources, on the one hand, and the synthetic scholarly constructs with which we attempt to impose order on them, on the other, I devoted decades of research and critical analysis to constructing the complex historical realities of Roman Palestine as comprehensively and precisely as possible. See my "alternative" constructions in the articles behind Horsley with Hanson, *Bandits, Prophets, and Messiahs*; Horsley, *Jesus and the Spiral of Violence*, chaps 1–5; Horsley, *Galilee*; Horsley *Archaeology, History, and Society in Galilee*; and Horsley, *Jesus and the Politics of Roman Palestine*. The discussions here in Part 2 presuppose and depend upon these works and others.

visions in Daniel 7, 8, 10–12; and the Animal Vision in 1 Enoch 85–90) as they address the looming crisis of the Judean temple-state under Hellenistic imperial rule, conclude that they do not attest such an "apocalyptic scenario." In these texts, rather, different circles of scribes involved in the temple-state are struggling to understand how the imperial military invasion and economic exploitation of Judea could have happened with "the Most High" still ultimately in control of history.[15] The interpretation of "Judaism" in Hellenistic and Roman Palestine as "apocalyptic" distorts Judean texts and historical movements by imposing a modern synthetic scholarly construct and leads to diversionary debates about whether Jesus was or was not caught up in "Jewish apocalypticism."[16]

Dispensing with the (distorting) synthetic constructs of (early) Judaism and (early) Christianity and Jewish apocalypticism will also enable us to discern how much the Gospels present Jesus' mission and movements as the continuation and fulfilment of the history and cultural tradition of the people of Israel. We thus cannot understand the Gospels without taking into account how they build on, adapt, and continue Israelite popular tradition that we know mainly indirectly from (elite) Judean texts.

Finally, it is essential to avoid the dominant individualism of modern Western culture and of Christian theology that is projected onto Jesus and the Gospels. In the dominant post-Enlightenment cultural atmosphere in which reality is defined by Reason, defensive Christian interpreters narrowed their scope and "data" to the individual sayings of Jesus. The result has

---

15. For attempts at "deconstruction," see Horsley, *Scribes, Visionaries*, esp. chaps 8–9; Horsley, *Revolt of the Scribes*.

16. See the application of the "deconstruction" of "apocalypticism" in Judean texts to studies of Jesus and the Gospels in Horsley, *The Prophet Jesus and the Renewal of Israel*, chaps 1–4. The shift of terminology from "apocalyptic" to "'millenarian" or the equation of the two terms may only be a further obfuscation of historical movements rooted in Israelite tradition in early Roman Palestine. Toward the beginning of the surge of anthropologists' and historians fascination with what they labeled "millenarian" movements, my grad-school friend John Gager presented an interpretation of the Jesus-movement and early Christianity generally on the model of anthropological studies of "millenarian" movements, mainly Melanesian "cargo cults," that burgeoned in the 1960s and 1970s, in *Kingdom and Community: The Social World of Early Christianity* (1975). Like "charisma/charismatic," however, this was yet another imposition of a synthetic composite social scientific construct onto diverse particular historical social movements. In particular, it obscured how different the popular Israelite movements led by Jesus and others that were rooted in the deep Israelite tradition of resistance to domestic and imperial rulers were from "cargo cults" and "nativist" movements that were reacting to the initial wave of European colonial invasion. Also, the nineteenth-century peasant movements in Italy and Spain that Hobsbawm studied in *Primitive Rebels* do not appear to have been historically analogous to the cargo cults and other movements being studied by the social scientists at that time.

been several versions of a religious "talking head" unengaged in political-economic interaction. The Gospel sources, however, present Jesus embedded in and always engaged in the historical social forms of Galilean and Judean society as a movement gathers around him in oppositional interaction with the rulers (and their representatives) of Roman Palestine. Insofar as the Gospel stories are narrating the interactive mission of Jesus inseparable from the origins of the communities in which they were composed, it is probably impossible to separate the one from the other and from the historical circumstances and forces in which they operated. But this is the case with any historically significant figure.[17] The clear implications are that we consider Jesus-in-interaction together with the movement(s) that resulted from his mission as the stories are told in the Gospel sources.

---

17. In Horsley, *Jesus and Empire*, 56–58, I outlined a relational-contextual approach to Jesus-in-interaction, in analogy with the historical figures of Abraham Lincoln and Martin Luther King, that considers five interrelated aspects. We can attempt to understand how, (1) in the particular historical conditions that had created a crisis for the ancient Judean and Galilean people (2) and working out of the Israelite cultural tradition in which those people were rooted, (3) Jesus emerged as a leader (4) by adapting particular social role(s) (5) in interaction with people who responded by forming a movement that became historically significant.

3

Historical Development of the Complex Context of Jesus' Mission

The historical context of Jesus' mission and movement(s) was complex, unstable, and rife with political-economic-religious conflict. This complexity has gone largely ignored because the synthetic modern construct of (early) Judaism hides the considerable diversity of regional history, the structural political-economic conflict, and the popular and scribal movements of resistance that led the Romans and their client rulers to take repressive action. The most effective way of presenting this diversity, instability, and conflict may be to trace briefly the historical development of the particular political-economic-religious structure and dynamics that are presupposed and attested in the Gospels and contemporary sources. In this way, step by step, it is possible to sketch the complex historical context of Jesus' mission and the resulting movement(s) that were obscured or simply hidden from view by the controlling synthetic scholarly constructs of standard New Testamen studies.

This survey of the historical development of the complex context of Jesus' mission may also serve to at least begin to address the gap, and often the disconnect, between study of books of the Hebrew Bible and books of the New Testament. Over the course of the twentieth century, "Old Testament Studies" and "New Testament Studies" developed into separate subfields of Christian theology. It was simply assumed that there was a centuries-long historical gap between the books of the Hebrew Bible and those of the New Testament. The mainly Judean "non-canonical" scribal texts produced in second-temple times were classified as Apocrypha or Pseudepigrapha. These were assumed to be expressions of an essentialist synthetic "Judaism." In the five centuries between the rebuilding of the temple and the Roman conquest, however, the Judean temple state had gone from a tiny territory in the hilly environs of Jerusalem to control of most of Palestine, from Idumea in the South to Samaria and Galilee in the North. The early history of the "second temple" period is often obscure because of the limited sources. It is clear, however, that the period involved a diverse regional history and intensifying political-economic-religious conflict, particularly under the Roman military conquests and economic exploitation, along with continuing resistance by popular leaders and movements.

The Base and Structure of the Agrarian Political-Economy in Ancient Palestine

The basis of the agrarian political-economy in ancient Judea, Samaria, and Galilee, as in virtually any agrarian society, were hundreds of village communities each comprised of many households.[1] Villagers labored on the land to produce crops and livestock that provided a subsistence living for themselves. Over many generations villagers had learned how to organize their labor for optimal use of their land to eke out a subsistence living in ways that required close cooperation and reciprocal aid and the spreading of risks. Textual and archaeological evidence indicates that village communities periodically (re-)allocated contiguous strips of land-shares to the constituent households on the common fields around their nucleated dwellings. Village households also shared a common pasture area beyond the cultivated field(s).[2] Both men and women worked the fields, and combined their long hours of labor at the urgent time of harvest and perhaps in plowing and sowing as well. While some households fared better than others, village communities had customary ways of trying to keep their component

---

1. A principal reason this has not been discerned is that biblical scholarship, like historical scholarship generally, has not recognized that extant written sources were produced by and represented the interests of the literate elite, who comprised a tiny minority at the top of any agrarian society. Peasants, like women generally, have been "hidden from history." Only recently are biblical scholars learning to extrapolate information indirectly from written sources. On the social-economic life and political-economic activities of villagers behind "biblical" texts, see, for example, Chaney, *Peasants, Prophets, and Political Economy*; Knight, *Law, Power, and Justice*, 70–74, 115–56; Boer, *Sacred Economy*, chaps 2–3; Horsley with Hanson, *Bandits, Prophets, and Messiahs*; Horsley, *Galilee*, esp. chaps. 6–12; and Horsley, "Introduction" and "Jesus Movements and the Renewal of Israel"; Herzog, "Why Peasants Responded to Jesus"; and Wire, "Women's History from Birth-Prophecy Stories," these last four all in Horsley, ed., *People's History of Christianity*, Vol 1: *Christian Origins*; Horsley, *Covenant Economy*, esp. chaps 2–4; and more generally, Scott, *Moral Economy of the Peasant*; Scott, *Domination and the Arts of Resistance*.

2. The concepts of "property" and "ownership" would thus appear not to be applicable to allotted field-shares of common village land, but the shares were heritable in multigenerational households.

household economically viable, e.g., with gleaning rights and interest-free survival loans. Households were patriarchal, under the authority of the senior male. But village communities were acephalous, without hierarchical social organization, with self-governance and cohesion from village assemblies, and local problems, accidents, and social conflicts handled by the village elders. With their communality of assent, economizing, and enforcement, the village communities, while operating at a subsistence level, had a considerable degree of resilience in adapting to changing conditions and in persisting through difficult circumstances.

Local and imperial rulers living in cities, however, extracted a portion of the villagers' crops to support their own lavish lifestyles, the artisans who served their desires, their scribal and other servants, and, at the imperial level, the military forces. They used their power to levy tribute and taxes and their authority to demand tithes and offerings. After yielding up tribute, taxes, and tithes to their imperial and local rulers, some households were unable to feed themselves and forced to take survival loans from neighbors. If their neighbors became unable to provide survival loans, they could be manipulated into debt by their wealthy and powerful creditors who could come to control their labor and even their fields ("woe . . . , because they add field to field," Isa 5:6; cf. Neh 5:1–13). Interpreters focused on text-fragments or on archaeological reports that do not take historical information and broader social patterns into account often miss the basic conflict in this political-economic structure that made it fundamentally unstable. Villagers resisted their rulers' extractions in various ways, and the rulers found further devices by which they could extract produce and labor.

The Emerging Temple-State in Jerusalem as the Local Representative of Imperial Rule

Following the Babylonian destruction of Jerusalem and devastation of the surrounding countryside, *Yehud* consisted of a tiny territory in the hills of southern Palestine with a population of perhaps 25,000 people settled mainly in a number of villages. At some point, the Persian regime allowed or sponsored a colony of the descendants of the previously deported Jerusalem elite, who claimed to be the true *Yehudim*, to return to the land and rebuild a temple, with the support of Persian governors in command of military forces. In the course of a struggle for power with some of the "big-men" in the area, such as the sheikh Tobias in the Transjordan and Geshem the Arab, a priestly aristocracy managed to gain the authority over the tiny territory to gather both tribute to the Empire and tithes and offerings to support the temple and priesthood, at least according to accounts in Nehemiah (5:4; 9:35–37; 10:32–39; 12:44; 13:10–13). Under this evolving arrangement, at least some of the "Judeans" were ostensibly serving "the god who was in Jerusalem" (Ezra 1:2–4) as directed by their own Judean priestly aristocracy. Sources such as the book of Haggai indicate that the people resisted the demands for revenues and labor to support the building and operations of the temple. Haggai's prophetic harangues sound like what could only be called religious-economic extortion: if you don't render up revenues to support the temple, God will cause your crops to fail (Hag 1:7–11). A succession of imperial regimes, Hellenistic and then Roman, kept the temple-state in place. Only by early Roman times it had greatly expanded the territory and population over which it had jurisdiction and influence.

Judean (Written) Scribal Texts and the Continuing Cultivation of Israelite Popular Tradition

The structural conflict, hence instability, of Judean society is evident in the texts produced by scribal circles of the temple-state. The (early versions of) books later collected in the Hebrew Bible, however, included legends and stories of how earlier generations of Israelites repeatedly asserted their independence of rulers who were coercing their crops and/or labor.[3] The paradigmatic legend of the origins of Israel as a people independent of rulers was the exodus, led by the paradigmatic prophet Moses. Texts of torah (teaching) also included the formation of Israel as a distinctive people in the covenant that Y H W H gave the people through the legendary prophet Moses as a binding mutual commitment with commandments for the people's exclusive loyalty to their transcendent divine king and for their social-economic interaction (in their village communities).[4] No mere rules of morality, these were principles of social-economic interaction that protected the people's (economic!) rights to a livelihood. The commandment of exclusive loyalty and that against "bowing down and serving" other gods (and their ruler-regents) in effect prohibited human rulers and their demands for tithes and taxes (implications evident in Judg 8; 1 Sam 12). Other commandments prohibited people from striving to take control of or stealing others' resources.[5] Included in the written texts that later became

3. The relation of popular Israelite tradition and their use and adaptation in scribal texts is discussed in Horsley, "Contesting Authority: Popular vs. Scribal Tradition in Continuing Performance" in *Text and Tradition* chap. 5.

4. Discussed in Horsley, *Covenant Economics*, 17–32.

5. Chaney, *Peasants, Prophets, and Political Economy*, 67–82.

books of the Hebrew Bible are collections of (scribal) adaptations of some of the customs and practices linked with the covenantal principles. These laws and customs extended the supposed protections of people's economic livelihood in the commands or exhortations of lending liberally without interest, sabbatical cancellation of debts and release of debt slaves, and collective aid for the destitute such as gleaning and leaving the land fallow in the seventh years so that the poor could gather what grew on the land. In the texts later included in the Bible, these law-collections were re-formulated and re-framed to support the centralization of political-economic-religious power in the (monarchy and) temple-state.[6]

Since literacy was limited to the circles of scribes who served the temple-state, it is unlikely that the villagers had direct contact with the scribal texts that included and adapted these traditions. But the Israelite popular tradition that had been adapted into the scribal texts would have continued to be cultivated orally in village communities that were semi-self-governing, with their elders and village assemblies. Local social-economic interaction continued to be guided by the popular customs and practices and covenantal commandments "underneath" the scribal adaptation the legal-collections that we are familiar with in the Hebrew Bible.[7] Age-old stories of resistance and liberation would have been told regularly, as when the Passover festival was celebrated. As evident in other texts later included in the Bible, memories of earlier resistance and its prophetic leaders inspired subsequent resistance such as that led by the prophets Elijah and Elisha. The covenantal commandments were the criteria on the basis of which later prophets such as Isaiah and Jeremiah pronounced judgment against kings, their officers, and high priests for exploiting the people.[8]

This Israelite popular tradition was distinctive but not unique. It was similar to the popular or "little" tradition that anthropologists and others have discerned and studied in other societies.[9] At the heart of such

---

6. Careful critical analysis and exposition of scribal shaping of collections of law in the interest of states in Knight, *Law, Power, and Justice*, esp. chaps 6–7.

7. See the extensive analysis and discussion in Knight, *Law, Power, and Justice*, chaps 2–5. "The population living in the rural villages had a flourishing tradition of customary laws . . . [that] lived on in oral form . . ." (96). "The people's customs constituted a body of practices and values into which [each successive] younger generation was socialized . . . (Collections of written 'literary laws' were) more the product and possession of the priests and leaders than a shared heritage of the people at large" (52–53).

8. This is the implication of the collection of articles by Chaney, *Peasants, Peasants*; some examples in Horsley, *Covenant Economics*, chap. 5.

9. The best cross-cultural analysis is Scott, "Protest and Profanation." The parallels and differences between the Judean "great tradition" embodied primarily in texts later included in the Hebrew Bible and the Israelite popular tradition that informed popular

popular traditions anthropological and historical studies have found core principles and customs of social-economic interaction that, in effect, protecting the people's rights to a livelihood, aimed to maintain the economic viability of each household in village communities. This has been called "the moral economy" of peasant village communities.[10] The popular customs and practices that lie behind or "underneath" the Mosaic covenant, its commandments, and other covenantal laws now included in the books of the Hebrew Bible are indications of the distinctive but similar "moral economy" that continued to function in Judean and other Israelite villages. With sources being scarce, we lose track of the Israelite popular tradition in the early second temple period, but it clearly became a motivating factor of resistance later in the period.

The book of Nehemiah narrates a political-economic crisis that indicates the continuing function of the ideals of this "covenantal economy" amidst the instability of the temple-state as representative of the imperial order in Jerusalem that required intervention by Persian governors such as Nehemiah (with military forces). Under heavy demands for "the king's tax" (tribute paid to the Persian Empire) the people were manipulated into spiraling debt and forced to yield control of their fields and houses and to surrender their children as debt-slaves to the Judean nobles and officials. The people appealed to the governor for relief (Neh 5:1–13). Presumably to preserve the empire's economic base in the territory of Judea, Nehemiah forced the nobles and officials to restore the people's houses and fields, along with the produce they had extorted. In doing this he was (at least ostensibly) enforcing the covenantal laws and customs according to which the religious political-economy in Judea was supposed to operate. But he did not relax the demands of the imperial system that still required dues to the temple and the tribute to the emperor that had forced the people into debt in the first place. Even though texts are limited for this period, they indicate that the people repeatedly faced such crises of debt and survival recurrently.[11]

That the fuller form of the Mosaic covenant along with its commandments continued to be cultivated as the guide and norm for social-economic relations among the people as well as their understanding that the

---

movements of renewal and resistance, including Jesus, informs Horsley, *Bandits, Prophets, and Messiahs* and the articles behind the book; and Horsley, *Jesus and the Spiral*, chap. 3–4. More recent general discussion in Horsley, "Contesting Authority: Popular vs. Scribal Tradition in Continuing Performance," in *Text and Tradition in Performance and Writing*, 99–122.

10. Scott, *Moral Economy of the Peasant*. Applied to Israelite popular tradition, particularly Mosaic covenantal teaching, in Horsley, *Covenant Economy*, 35–43.

11. See Gottwald, "The Expropriated and the Expropriators in Nehemiah 5."

impositions by human rulers were against the will of God is vividly indicated by key texts found at Qumran, especially the Community Rule (1QS). The Rule includes instructions for the ceremony of covenant renewal for a new-exodus community in its withdrawal from the rule of the Jerusalem temple-state in which the traditional *sanctions of the blessings and curses* have been transformed into (part of) the new *declaration of deliverance* that provided a basis for the covenantal *commandments* and more specific regulations of community life.[12] That the Mosaic covenant in its fuller form continued to be cultivated in scribal circles where it could provide the political-economic charter for a "breakaway" scribal-priestly group suggests strongly that the covenant form and its commandments continued to function prominently in village communities as well—and could later come to public prominence in John's "baptism of repentance for the remission of sins" that was also symbolically located as a new exodus in the wilderness.

Hellenistic Imperial Invasion and the Hasmonean Take-Over of Galilee

The temple-state was kept in place by successive empires as the local representative of imperial rule, with considerable expansion and intensification, along with continuing resistance. While sources for what was happening among the vast majority of people are limited, they are sufficient for the three hundred years under Hellenistic and early Roman imperial rule (from early second century BCE to early second century CE) to warrant two important interrelated generalizations. (1) Under Hellenistic imperial rule, there was increasing interference and military invasion by the imperial regimes. This continued, indeed escalated under Roman rule, with military conquest and repeated reconquest. (2) The Israelite people(s), however, having inherited a passion for independence, mounted resistance with increasingly frequent widespread revolts.

Under the Hellenistic regimes the high priestly aristocracy gradually consolidated its command of the temple-state as the local representative of imperial rule and accumulated considerable wealth in the temple. Leading figures at the head of the dominant faction in the aristocracy, Jason and then Menelaus, usurped control by paying ever-higher, exorbitant amounts from the temple treasury for the high priesthood to the

---

12. Fuller discussion in Horsley, *Covenant Economics*, 100–103, drawing on Baltzer, *The Covenant Formulary*; extensive analysis and discussion of what could be called covenantal economic practices evident in the Dead Sea Scrolls in Murphy, *Wealth in the Dead Sea Scrolls*.

Seleucid regime that was desperate for resources (2 Macc 4–5). Evidently seeking fuller participation in the imperial "political" culture, they then transformed Jerusalem into a *polis*, the distinctively Hellenistic form of political-economy in which powerful elites dominated indigenous villagers. When the Seleucid emperor, Antiochus Epiphanes, sent troops to enforce the "reform" against resistance by some scribal groups, widespread popular revolt erupted that fought the Seleucid army to a stand-off with sustained guerrilla warfare (2 Macc 7–15).[13]

The Hasmonean brothers who led the popular revolt, who were not of a high priestly family, then arranged with a weakened Seleucid regime to be appointed high priests in a reinstated temple-state. This was evidently the point at which a group of priests and scribes withdrew in protest to the wilderness at Qumran in a new exodus and established a renewed Mosaic covenantal community, deeply informed by the fundamental parts of Judean scribal tradition derived from earlier Israelite popular tradition. The Hasmoneans, after consolidating their power and wealth, hired Greek mercenaries and conquered first the Samaritans to the north, destroying their temple, and then took control of Galilee as well (Josephus, *Ant.* 13.318–319). The Hasmonean high priesthood in Jerusalem thus expanded its rule from a limited area around the city to nearly all of Palestine, including all of the principal areas of Israelite cultural heritage (Samaria and Galilee as well as Judea). For the first time in many centuries the area of Galilee came under Jerusalem rule, although it lasted for only the hundred years prior to the lifetime of Jesus.[14]

According to Josephus, the Hasmoneans forced the inhabitants there to obey "the laws of the Judeans" (meaning presumably to submit to taxation?). The Hasmoneans, followed by Herod after them, established fortresses in Galilee garrisoned by Judean officers and soldiers (*War* 1.303; for example, at Sepphoris and probably Gabara, *Life* 246) to enforce their rule and, presumably, gather revenues.[15] Some of these Judean officers would have been "the power-holders in the region" that the Galileans revolted against sixty years later (*Ant.* 14.450). But there is no good evidence that

13. For my own analysis and presentation see further Horsley, *Scribes, Visionaries*, chap. 2. There are many and varied constructions of this history, some of which avoid the political-economic aspect, while others downplay the scribal resistance.

14. An attempt to critically reconstruct this history on the limited evidence available in Horsley, *Galilee*, 39–52. Freyne, *Galilee*, and some of the studies based on surface-survey archaeology in the 1980s and 1990s were still working with the synthetic construct of "the Jews" and "Judaism" without analysis of the sources for the Hasmonean take-over of Galilee and who the "inhabitants" were.

15. For a fuller discussion, with references, of the Hasmonean and Herodian "administration" of Galilee, see Horsley, *Galilee*, 137–44.

large numbers of Judeans suddenly flooded into Galilee to become settlers, as is simply assumed by many scholars. Several generations after the Hasmonean take-over of Galilee, Josephus still refers to the Israelite people according to geographical area: the people in or from Judea proper as "the Judeans," the people in Samaria as "the Samaritans," and the villagers in Galilee as "the Galileans."[16] The Galileans, like the Judeans and Samaritans, were people of Israelite heritage. While the Galileans were not (yet) necessarily hostile to Jerusalem rulers, as were the Samaritans, whose temple the Jerusalem rulers had destroyed, it seems likely that they would have been ambivalent at best about the temple and high priesthood as the dominant political-economic-religious institutions.

Roman Imperial Rule in Palestine: Intensification of Exploitation

Roman conquest and imperial rule further complicated the overall political-economic structure and dynamics and intensified the economic circumstances and burdens of the people.

Roman warlords, having already launched their conquest of the eastern Mediterranean, now also conquered Palestine, which had become highly unstable under rival Hasmonean factions. Pompey plundered the considerable wealth that had accumulated in the temple, and confirmed the Hasmonean high priest Hyrcanus as Rome's client ruler in Palestine. The Romans required the subjugated people to render tribute, a principal purpose of imperial conquest, to be collected by the Hasmonean high priesthood. The people, already paying tithes and other dues to the temple and high priesthood, were (again) required to yield up another percentage of their produce to their imperial rulers (25% every second year, or perhaps every year; Josephus, *Ant.* 14.202–203).[17] Recurrent war between rival Hasmonean factions and the extension of the empire-wide Roman "civil war" into Palestine brought considerable destruction in the countryside, including crops, and further extraction of villagers' economic resources, including a special levy of tribute imposed by Cassius, the Roman warlord.[18]

16. Occasionally in his accounts of the great revolt in 66–70, Josephus uses "Judeans" with reference to the rebels more generally. Of course, insofar as the Hasmoneans and Herod controlled Galilee by means of several garrisoned fortresses, there were Judeans in Galilee. At one point in the resistance to Herod's conquest of his subjects, Josephus mentions that the Galileans drowned the (Judean) *dynatoi* (powerful ones) in the Lake (*War* 1.326).

17. See further Udoh, *To Caesar What Is Caesar's*, 41–57.

18. Josephus devotes most of *Antiquities* book 14 to these events.

Wanting to exert far more decisive control over Palestine, the Roman Senate appointed the military strongman Herod as "King of the Judeans" in 40 BCE.[19] It took him three years to subdue his subjects, the widespread popular resistance being particularly strong in Galilee. Herod made heavy economic demands on his subjects to fund his extensive building projects and lavish expenditure. In addition to erecting temples in honor of Caesar, he built two new cities named for the emperor, Caesarea as his seaport on the coast and Sebaste (Augustus) in Samaria.[20] In addition, he mounted a massive reconstruction of the temple in grand Hellenistic imperial style. He also appointed a succession of his own creatures as high priests, thus expanding the priestly aristocracy that continued as one of the layers of rulers supported by the producers. The funding of all of these grandiose building projects came on top of the expenses of his lavish court, massive military fortresses, and unmatched benefactions to other cities of the empire and gifts to Augustus and others in the imperial family. He did recognize that his exhausted economic base could not survive a famine exacerbated by a drought, and imported grain from Egypt to tide them over to the next harvest and round of extractions (Josephus, *Ant.* 15.299–312).

After Herod's death in 4 BCE widespread revolt erupted in the major districts of Israelite heritage, Judea, Galilee, and the Jordan valley and beyond (Perea). In their reconquest (*War* 2.66–75; *Ant.* 17.286–295), the Romans exercised the extreme brutality with which they terrorized subjected peoples into submission.[21] In systematically suppressing resistance, according to Josephus, the Roman legions destroyed the fortress town of Sepphoris in Galilee and enslaved the people, then plundered and destroyed villages, including Emmaus, in a widespread "scene of fire and blood" through the hill country of Judea. There the warlord Varus sent his soldiers out to round up fugitives and crucified about 2,000 of them as supposed leaders of the insurrection. There may be at least representative significance in the destruction of villages and the enslavement and crucifixion of Galilean and Judean villagers right at the beginning of the lifetime of Jesus and his followers in the area of Nazareth and in the area of Emmaus (where the Jesus movement

---

19. Herod had impressed the Roman warlords as the ruthless young military commander of Galilee who had exacerbated the already acute economic distress of the Galileans in the wake of the Roman conquest. He brutally suppressed the bands of brigands continuing the resistance to Roman rule and then ruthlessly collected the special levy of tribute decreed by Cassius (*War* 1.204–209; *Ant.* 14.159–160, 271–274).

20. See Netzer, *Herod the Builder*.

21. Only recently have Roman historians become more candid about the devastating effects of Roman legions' terrorization of peoples they subjected by slaughter and enslavement of people, devastation of villages, and crucifixion of those viewed as leaders of resistance. See, for example, Mattern, *Rome and the Enemy*.

apparently spread, Luke 24:13-43). The brutal destruction and slaughter of such reconquest left economic devastation of households and villages and collective trauma for survivors in these areas.

After reconquering the Galileans and Judeans, the Romans set different client rulers over separate districts of Palestine. Galilee and Perea they placed under the rule of Herod's son Antipas (4 BCE—37CE?), who had been "educated" at the imperial court in Rome (4 BCE). Within twenty years, Antipas built Sepphoris as one capital city and then also built Tiberias along the Sea of Galilee as a second capital city. With less than a quarter of the revenues commanded by his father, he undertook these two massive projects, which would have meant a further intensification of extraction from Galilean villagers. Tax collection would have been far more "efficient" with the ruler of Galilee now located directly in the area, nearly all of the villages of lower Galilee now within (over)sight of one or another of the capital cities.

In Judea (as of 6 CE) the Romans placed the priestly aristocracy in charge of maintaining order and collecting the tribute as well as tithes and temple dues, only now under appointment and oversight by a Roman governor. During the next several decades the priestly aristocracy became ever more oppressive of their people.[22] They used the surplus wealth building up in the temple to make loans to needy peasants, manipulated them into spiraling debt, and forced them into tenancy, for example, on estates in northwest Judea,[23] meanwhile building ever more lavish mansions for themselves in Jerusalem.[24] Eventually high priestly families even became predatory on their people, sending strong-armed gangs out to seize grain from the village threshing floors, leaving the ordinary priests as well as the people to starve (*Ant.* 20.180-181, 206-207). Later rabbinic texts contain memories of the widespread resentment of the high priestly families' rule, in which the economic dimension is clear.[25]

---

22. See the surveys by Goodman, *The Ruling Class of Judea*; and Horsley, "The High Priests."

23. See especially Broshi, "The Temple in the Herodian Economy"; and Goodman, "The First Jewish Revolt: Social Conflict and the Problem of Debt."

24. See Avigad, *Discovering Jerusalem*, 77, 83.

25. Woe unto me because of the house of Baithos;
    woe unto me for their lances!
    Woe unto me because of the house of Hanin (Ananus) . . .
    Woe unto me because of the house of Ishmael ben Phiabi,
    woe unto me because of their fists.
    For they are high priests and their sons are treasurers
    and their sons-in-law are temple overseers,
    and their servants smite the people with sticks! (b. Pesaḥim 57a)

Economic Pressures on Villagers and Popular Movements of Resistance and Renewal

The eruption of pent-up resentment after Herod's death, however, began a period of several generations in which popular resistance drove the history of Palestine, leading to the collapse of the temple-state, the great revolt throughout most of Palestine, and the brutal Roman destruction of people and their villages in much of the countryside. Set up by the historical development of the previous centuries just outlined, this period of increasingly frequent popular renewal and resistance movements was the immediate context of the emergence of Jesus' mission and movements in Galilee and beyond.

In the face of economic pressures from imperial regimes and their client local rulers, (Israelite) village communities of Israelite heritage had been remarkably resilient as well as resistant. At least some of the customs that helped the component families of village communities remain economically viable persisted under early Roman domination. Given the periodic droughts and resultant famine, destruction of villages and killing or enslavement of people by conquering armies, and seizure of family members as debt-slaves, the people maintained at least the ideal of community responsibility for the widow, the orphan, and the refugee "resident alien." Rulers periodically cultivated popular support by promising aid for these marginal folks. The practice of allowing the land to lie fallow every seventh year, enabling the destitute to harvest whatever grew in the uncultivated fields was evidently widely observed, judging from Josephus' accounts of how it figured in famines and in payment of the tribute to Rome (Exod 23:10–11; *Ant* 3.280–281; 12.378; 13.235; 14.202, 206, 475; 15.7). Similarly, the cancellation of debts every seventh year must still have been a widespread practice, at least among villagers and perhaps by better-off creditors as well (see just below on the *prosbul* promulgated by Hillel).

The effects of military conquest and the political-economic pressures of multiple layers of rulers, however, were disintegrating families and village communities and their traditional mechanisms of mutual support. Limited by the standard academic separation of economy from politics, historical studies have largely ignored the economic effects of the Roman conquest and reconquest. But the cumulative effect of two or three generations of Roman, Hasmonean, and Herodian devastation and slaughter on household and village life must be taken into account in assessment of the largely subsistence economic circumstances of the Galilean and Judean people in the lifetime of Jesus and his movement(s).

Less sudden and more sustained, demands for tribute, taxes, and tithes and offerings from the different layers of rulers left many villagers without enough of their crops to feed their families.[26] Under Herod's regime one of the principal mechanisms of temporary relief was undermined. The scholar-teacher Hillel promulgated the *prosbul* as a device (supposedly to ease credit) to allow creditors to avoid the sabbatical cancellation of debts by placing the records of debts in the hands of a court (m. Shebi'it 10:3-7; cf. Deut 15:1-6).[27] This would have led to peasants falling ever more deeply into debt. The cumulative pressures were such that village practices of mutual aid and cooperation could not cope with them. Desperate peasants had borrowed from their neighbors, but those neighbors would have come under ever more stress themselves. Although the particular circumstances would have varied from area to area and village to village, what were already subsistence conditions for many would have deteriorated, with hunger, debts, loss of control over land, and decline into tenancy or increasing dependence on day-labor, with the corresponding disintegration of family and village community.

The economic deterioration of the villagers in Galilee and Judea and the passion for independence from rulers' extractions deeply rooted in Israelite tradition would have been major factors in the widespread popular revolts and resistance movements that were the driving force in the history of early Roman Palestine. Cross-cultural studies of peasants in other times and areas of the world have shown that it is when peasants sense that their subsistence livelihood is threatened, rather than when they have sunk completely into tenancy and dependency, that they form movements of resistance and mount wider revolts. Just such conditions were developing under the impact of Roman conquest and Herodian and high priestly rule. The lifetime of Jesus and the early development of movements of Jesus-loyalists were framed historically by two widespread popular revolts: the sudden eruption of revolt in Galilee, Judea, and the Transjordan from the pent-up resentment when Herod finally died in 4 BCE; and the great revolt that climaxed the steady deterioration of the political-economic order in 66-70 CE. In between were significant protests and a highly significant series of popular movements of resistance and renewal toward mid-century.

According to the accounts in Josephus (*War* 2.56-65; *Ant.* 17.271-284), the popular revolts in 4 BCE took a distinctively Israelite political-economic form (that is highly relevant to the mission of Jesus, judging from

26. Solid analysis with mainly textual evidence in Hanson and Oakman, *Palestine*, 101-25.

27. Good discussion in Goodman, *The Ruling Class of Judea*, 57-58. Critical analysis of the rabbinic accounts in Neusner, *Politics to Piety*, 14-17.

a few Gospel passages).[28] In their revolt, villagers in each area acclaimed their leader as a popular "king," a move informed by (evidently) still-cultivated stories of how earlier Israelites had "messiahed" the young David to be their leader in resistance to the Philistines (2 Sam 2:1–4; 5:1–4). The Judean historian Josephus, who despised peasants, especially when they engaged in resistance, focuses on their attacks against royal fortresses, palaces, and troops and their raids against Roman supply trains. His accounts, however, also indicate the political-economic agenda of these popular "messianic" movements. In Galilee, he says, the movement led by Judas, son of the brigand chieftain Hezekiah, killed by Herod a generation earlier, attacked the royal fortress at Sepphoris (near Nazareth), and took the arms and the goods stored there. These movements were in effect local declarations of independence, an age-old peasant ideal narrated in many stories in Israelite popular tradition, some of which were adapted in the books of Judges, 1–2 Samuel, and 1 Kings. By holding at bay the Herodian troops (before the massive Roman reconquest), these movements and their kings were able to maintain their independent village life free of rulers' extractions for many months and even, in the movement led by the shepherd Athronges in Judea, for three years. Josephus provides a somewhat fuller account of the most significant of these "messianic" movements, led by the popularly acclaimed "king of the Judeans," Simon bar Giora, seventy years later during the great revolt of 66–70 CE. In establishing independent self-rule in much of Judea, he and his movement were evidently striving to re-institute the just political-economic relations for which Israelite peasants yearned, including the release of debt-slaves (*War* 4.507–510).

Some dissident scribes and Pharisees also mounted significant resistance. As noted above, dissident scribal circles mounted active resistance to the Hellenizing "reform" by the high priestly aristocracy. Continuing conflicts between the high priests and scribal groups who were supposedly servants of the temple-state further complicated the dominant conflict between rulers and ruled. As they faced the increasingly invasive Roman imperial rule, at least a minority of the scribal and Pharisaic guardians of the "great tradition" could no longer compromise the covenantal principles they viewed as the very basis of the people's (social-economic) life under the rule of God. In 6 CE a group that Josephus calls "the Fourth Philosophy," who agreed basically with the views of the Pharisees, organized resistance to payment of the tribute to Caesar, insisting that the people already had

---

28. See further the critical analysis and discussion of Josephus' accounts in Horsley, "Messianic Movements"; Horsley with J. S. Hanson, *Bandits, Prophets, and Messiahs*, chap. 3; and Horsley, *Hearing the Whole Story*, chap. 10.

God as their lord and master (Josephus, *Ant.* 18.23).[29] That this group led by a scribal teacher and a Pharisee were willing to organize resistance to the tribute in defiance of Roman rule is evidence that some scribal circles were deeply committed to, indeed ready to die for the first two Mosaic covenantal commandments that formed the basis of the people's political-economic life.

Popular resistance became ever more frequent from the end of Antipas' reign in Galilee and from the time of Pontius Pilate in Judea and Samaria, according to the accounts of Josephus, on which we are largely dependent. More or less contemporary with Jesus' mission and movement(s), a series of popular movements emerged in the countryside that took yet another distinctively Israelite social form.[30] In each of these movements people from many villages responded to a prophet who promised to lead a new act of divine deliverance patterned after one of the formative events of Israel. The best known of these was the renewal of the Mosaic covenant led by John the Baptist symbolized by the ritual of baptism, accompanied by sharp prophecy against the injustice of Herod Antipas (Mark 6:16-29; Josephus, *Ant.* 18.116-119). In addition to a generalization that there were several more of these popular movements (*War* 2.259; *Ant.* 20.168), Josephus offers at least a brief account of particular cases (*Ant.* 18.85-87; 20.97-98, 169-171; *War* 2.261-263). The prophet Theudas, in imitation of Moses and/or Joshua, led a large group of villagers out into the wilderness of the Jordan where the waters would be divided, giving them access to the land, again a movement of renewal patterned after events of the origins of the Israel. Somewhat later in Judea, a prophet recently come from Egypt led followers to the Mount of Olives where they would see the walls of Jerusalem collapse, giving them access to the city, a renewal of the people and recovery of their land in the mold of the legend of Joshua and the fall of Jericho. Viewing these movements of renewal of Israel as popular uprisings, the Roman governors sent out the military to suppress them.

The mission and movement(s) of Jesus emerged just in this historical context and fit somewhat the same pattern, of a prophet (like Moses or Elijah) leading a renewal of Israel. The mission and movement(s) of Jesus,

---

29. See further Horsley with J. S. Hanson, *Bandits, Prophets, and Messiahs*, 190-99. While Israelite popular tradition developed and continued in opposition to rulers and their economic extractions, Israelite scribal tradition included principles and texts that objected to imperial rule, even though the scribes themselves were compromised by it.

30. See further the critical analysis and discussion of Josephus' accounts in Webb, *John the Baptizer and Prophet*, esp. chap. 10; Horsley, "Popular Prophetic Movements"; and Horsley with J. S. Hanson, *Bandits, Prophets, and Messiahs*, chap. 4; and of how these movements are pertinent to our understanding of Jesus and the Gospels in Horsley, *Hearing the Whole Story*, chap. 10.

however, were not caught up in an expectation of a new act of divine deliverance, but focused on the more concrete political-economic-religious renewal of covenantal community in the villages of Galilee and beyond (as should become clear in the discussion below).

Until a generation ago, interpreters of Jesus had difficulty imagining that villagers had more than two diametrically opposed options of open revolt or humble acquiescence in their rulers' oppression.[31] To appreciate that villagers were capable of organizing disciplined resistance in which they "held their ground" precisely in asserting—and risking—their economic subsistence it is important finally to attend to the Galilean "peasant strike" in resistance to payment of the Roman tribute (see esp. Josephus, *Ant.* 8.261–288; cf. *War* 2.185–203; Philo, *Legat.* 222–224).[32] The emperor Gaius (Caligula) had ordered his image/statue to be erected in the temple in retaliation for the way Judeans had disrespected his divinity in Alexandria (again note that "politics" and "economics" and "religion" were not separable). As Petronius, legate of Syria, led the Roman troops through Galilee, peasants in many villages refused to plant their fields. They were evidently willing to suffer the consequences (famine) of using what little leverage they had: deny the Romans the tribute by not planting their crops. This is a bold collective action in obedience to the first and second commandments, indicating that the Mosaic covenant was still operational among Galilean villagers. As Herodian officials pointed out to Petronius in their emergency consultation on how to respond: instead of a harvest from which the Romans could extract their tribute, the result would be "a harvest of banditry," that is, serious political-economic disruption for years to come. Petronius backed off—and was spared suicide by the (un)timely death of Gaius.

The Cumulative Effect:
Escalating Political-Economic-Religious Conflict

From its foundation under the Persians, there was structural political-economic conflict between the people and the temple and high priesthood as the ruling institutions. The conflict was complicated under the Hellenistic empires by serious scribal opposition to imperial invasion and further complicated by the Hasmonean high priesthood's conquest of Idumea and

---

31. For further discussion of the various forms of "peasant politics" (resistance), see Horsley, *Jesus and the Politics of Roman Palestine*, 36–43.

32. See further the critical analysis and discussion of the sources and the protest in Horsley, *Jesus and the Spiral of Violence*, 110–16.

Samaria and its take-over of Galilee. The conflict was intensified by the Roman conquest, imposition of Herod's kingship, and more direct Roman rule through the high priesthood in the first century CE, on the one hand, and the many popular movements of renewal and resistance, on the other. In the decades during which the Jesus movement(s) expanded rapidly in Palestine and beyond, the political-economic order further disintegrated until widespread insurrection erupted in Galilee and Judea as well as in Jerusalem in the great revolt of 66-70.[33]

This complex situation of political-economic-religious conflict, with escalating economic pressures on the villagers and their formation of movements of renewal and resistance rooted in Israelite popular tradition, is the context in which the Gospel sources can be read in order to discern the political-economic-religious program of renewal and resistance in Jesus' mission and movement(s).

---

33. It is often claimed that in the time of Jesus' mission and movement, Galilee was generally prosperous and peaceful. Such claims ignore the Galileans' intense opposition to the ruling cities of Sepphoris and Tiberias, as narrated at length by Josephus, that cannot have emerged only suddenly in 66-67 CE. Josephus proudly admits that he and Herodian officers took actions to secure the grain and other resources that had been taken from the villagers in taxes and tribute (*Life* 70-73; 119-120). He also recounts bold actions by Galileans, such as the raid on the royal palace in Tiberias (*Life* 65-66) and an ambush of a convoy under military escort transporting some of the huge quantities of wealth accrued by the ruler of eastern Galilee, Agrippa II, from taxation of his subjects (*War* 2.595; *Life* 126-131). These accounts indicate the economic roots of the revolt in Galilee as well as in Judea. Some of the incidents, moreover, indicate that the Galileans were motivated by their adherence to covenantal principles of economic justice. Critical analysis of Josephus' accounts of the conflicts in Galilee during the great revolt in Horsley, "Power Vacuum and Power Struggle."

4

The Political-Economic Project of Jesus' Mission and Movement(s)

Jesus' mission, his movement(s), and the Gospels that they produced did not stand apart from concrete political-economic life in Palestine, with distinctive religious values and perspectives. They were rather unavoidably embedded in the deepening political-economic-religious conflict between the rulers and the people. Jesus and his movement(s) condemned and actively opposed the ruling institutions and their exploitation of the people as they generated the social-economic renewal of the people in their village communities. As laid out in the Gospels, if we have eyes to see and ears to hear, *Jesus and his movement(s) were engaged in concrete renewal of covenantal community that fostered economic subsistence and justice for component families in opposition to the Roman imperial order in Palestine headed by the high priestly and Herodian rulers.*

Renewal of Covenantal Social-Economic Cooperation in Village Communities

As noted at the outset, recent interpretation of Jesus focused on separate sayings remains limited by its modern individualism and separation of religion from political economy. The Gospels as whole stories, however, present a dramatically different picture, portraying Jesus-in-interaction in fundamental socio-economic forms.

The Gospels present Jesus' mission as focused on village communities, each comprised of many families. As noted above, these were the fundamental social forms in which people's lives were embedded in Galilee or Judea or any traditional agrarian society. In the early episodes of the Markan story (1:21; 2:1; 6:6) and their parallels in Matthew and Luke, Jesus seems to have a base in the village of Capernaum, from which he could access other villages in the area that were only a few kilometers apart. Similarly, when he moves into nearby "regions" subject to other Roman client rulers, he works, for example, "in the villages of Caesarea Philippi." The Gospel stories, moreover, have Jesus going into the "synagogues" of Capernaum and other villages on the sabbath. Contrary to the standard (but anachronistic) assumption, *synagogai* in the Gospel stories refers not to religious buildings but to village assemblies, the form of local self-governance and community cohesion that gathered at least once a week.[1] Jesus carried out his work in village communities, often when the people were gathered in their assemblies. His mission was directed to whole communities, not just individuals, and he was dealing not just with what we moderns call "religious" matters, but with the more general political-economic(-religious) concerns of village communities.

Jesus' work in these villages is primarily two-fold: He proclaims and teaches about the direct rule (kingdom) of God; and he carries out exorcisms and healings that manifest the direct rule of God. The two are closely related in the Gospel narratives, are directly addressed to the tensions and sufferings of the village communities, and both have an economic as well as religious dimension. The teachings will be treated extensively below. Because the exorcisms and healings have been distorted and misunderstood as miracles, however, it is important at least to recognize their social-economic aspect.[2]

The healings and exorcisms are not simply individual interactions between Jesus and someone with a sickness or possessed by a spirit. Sickness and spirit-possession affect whole villages, especially component households/families. Paralysis, blindness, spirit-possession all mean loss of labor essential to subsistence that compounds the suffering. Family members or support groups bring sick people for healing. Exorcisms and healings evoke trust (*pistis*) among the people that enables further healing. Jesus sends the healed back into their communities. Some cases of sickness and healing, most clearly the twelve-year-old girl and the woman who has been hemorrhaging for twelve years, are clearly representative of the people of Israel as a whole. The mission of Jesus is bringing renewed life to a people that was nearly dead from hemorrhaging its economic life-blood.

---

1. Archaeological explorations have found buildings for the gathering of local assemblies that date mostly to late antiquity, suggesting that there were few or none yet in Galilean villages at the time of Jesus. Horsley, *Galilee*, chap. 10; Horsley, *Archaeology, History, and Society in Galilee*, chap. 6.

2. See Horsley, *Jesus and Magic*, chaps 9–10; and the forthcoming book on Jesus' healings and exorcisms: Horsley, *Empowering the People*.

Jesus' appointment of the Twelve as representative of the people of Israel indicates that what is happening in the direct rule of God and its manifestation is the renewal of the people (as noted above). He commissions his disciples to expand his mission in village communities (Mark 6:7–13 and par.; Luke 10:1–16). And his commissioning speeches give several indications that the proclamation and exorcism and healing were addressed to whole communities. The disciples are instructed to stay, in pairs, in one of the households of a village. Insofar as the dwellings in a village were packed closely together, the envoys unavoidably interacted with the other villagers. Their reception or rejection by the village ("place" or "town") is to determine how the envoys respond: i.e., with the peace and healing of the kingdom of God for any and all in the village or by calling down judgment on the whole village. If they are well received, moreover, they are to continue working in that village for a period of time (what today might be called community-organizing). Not only are villages the focus of the mission of Jesus and his disciples. But Jesus' project in his proclamation, his healings, and his commissioning the disciples is evidently the renewal of the people of Israel in their village communities.

As we learn to take seriously the episodes and their sequence in Gospel narratives for the historical information they may supply, serious attention should be given to the episodes of Jesus pointedly recruiting disciples from fishing families on the shores of the Sea of Galilee. The Markan story, followed to an extent by both the Matthean and Lukan stories, portray Jesus as working from a base in the village of Capernaum in the northwest corner of the large lake more or less across from the newly built city of Tiberias, which was topped by the palace of Herod Antipas. Presumably with his close relations with fishing families, Jesus has access to boats with which he moved from village to village around or across the lake. Many families in these villages would have made their living by "farming" the sea in addition to or instead of the land.[3] It is surely significant that Jesus evidently recruited disciples to assist in his mission in the villages of Galilee and beyond from fishing families. In contrast with cultivating the land that required villagers to work regularly on their crops, those engaged in fishing may have had more flexibility to move about from village to village, and may even have become acquainted with other villages around the lake.

---

3. In a carefully researched article, "The Galilean Fishing Economy and the Jesus Tradition," K. C. Hanson has explained the importance of fishing in the Galilean economy, including how Herod Antipas was exploiting it to enhance his income to fund his city-building and lavish court life and how Jesus used the fishing villages and harbors in carrying out his mission.

That households/families have an integral role in Jesus' mission focused on village communities suggests, contrary to assertions of recent liberal interpreters, that Jesus and the Gospels were not anti-family.[4] In many episodes of the Gospel stories, households/families are presupposed and renewed. Sick and spirit-possessed people are restored to their families (as noted above). In what seems to be a response to the disintegration of households and villages that was happening as a result of increased economic pressure, Jesus declares that those who do the will of God are his mother and sisters and brothers (Mark 3:31-35; cf. 10:2-45), that is, a renewed village community that can also serve as supportive household/family (which had, in effect, been an aspect of covenantal mechanisms of mutual aid).

Jesus' preaching and healing in many village communities and commissioning disciples to extend his mission in villages is thus Jesus generating a movement. As he proclaims the direct rule of God and manifests it in healings and exorcisms, the word spreads and crowds of people come from other villages in trust (*pistis*) that he can and will heal. He goes on to preach and heal in those other villages to which he sends his disciples, in effect, as a cadre of catalysts who expand and deepen the movement comprised of those village communities. In contrast to the other popular prophets of the renewal of Israel, who called people out of their villages to experience a new act of deliverance, Jesus was generating a renewal of the people in their village communities.

Renewal of Covenantal Community

At the center of Jesus' renewal of the people/Israel, according to the Gospels' portrayals, was his renewal of the Mosaic covenant that for centuries had

---

4. In the last several decades, theological liberals (especially the leaders of the Jesus Seminar) have pressed an individualistic interpretation of Jesus and his followers that blocks recognition of the political-economic project of his mission. They took over a construction of Jesus and his followers based on a literalistic reading of isolated individual sayings of Jesus: Theissen, *Sociology of the Early Jesus Movement*; cf. the criticism in Horsley, *Sociology and the Jesus Movement*. In Theissen's construction, Jesus was calling individuals to abandon their families and possessions to pursue an itinerant life that included begging for food. Given the historical circumstances, Jesus would thus have been making life much worse for those abandoned families left without a major contributor of the labor necessary to feed the family, pay tribute, taxes, and tithes, and hold off the creditors, dooming them to debt-slavery or worse. The sayings that Theissen and others cite as proof-texts (e.g., "whoever does not hate father and mother . . . cannot be my disciple"), however, are hyperbolic statements of the extreme demands of loyalty to Jesus and his mission.

guided social-economic interaction in the villages.⁵ In both Matthew and Luke (both presumably drawing on the covenant renewal speech in "Q") Jesus begins his mission among the people with a long speech that appears to be programmatic. Particularly striking is Jesus' declaration in the covenant renewal speech in Matthew, "Do not think that I have come to abolish the law or the prophets; I have come not to abolish but to fulfill," followed by the admonition to keep the covenantal commandments in order to maintain justice (the translation "righteousness" is too weak and individualistic; Matt 5:17–20). Jesus then exemplifies specifically what he means in what have been called, misleadingly, "antitheses" (5:21–48). In a patterned series, he first cites one of the commandments (of Moses), then intensifies it by moving into the motivation behind keeping the commandment.

Luke has a parallel but shorter speech (still the longest speech in the Gospel) at the beginning of Jesus' mission (6:20–49). Comparison shows that these are speeches of Mosaic covenant renewal.⁶ They both contain many references and allusions to covenantal commandments and exhortations that we know from Exodus, Leviticus, and Deuteronomy. They both proceed according to the traditional components of the Mosaic covenantal structure:

- a declaration of (God's) deliverance;
- covenantal demands of exclusive loyalty to God as ruler and of justice in social-economic interaction (in village communities); and
- sanctions on keeping those demands (e.g., blessings and curses).

---

5. Scholars of Jesus and the Gospels have tended to miss or ignore the prominence—indeed centrality—of Mosaic covenant renewal in the Gospels and Jesus' teaching for several interrelated reasons. Protestant theology identified the message of the Old Testament generally as Law and that of the New Testament as Gospel. Then New Testament studies developed as a separate subfield from Old Testament/Hebrew Bible studies in which the Mosaic covenant and covenantal laws are central, particularly in the books of torah. The Christian theological agenda was to discern how different the teaching of Jesus was from Judaism, which was (supposedly) focused on the Law, with which the Mosaic covenant was closely interrelated, often virtually synonymous. Jesus-interpreters, moreover, as mentioned before, tended to focus narrowly on individual sayings taken out of their contexts in the Gospels, so that they missed the broader cultural patterns evident in Gospel narratives and especially in Jesus' speeches and dialogues. See Horsley, *Jesus and the Spiral*, chaps 8–9; Horsley with Draper, *Whoever Hears You Hears Me*, chap. 8; Horsley, *Covenant Economics*, chap. 7.

6. Horsley, *Jesus and Empire*, chap. 5; Horsley, *Covenant Economics*, esp. chaps 7 and 10.

As in the covenant ceremony prescribed in the Community Rule of the Qumran community that had withdrawn to the Dead Sea wilderness, the sanctioning blessings and curses have been transformed into a new opening declaration of deliverance: "Blessed are you poor, for yours is the kingdom of God/heaven." The original sanction of blessings and curses have been replaced by the double parable of the houses on the rock and the sand (if you keep or do not keep Jesus' "words," that is, his covenantal commands).

In both Matthew and Luke, moreover, the narrative sets up the speeches as renewals of the Mosaic covenant, which in turn set up the rest of the Gospel story and shorter speeches. In Matthew, after Jesus proclaims the kingdom and heals all kinds of sicknesses in village assemblies, leading crowds to come to him from all areas of Israelite heritage (Galilee etc.), he went up on *the mountain* (as had Moses) and taught his disciples.[7] In Luke, Jesus is up on *the mountain* where he appoints the Twelve as representatives of Israel (undergoing renewal), then comes down where he teaches a great multitude of his disciples.

In the covenantal renewal speeches parallel in Matthew and Luke, Jesus addresses directly the disintegration of village communities under the pressures of Roman imperial rule. The people were evidently blaming themselves for their poverty and illnesses. While the blessings and curses were supposed to function as sanctions to motivate the people to obey the commandments, they had become an explanation of people's fortune or misfortune. If people were suffering sickness, poverty, and hunger, it must be because they or their parents had sinned, that is, broken the covenantal laws and were therefore receiving the curses, illustrated in the episode of Jesus' healing of the paralytic (Mark 2:1–12; John 9:1–3). Jesus' response dealt not just with the paralysis but with the people's assumption about its cause. In declaring that the paralyzed man's sins are forgiven, he addressed the debilitating collective self-blame, releasing healing powers that enabled the man to "take up his bed and walk."

Similarly, in the blessings (and curses) with which the covenant speech in Matthew and Luke begins, Jesus first addresses the people's broken spirit, their assumption that their poverty and distress are the result of their having disobeyed the covenantal laws. In the renewal of the covenant, he transforms the blessings and curses into in a new declaration of deliverance that addresses precisely the way the people have become dysfunctional. In addressing the people's self-blame and despair, Jesus pronounces God's blessing for the poor and hungry.[8] In the Lukan version, he

---

7. See K. C. Hanson, "Jesus on the Mountain."
8. The blessings are *not* spiritualized in Matthew, contrary to a common

correspondingly pronounces woes on the wealthy, reminding the villagers that the wealth of the rich derived from their extraction from the crops of the villagers, leaving them poor and hungry.

After declaring the new deliverance-in-process in the direct rule of God, Jesus presents covenantal demands specifically aimed at overcoming the internal economic and social conflicts that were weakening village communities, threatening their economic viability (Luke/Q 6:27–42). As summarized above, the Roman conquests and demands for tribute, tithes, and taxes by multiple layers of rulers under Roman rule had intensified the economic pressure on the Galilean and other peasants during the several preceding decades. The "moral economy" of the Galilean and other villagers operated according to Mosaic covenantal commandments, customs, and principles aimed at keeping the component households of the village economically viable. Villagers would have been attempting to share their ever-shrinking resources, borrowing from and lending to one another according to the covenantal laws and customs of generous lending at no interest and periodically cancelling debts (Exod 22:25–27; Lev 25:35–37; Deut 15:1–2, 7–8, 12–15). The economic pressures, however, were so heavy that the ability of the people to maintain their commitment to mutual aid had begun to break down.

In restating the demands of the Mosaic covenant, Jesus is focusing on just this disintegration of the village community. He focuses first on economic relations and then on related social interaction in the village. Taken out of the contexts of the covenantal structure and the fundamental social form of the village, "love your enemies" and the associated sayings that Matthew uses in the fifth and sixth "antitheses" of the Sermon on the Mount (Matt 5:38–48) have traditionally been read as commands of nonretaliation against hostile enemies, especially the Roman soldiers. From the context indicated in the content of the sayings, however, it is clear that Jesus is addressing economic and social conflicts in local village life.[9] Lender families, themselves under pressure of the heavy tax burdens, would have been seeking repayment of the loans, but the debtor families would have been unable to pay, leading to local conflicts. Jesus addresses these conflicts with the general principle,

---

interpretation. Rather in the opening of Jesus' covenant renewal speech, Matthew has further transformed the covenantal blessings into the desired interaction among participants in the renewed community: "blessed are (you who are) the meek/peacemakers/ etc."

9. Thus in these commands Jesus is not addressing relations with Roman soldiers, who would not have been present in Galilean villages as occupying troops during the rule of Herod Antipas. Those of us looking for a paradigm of nonviolent direct action might well focus on Jesus' confrontation with the rulers and ruling institutions.

"love your enemies, do good, and lend," and he applies the principle in some typical cases of borrowing and lending that focus the covenant renewal on concrete local conflicts. Since the Matthean version divides the sayings in order to conclude the "antitheses" with a general principle ("Love your [local] enemies"), we will focus on the Lukan version that focuses more on concrete economic interaction throughout 6:27–36.

Many villagers would have been indebted to their neighbors, perhaps partly because they had previously aided them with survival loans and become economically vulnerable themselves. The command (Luke/Q 6:29), "If someone sues you for your cloak, let him take your shirt as well," addresses the desperately needy. The implication, of course, was that the debtor would be standing stark naked, embarrassing the neighbor in front of the whole village (Jesus had a sense of humor!—and a sense of how a neighbor could be motivated by threat of local public embarrassment). The reference to the age-old covenant command is unmistakable: "You shall not deal with others as a creditor. If you take your neighbor's cloak in pawn, you shall restore it before the sun goes down, since it is your neighbor's only covering at night" (Exod 22:25–27; Deut 24:10–13).

In these economic commands (that "update" covenantal commandments), Jesus addresses mainly people in their perpetual role of aiding needy neighbors, insisting that they continue their sharing and generosity (6:30–36). "To the one who asks from you, give, and from the one who borrows, do not ask back . . . But love your enemies, and do good and lend." Having declared the direct rule of God for the people, with its sufficiency for the hungry, Jesus delivers demands for local economic cooperation and sharing that apply traditional covenantal commandments and customs (e.g., Deut 15:7–11) to the economic difficulties of village communities. In the command to "be merciful as your Father is merciful," Jesus calls community members to pattern their generosity on God's generosity. This command also resonates with age-old covenantal tradition, particularly with the similar principle cited in the Levitical scribal collection of customs and laws (Lev 19:2). The principles implicit in these focal cases and the accompanying general exhortation also bear a remarkable resemblance to the third petition in the Lord's Prayer: "Cancel our debts, as we herewith cancel the debts of our debtors."

These commands and rhetorical questions of Jesus that begin with "love your enemies" thus stand directly in the Mosaic covenantal tradition, build on it, and renew the people's commitment to the covenantal demands. The focal instances of lending and borrowing here would have recalled the whole range of such traditional covenantal teachings to the minds of the listeners. To counter the local conflict over borrowing and lending, Jesus thus commands villagers to recommit to the time-honored principles and practices of mutual sharing and cooperation central to covenantal teaching. In an "updating" of the Mosaic covenant, he intensifies the covenantal demands of mutual aid, cooperation, and support, even in the circumstances of intensified economic pressures that probably left most in the village with insufficient resources.

Jesus then speaks to the social disputes that were evidently rooted in the economic conflicts among neighbors in the communities (Luke/Q 6:37–42). "Do not judge and you will not be judged." These instructions are also rooted in the Mosaic covenantal tradition, as can be seen through the window provided by Lev 19:17–18. The appended "parable" and rhetorical questions insist that the people stop accusing one another and return to mutual support in the community.

In accordance with the traditional pattern of the Mosaic covenant, the motivating sanction forms the concluding step (6:43–49//Matt 7:21–27). Since the blessings and curses had become problematic, inducing people to blame themselves, Jesus tells a double parable of houses built on rock and sand (6:46–49). The admonitions that precede the double parable (6:43–45) function somewhat similarly to the Matthean intensification or sharpening of the covenantal commandments (Matt 5:20–48), to probe the motivational bases of covenantal behavior. In this regard, Jesus' renewal of the Mosaic covenant stands in a long prophetic tradition that goes back at least as far as Jeremiah's prophecy of the new covenant written on the heart rather than on stone tablets (Jer 31:27–34).

In his covenant renewal speech, Jesus thus addresses economic and social conflicts among households/families under the economic pressures of Roman imperial rule that were disintegrating the fabric of reciprocal economic support that had traditionally held village communities together. The covenant renewal speech, however, was more than mere teaching of economic ethics or values. It was a reenactment of the covenant, in "performative speech," which enacts what it states. In the role of a prophet like Moses, Jesus-in-community enacted renewed commitment to the practice of mutual support among the component families of the villages. This renewed mutual support, moreover, would have strengthened the solidarity of the community to better withstand and resist the economic pressures from the rulers.

Renewal of the Mosaic covenant is also central in the Markan story, although the structural components are not so explicit as in the covenant speeches in Matthew and Luke.[10] As Jesus is completing his mission of

---

10. More fully discussed, in connection with the covenant renewal that runs

healing and proclamation in the villages of Galilee and beyond, he engages in a series of dialogues, each of which climaxes in a law-like principle (Mark 10:2–45; followed to an extent by the Matthean and Lukan stories). In the course of the dialogues, Jesus cites nearly all of the covenantal commandments, insisting that they must be faithfully observed. The dialogues, moreover, focus on subjects that the Mosaic covenant and covenantal laws and customs were meant to guide and protect: marriage as the basis of households/families that constituted the community, membership in the community, the economic exploitation that the commandments prohibited to protect people's livelihood, and leadership of the movement (of communities) that was to serve and not dominate. Just as the covenant renewal speeches in Matthew 5–7 and Luke 6:20–49 are addressed to the villagers' concrete circumstances of poverty and disintegration of community, so also the covenantal dialogues in Mark are addressed to concrete economic difficulties facing the people.

The Pharisees' question in the first dialogue signals the move into covenantal issues. Two of the six covenantal commandments pertaining to social-economic relations focused on marriage and the family (no adultery and honor father and mother). The command prohibiting divorce-and-remarriage that concludes this dialogue is one of many indications in the Gospels that Jesus, far from being anti-family, was renewing the household/family, the fundamental (social-economic!) unit of production, consumption, and reproduction in any agrarian society. Presupposed here and evident in later rabbinic discussions, marriage and divorce concerned not merely marital relations, but economic rights, especially for the wife-mother, and use and inheritance of the land that was the basis of household/family livelihood. Lax laws on divorce, like the Deuteronomic provision referred to here (Deut 24:1–4; Mark 10:3–4) could enable ambitious men to consolidate their control of land through divorce and remarriage to the detriment of others.[11] Jesus here again (as in Matthew 5:20–48) intensified the covenantal commandment on adultery: divorce for the purpose of remarriage is tantamount to adultery. This command reinforces the patriarchal family, including the subordination of the wife.

---

through the Markan story, in Horsley, *Hearing the Whole Story*, chap. 8; and again in Horsley, *Covenant Economics*, chap. 8.

11. Might Jesus and/or those in his movement(s) have been thinking of Herod Antipas, whom John the Baptist had condemned for divorce and remarriage to Herodias, the wife of his brother (Mark 6:17)? See the role of John as prophet summarized by Josephus (*Ant.* 18.106–118), which helps fill in a bit of background to the legend of his imprisonment and beheading in Mark 6. Excellent critical discussion in Webb, *John the Baptizer*, 366–70. Whatever Antipas' motives and expectations, the scheme backfired.

In the historical situation in which families were struggling under economic pressures from their rulers, however, the principal concern of this command would probably have been to reaffirm the economic rights of women in marriage and household in the patriarchal society.

This dialogue about divorce and remarriage should probably be read in connection with Jesus' earlier reaffirmation of covenantal community at the conclusion of the first narrative step in the Markan story. The appearance of Jesus' mother and brothers outside the house (in Mark 3:31–35) sets up his rhetorical question, "Who are my mother and brothers and sisters?" His answer that they are "those who do the will of God," that is, those who keep the (Mosaic) covenant, suggests that the mission of Jesus aims to renew (local) covenantal community in ways that would function as a replacement or aid for families that were disintegrating. Is the absence of the patriarchal head of household significant in this conceptualization of renewed familial-covenantal community?

The foil for the next dialogue (10:13–16) is the disciples' discussion about who is the greatest and their rejection of children immediately following Jesus' second announcement that he must be martyred. A reminder that "childhood" is an invention of modern Western society may help in guarding against the frequent sentimentalizing of the principle that one must receive the kingdom of God "like a little child." In a traditional agrarian society, children were the lowest-status members of families and village communities, not necessarily recognized yet as persons. Children hence would have been the opposite of the wealthy and powerful that the disciples appear to be thinking of in trying to imagine living in the kingdom of God (as in the request of James and John, Mark 10:35–37). The principle that concludes this dialogue thus has a similar effect to the declaration in the covenant renewal speech in Luke, that the kingdom of God is offered to the poor, as opposed to the wealthy.

It is significant that in the Markan dialogues of renewal of covenantal community the economics of renewal receives the most attention, in a series of three steps (Mark 10:17–22, 23–25, 26–31). Though the "man" is not identified further in the Markan story (only Luke 18:18 presents him as "a ruler"), his question identifies him as wealthy. While peasants would be worrying mainly about where the next meal is coming from, only a wealthy person would be looking for "eternal life." Jesus makes a point of walking him (and the audience) through the covenantal commandments that govern social-economic relations. "You shall not defraud" is a pointed substitution for "you shall not covet-and-seize."[12] Jesus' audience of peasant villagers

---

12. Again, see Chaney, "Coveting Your Neighbor's House," in *Peasants, Prophets,*

would have recognized that the only way the man could have gained his wealth was by "defrauding" (other) needy peasants desperate for a loan or day-labor when what remained of their crops after taxes and tribute were insufficient to live on. His wealth indicated that he had obviously not been observing the commandments but had been flouting the commandments not to covet and steal. Jesus makes the (wealthy) man questing for "eternal life" into an example of what not to do in the community's economic relations, that is, not to take advantage of one another's need.

In the second step, Jesus presents the appropriate renewed covenantal principle: it will be impossible for the wealthy to enter the kingdom. The further statement of the principle, "it is easier for a camel to go through the eye of a needle than for someone who is rich to enter the kingdom of God," is a great example of caustic peasant humor. The hostility of the villagers to the wealthy is not even veiled.

The third step in the focus specifically on covenantal economic relations brings the dialogue directly to bear on the concrete circumstances and project of the communities of the movement in which the Markan story was produced. Peter articulates the puzzlement of the astonished disciples who are wondering, "then who can be delivered? Look, we left everything and followed you." Jesus' response is one of the key passages in the Gospels that indicates how concretely economic the program of Jesus' mission and movement(s) was in the circumstances in which they lived in the Roman imperial (dis-)order in Palestine. Understanding what Jesus is saying enables us to recognize that "and in the age to come eternal life" is a "throw-away" line (mocking the man who was seeking eternal life). The disciples (and Jesus-communities) are to anticipate restoration of their families/households as villagers working on their lands. Jesus declares that they will most certainly have economic sufficiency—conveyed in the hyperbole of "a hundredfold." This is to happen "in this time," that is in the future of the movement, but "with persecutions." The rulers in the Roman imperial (dis-)order that feel threatened by the resistance of the movement of renewal will be taking measures to suppress them. The renewal of village communities included at its foundation the economic renewal that was happening in the coming of the direct rule of God. Mutual commitment to observing the economic principles of the covenant, in which no one takes advantage of others' circumstances, would result in economic sufficiency for all in the community. But they were to have no illusions about the continuing political-economic power of the hostile Roman order in Palestine and Syria.

---

and Political Economy, chap. 3.

The final dialogue of the series focuses on leadership in the movement that is to be diametrically the opposite of the Roman imperial order. The request of James and John for highest positions of power in the kingdom, following Jesus' third announcement that he must be martyred, is the foil. Jesus' response, that focuses attention again on his impending martyrdom, declares that leadership in his movement is to be just the opposite of the "great ones"/rulers of the nations (the Romans) who lord it over their subjects, becoming hyperwealthy as well. The leaders of his movement(s) are to be servants of the movement. In the Markan narrative, and evidently in the Matthean as well, this dialogue includes an economic aspect in Jesus' reference to his own martyrdom, which had become a powerful motivating factor in the expansion of his movement(s). His death would be a ransom for many, "ransom" referring to the covenantal mechanism by which those who had fallen into debt-slavery could be ransomed and their land, which had fallen into others' control, be redeemed. It may have been unrealistic, but the story seems to be anticipating that, by energizing the movement, Jesus' martyr death would enable the renewal of community to gain sufficient cooperation that it could redeem debt-slaves and families' land. Also in the Markan narrative, this ransom fits with Jesus' promise at the end of the dialogue on economic life in the renewed community (10:28–30) that those (the disciples) who left their family and land would receive back (in the hyperbole of "a hundred-fold") family and land in this time/age.

Other Episodes of Covenant Renewal

While it is not possible to comment on every episode in the Gospels, it should be noted that a number of other episodes in the Markan Gospel story and/or in the Matthean and Lukan stories and speeches form parts of the focus on renewing the Mosaic covenant as central to the social-economic renewal of the people of Israel. John's baptism of repentance introduces covenant renewal in the overall Gospel story. Then, in the climax of the Gospel story in both Mark and Matthew, Jesus transforms the celebration of the Passover meal he shares with his disciples into a ceremony of covenant renewal (the central symbol of the blood of the covenant in his words refer to the original covenant ceremony on Sinai, in Exod 24), which continued in the communities of Jesus-loyalists. Among the speeches parallel in the Matthean and Lukan Gospels (but not in the Markan), Jesus' exhortation to "seek first the direct rule of God" and subsistence food and clothing would take care of themselves presupposes the recommitment to cooperative sharing enacted in the covenant renewal speech.

Some key episodes included only in the Lukan story should disabuse us of the previously standard (and still influential) theological scheme in which Christianity originated in Jesus' criticism or even attack on "the Jewish Law." Heard/read in narrative context, moreover, these episodes indicate that the Lukan Gospel as well as the Markan and Matthean, like the mission of Jesus whose story they tell, was addressed to movements of ordinary people. Both the parable of the "good Samaritan" and the story of the obscenely rich man and the beggar Lazarus, in narrative context, set up elite figures as "straw men."

The parable of "the good Samaritan" follows closely upon Jesus' commission of his disciples to extend his proclamation of the direct rule of God in village communities and his thanksgiving that his "Father" had revealed his renewal of Israel to ordinary folks ("children") and not to "the sages" (the scribal elite). "Behold," up pops a scholar of torah/law. Mocking his literacy and learning, Jesus asks what he finds "written" in the torah/law. He answers with what had by late second-temple times become the standard summary of the torah, the "double" command, the very elaborate command to love God and the almost incidental second, to love neighbor. The torah-scholar, who almost certainly did not live in the close social-economic interaction of a village community, naively asks, "So who is my neighbor?" In the parable, the priest and the Levite, staff of the temple-state and both presumably well-versed in the torah, see the beaten man and pass on by. Astoundingly a Samaritan, despised by the Judeans, especially since the Judean high priests had conquered the Samaritans and destroyed their temple, came to the beaten man's aid. The parable forces the torah-scholar to recognize that it was the Samaritan who responded to the obvious need of the man who proved neighbor to him. The command to "go and do likewise"—respond to people's needs, as in the demands of the covenant renewal speech—is directed through the dense torah-scholar to the disciples and hearers/readers of the Gospel story.

Following Jesus' declaration that "you cannot serve God and wealth" and, further, the declaration that the torah and the prophets led to John (presumably his renewal of covenant in the baptism of repentance) after which the direct rule of God is proclaimed, comes the statement that the whole (Mosaic) torah is still in effect (16:13–18). This stands parallel to the similar statement toward the beginning of the Matthean covenant renewal speech (Matt 5:17–20). The ensuing story of the obscenely wealthy man who utterly ignores the desperate beggar at the gate of his mansion illustrates that social-economic relations should and must be regulated by "Moses and the prophets." The direct rule of God consists in social-economic relations being guided by the covenantal torah of Moses and the pronouncements of the prophets.

As portrayed in the Gospels of Mark, Matthew, and Luke, Jesus in his mission of renewal healed and pronounced the direct rule of God in the villages of Galilee and beyond, households and village communities that were disintegrating under the impact of Roman conquest and the demands of multiple layers of rulers for tribute, taxes, and tithes. The focus of his mission was the renewal of the Mosaic covenant, especially its commandments of no exploitation of one another and its commands and customs of mutual aid and cooperation, even in the circumstances in which all were struggling for subsistence. The promise was that if the people gave priority to "seeking the direct rule of God" (as articulated in the covenantal commandments) and engaged in mutual aid (generous giving to the needy) and cooperation (mutual cancellation of debts), all would have sufficient food and clothing. And this would strengthen the village communities in their efforts to resist the intensified exploitation by their rulers.

5

Prophetic Condemnation of the Rulers' Control and Extraction

The Gospels also present Jesus' mission as a rejection of and resistance against the high priestly rulers in Jerusalem and their extractions from the people. This has been interpreted—tragically—as opposition to Judaism. What could intelligibly be referred to as Judaism, however, did not emerge until well after the Roman destruction of the temple and high priestly aristocracy in Jerusalem. When something that could more appropriately be referred to as Christianity did develop, some of its texts did blame, reject, and condemn "the Jews." And (at least until recently) modern Christian biblical scholarship, as a branch of Christian theology, framed its interpretation of Jesus and the Gospels as opposed to Judaism. The Gospels, however, present Jesus as engaged in the renewal of the people of Israel in proclaiming the direct rule of God and performing exorcisms and healings, starting in the villages of Galilee. The Matthean story even has Jesus instruct the disciples to "go only to the lost sheep of the house of Israel." In the Gospel stories one finds no rejection of "the Jews" and no indication of a mission to "the Gentiles." The Gospels present Jesus' mission as the renewal of the people of Israel, indeed as the fulfillment of Israelite tradition and history.

The Gospels, however, present Jesus as adamantly opposed to the rulers of Israel, who were appointed and backed by the Romans, and evidently the temple-state they headed, mainly because of their economic extractions from the people. The gospels' presentation of Jesus' mission fits the historical context of the intensifying conflict between the high priestly rulers and the people in Roman Palestine, as known from Josephus' histories and memories in rabbinic texts, as discussed in chap. 3. As the dominating political-economic-religious institution in Judea, the temple-state with its high priestly heads, was the face and representative of imperial rule of the (Judean and by the end of the second century BCE the general Israelite) people. The temple itself Herod had rebuilt in grand Hellenistic style, with a Roman eagle over a main gate and daily sacrifices for (the divine) Roma and Caesar. Wealth continued to pile up in the temple, tempting Pontius Pilate, for example, to expropriate some of the sacred treasure known as *qorban* to pay for an aqueduct (Josephus, *War* 2.175–177). The expanded high priestly aristocracy consisted of four principal families, all inherited from Herod, from which Roman governors appointed figures to the high priestly office. And, as noted in chap. 3, these families had been using their positions of power to considerably expand their own wealth.

Condemnation of the Pharisees, Servants and Representatives of the Temple-State

While Jesus' opposition to the rulers in Jerusalem comes to a dramatic climax in his confrontation with the high priestly heads of the temple-state, the Gospel stories present his mission as independent of and objectionable to the temple-state from the beginning. It seems as if his healings and exorcisms (and giving the people authority to forgive one another's sins) might displace the functions of the priests and scribes in temple-system (e.g., sin-offerings in the temple, Mark 2:1–12; stated more explicitly, Matt 9:1–8). In what became the standard theological scheme of the origins of "Christianity," the scribes and Pharisees were misunderstood as the principal representatives of the supposedly overly legalistic and ritualistic old religion of Judaism. If we consider the Gospels as whole stories, including the speeches of Jesus, it is clear rather that they, in agreement with the Judean historian Josephus (e.g., *Ant.* 13.296–298), present the scribes and Pharisees as the representatives of the Jerusalem temple and its heads, the priestly aristocracy. In the Markan narrative, for example, the scribes and Pharisees "come down from Jerusalem" to condemn Jesus' actions and those of his loyalists. While Jesus' direct confrontation with the high priestly rulers in the temple forms the climax of the Gospel story after his mission in the villages of Galilee and beyond, the opposition to his actions by the representatives of the rulers begins early in the story, as the Pharisees (and Herodians) plot how to destroy him (Mark 3:6 and parallels).

In response to their opposition, Jesus declares God's condemnation of the scribes and Pharisees, mainly for their role in the rulers' extractions from the resources the people need for their own subsistence. The long-standard Christian theological misunderstanding of Jesus as opposed to Judaism and the Jewish law was focused on what is only the rhetoric of Jesus' counter-attacks on the scribes and Pharisees. He mocks their focus on particular purity concerns and ritual requirements. But he then zeroes in on their role as representatives of the temple-state and its effects on the people. This can be seen most clearly in three particular episodes in the Gospels.

Both Matthew and Luke include a series of prophetic woes against the scribes (lawyers) and Pharisees (Matt 23; Luke 11:37–52).[1] Following a traditional form known from Israelite prophets such as Amos, Isaiah, and Habakkuk, these are indictments for actions that exploit the people followed by declaration of God's judgment. After mocking their cleansing the outside of the cup and dish, he charges that inside they themselves are full of extortion and wickedness. After mocking them for being so scrupulous as to tithe even herbs not clearly subject to tithing requirements, he charges them with neglecting the weightier matters of (covenantal) torah (the law), such as justice and mercy. He indicts them for laying heavy (economic) burdens on people's shoulders and not being willing to alleviate them with (the flick of the pen in) their scribal fingers. These indictments lead to the declaration that the blood of all the prophets killed by their ancestors will be required of "this generation," that is the scribes and Pharisees and their high priestly patrons.

In the Markan story (7:1–13), when the Pharisees and some scribes (again) "come down from Jerusalem" and observe Jesus' disciples eating with unwashed hands, they charge them with not observing "the traditions of the (Pharisaic) elders."[2] Jesus first castigates their laws supplementary to the written (scriptural) laws of purity as not being of divine origin. But then he changes the subject from purity to economic subsistence. He charges that by pressing their traditions of the elders the Pharisees are rejecting the very commandment of God. He focuses on the commandment that was surely the most sensitive to peasants, that is, being able to feed their families. By urging the people to "devote" (*qorban*) a portion of their crops to God (i.e., the temple), the Pharisees cause the people to violate the commandment to "honor your father and mother." That is, Jesus condemns the Pharisees for insisting that the people "devote" to the temple economic resources needed locally to feed their families.[3]

---

1. More extensive analysis and discussion in Horsley with Draper, *Whoever Hears You Hears Me*, 285–91.

2. This and the next paragraph are dependent on the fuller analysis and discussion in Horsley, *Hearing the Whole Story*, 161–76; and Horsley, *Jesus and the Politics of Roman Palestine*, chap. 6.

3. Unless it is purely a rhetorical device, the location of this episode in Galilee adds another dimension to the Pharisees' urging the people there to "devote" a portion of their crops to God (the temple). After 4 BCE, the Romans had appointed Herod Antipas as ruler of Galilee. Presumably the Jerusalem rulers no longer had jurisdiction to impose taxation on Galileans during the lifetime of Jesus and thereafter. Jesus' charges

At the end of the Markan and Lukan narratives of Jesus' confrontation with the high priests in the Jerusalem temple (12:38—13:2; par. Luke 20:43—21:7), Jesus warns, "Beware of the scribes, . . . who devour widows' house(hold)s." In the immediately ensuing narrative sequence, a widow gives two copper coins to the temple treasury. This is all that remains of her "household," that is all that remains of her living, which has thus been "devoured" by the scribal staff of the temple-state who were urging the people to support the temple. And this is what leads immediately in narrative sequence to Jesus' announcement that the temple is about to be destroyed.

Jesus' Prophetic Condemnation and Direct Action against the Temple-State

All four Gospels present Jesus as an Israelite prophet acting out God's condemnation of the heads of the Jerusalem temple-state that the Romans had imposed as rulers of Judea. Near the outset of its narrative of Jesus' mission, the Gospel of John presents Jesus as carrying out a prophetic demonstration against the temple, announcing that it would be destroyed (John 2:13-22). This is often missed because John has traditionally been taken as a "spiritual" Gospel. The depoliticizing interpretation of the Johannine story according to a standard Christian theological scheme has had particularly tragic consequences insofar as "the Judeans" in John have been taken as a reference to "the Jews" (and Judaism) in general. A careful reading of the Johannine narrative with attention to context (setting), however, indicates that while "the Judeans" sometimes refers to those who live in Judea generally (many of whom the story portrays as responding positively to Jesus), more often the term refers to the heads and staff of the temple-state in Jerusalem, and is sometimes even synonymous with "the high priests and the Pharisees." In the Johannine story Jesus does not oppose "the Jews" and "Judaism" generally, but the rulers in Jerusalem who head the temple and its festivals, and who are beholden to the Roman governor.[4] His forcible demonstration in the temple is the first and most dramatic in a series of confrontations with the high priests and the Pharisees.

In the "Synoptic Gospels" the stories come to their climax in Jesus' sustained confrontation with the high priestly rulers and the temple they headed

---

suggest that *qorban* was a device by which the Jerusalem temple-state could attempt to continue some economic support from the Galileans, further threatening their economic viability.

4. For fuller elaboration of this reading of John, see Horsley and Thatcher, *John, Jesus, and the Renewal of Israel*, esp. 39–41, 111–12, 122, 127, 161–66.

in Jerusalem. Jesus' direct action against the temple leads the high priests to have him arrested and to hand him over to the Roman governor for execution as a leader of insurrection ("king of the Judeans"). Jesus' prophetic pronouncements against the rulers, moreover, like his woes against the scribes and Pharisees, stand in a deep tradition of Israelite prophets such as Amos, Micah, Isaiah, and Jeremiah. In the earliest prophecies attributed to them,[5] these prophets had pronounced God's indictment and judgment of kings, their officers, and/or the Jerusalem temple and the Bethel temple for their economic exploitation of the people. In comparison with the contemporary popular prophets (and kings/messiahs), such as Theudas, Jesus in the Gospels engaged in a bolder and more direct confrontation and condemnation of the rulers and ruling institution in the Jerusalem temple.

In the Gospels, Jesus stages his sustained confrontation with the rulers at the Passover festival in Jerusalem, perhaps the principal expression of the irreconcilable contradiction and conflict between Israelite tradition and the Roman imperial order that focused on the rulers' extraction of the people's produce and resources. Passover was the annual celebration of the liberation of the people from political-economic bondage under Egyptian imperial rule. Originally observed in the local family setting, it had long been institutionalized as a pilgrimage festival in the Jerusalem temple, a key concrete as well as symbolic component of economic centralization that extracted resources from the people.[6] For the people, however, Passover remained a celebration of their formative liberation. Under Roman imperial rule, Passover became the occasion for peoples' protest of their current subjugation. Fearing that the celebration by crowds who came in from the villages might get completely out of hand, the Roman governors made a practice of bringing their troops into Jerusalem and posting them on the porticoes of the newly constructed Herodian temple. But that only exacerbated the symbolic face-off that dramatized the structural political-economic-religious conflict. In the most overt manifestation of the conflict, under the governor Cumanus, when the crowd erupted into protest, the governor unleashed his troops against them (Josephus, *Ant.* 20.105–109; *War* 2.223–226).[7] The Gospels place Jesus' confrontation with the rulers precisely in this volatile situation of conflict.

---

5. Coote, *Amos among the Prophets*.

6. The centralization of the Passover celebration (and other sacrifices) in the temple required peasants to sell produce for coins and then buy animals (at mark-up) suitable for sacrifice in the temple and expend other resources required for pilgrimage festival(s) in Jerusalem.

7. On popular protests in Jerusalem, particularly Passover protests, see Horsley, *Jesus and the Spiral of Violence*, 34–35, 90–99.

The Gospels' portrayal of Jesus' prophetic demonstration and pronouncements against the temple and high priests is highly significant in yet another way. The crowds at the Passover festival provided a kind of protection for the prophet. In preindustrial capital cities, the rulers were hesitant to take direct action against protests and demonstrations lest their repressive action provoke wider protest or prolonged rioting. The Gospels portray Jesus as protected during the day by the crowds that viewed him as a prophet with divine authority, then leaving Jerusalem at night for a hiding place on the Mount of Olives (see esp. the narrative in Mark 11:11, 18–19; 13:3; 14:1–3, 12–17, 26, 43–49; and parallels).

The sheer number of episodes in the Gospels in which Jesus pronounces God's condemnation of the temple and high priests attests to how prominent this was in his mission and for the movements that produced the Gospels.[8] While it has often gone unnoticed in previous interpretation, the economic dimension is clear and even focal.

Jesus' confrontation with the rulers begins with his forcible *demonstration in the temple*, "overturning tables of the money changers" and "not allowing anyone to carry anything through the temple [courtyard]." This can hardly be construed as a mere "cleansing" of a house of worship from "corruption." He was effectively blocking operations integral to (not "corruptions" of) the functioning of the religious-political-economy of the temple. In interpretation of his disruptive action, Jesus recites (appeals to the "written" authority of) an unidentified "prophecy." That it is a combination of lines from two different prophets (what modern scholars recognize from printed editions of canonized books), Isaiah (56:7) and Jeremiah (7:11), suggests that the prophecy was probably being recited from (oral) popular tradition (not from written scrolls). The second line, "you have made it a bandits' den," would have been an unmistakable reference to Jeremiah's famous prophecy against the temple (7:1–15): God had condemned the temple because, in taking tithes and offerings (and perhaps interest on loans) from the people, its officials were stealing from them, in violation of the Mosaic covenant commandments, confident that their sacred position and space would keep them secure. Thus they were like brigands who stole from people and then headed for safety to their hideout.[9]

---

8. The interpretation of Jesus' prophetic action and speech of God's impending judgment of the temple here depends somewhat on earlier analysis in Horsley, *Jesus and the Spiral*, 285–300. See also the insightful discussion emphasizing the economic dimension of the temple and Jesus' prophetic action in Herzog, *Jesus, Justice, and the Reign of God*, esp. 137–43.

9. The first line of Jesus' prophetic statement, "my house shall be called a house of prayer for all peoples," as indicated by its original context in Isaiah 56, was part of

CONDEMNATION OF THE RULERS' CONTROL AND EXTRACTION

Jesus' dramatic disruption of temple business was a symbolic prophetic demonstration, in the tradition of Jeremiah having walked around Jerusalem with an ox-yoke on his neck (Jeremiah 27-28). Jesus was symbolically acting out God's condemnation not just of the building (so massively rebuilt by Herod) but of the temple system, because of its exploitation of the people indicated in the reference to Jeremiah's well-known prophecy. The high priests and scribes knew what Jesus had just done: from this point, "they kept looking for a way to kill him."[10]

Jesus tells the Parable of the Vineyard and Tenants as a prophecy against the high priests (Mark 12:1-12 and par.). The vineyard parable builds on a well-known prophecy of Isaiah (Isa 5:1-10) that began as an ironic, almost sarcastic "love song" about a vineyard that turned into a prophetic condemnation of the rulers. In both the historical context of Isaiah and again in that of Jesus, a vineyard was a significant symbol of the dynamics of the political-economic structure in which the rulers used their wealth and power to exploit and impoverish the peasants.[11] The lines of indictment of the rulers in Isaiah's prophecy (5:6) indicate how "a man" went about building a vineyard: by "joining house to house and adding field to field." That is, by manipulating needy villagers into debt, he came to control their fields on which he planted vines — and dug a pit for a winepress, built a storage tower, and hired tenants (perhaps the very peasants whose fields he now controlled). This is just what high priestly figures (and probably Herodian figures as well) had been doing in the hill country of northwest Judea at the time of Jesus (as mentioned above). This process was only too familiar to the high priests who were listening to the story about the vineyard; but also to the wider audience of Passover pilgrims who may have lost control of their

---

a prophetic appeal to make the (second) temple a center where God could gather the outcasts of Israel and other peoples (Isa 56:8). This would have been virtually the opposite of the actual political-economic-religious function of the temple as known from other sources.

10. Just as the earlier officers of the temple sought to kill Jeremiah after his oracle pronouncing God's judgment against the temple (Jeremiah 26). That the point of Jesus' action is indeed that God is about to destroy the temple is confirmed from the way the Markan and Matthean narratives frame the demonstration with the analogy of his cursing the fig-tree (Mark 11:12-14, 20-24 //Matt 21:20-22). Jesus makes the connection in an ominous declaration: "Have faith in God. Truly I tell you, if you say to this mountain [on which the temple stands], 'Be taken up and thrown into the sea,' and . . . trust that what you say will come to pass, it will be done for you."

11. Herzog places interpretation of the parable squarely into this historical context (*Parables as Subversive Speech*, 98-113), which is further sketched out in Horsley, *Galilee*, 132-37, 205-21. The mistranslation of "lord of the vineyard" as "owner of the vineyard," which suggests private property, is a later economic concept that should not be projected onto land-tenure in late-second-temple Judea.

fields/land and would have silently cheered at the resistance of the tenants and even their scheme to retake control of their fields once the heir was out of the way, as Jesus shifts the focus to the tenants. The high priests, however, knew very well that (in the official ideology of the temple-state) they held their positions of power and privilege as regents of God but, instead of producing "justice," had exploited the people. They would have recognized that they were the analogue of the tenants in the parable. Probably from their own practices, they knew very well what "the lord of the vineyard" would do to such tenants, drew the analogy, and recognized that Jesus had told the parable as a prophecy of God's condemnation of them.[12]

Just as Jesus completes his confrontation with the high priests and scribes in the Gospel stories he declares that the temple will be destroyed. Then in his trial before the high priestly court he is accused of having declared:

> I will destroy this temple that is made with hands,
> and in three days I will build another not made with hands.
> (Mark 14:58 and par.)

As he is hanging on the cross he is mocked with the same charge of destroying the temple (15:29). This accusation in the Gospel texts is an adaptation of what would have been a double saying in Israelite prophetic tradition in which the prophet speaks for God (the "I" is God speaking). The prophecy of destruction is clear enough: the temple made with hands would have been the massive edifice rebuilt by Herod (still under construction at great cost at the time of Jesus' mission and the formation of the Gospel story). As for "the temple not made with hands,"[13] the clue to this prophetic statement by Jesus may lie in the parallel to this saying in the Gospel of Thomas 71, where "house" of God, a synonym for the temple, appears. In Judean scribal texts (e.g., the Animal Vision in 1 Enoch 85–90) "the house of God"

---

12. Christian interpreters, some keying off the cornerstone in the lines from Psalm 118, take this parable as an allegory, with the lord of the vineyard as God, "his son" as Jesus Christ, the tenants as "the Jews," and "the others" to whom the vineyard is given as (Gentile) Christians. This allegorization is forced; it does not quite work, certainly not in the context of the whole Markan or Matthean or Lukan Gospel story. Certainly the Lukan narrative does not take the stone as Jesus Christ. This allegory not only became one of the principal textual bases of the Christian doctrine that Christianity had replaced (superseded) Judaism, but also left Christians with an image of God as a punitive absentee landlord. That the Gospel stories and their parables were not (yet) biblical relativizes their authority claims as "the Word of God" so that authoritarian images of God need not be perpetuated.

13. Sanders argued in *Jesus and Judaism* that this refers to a rebuilt temple in the future. But there was no such tradition, even in scribal texts, of a rebuilt temple; see the critical survey of key Judean texts in Horsley, *Jesus and the Spiral of Violence*, 286–92.

referred to *the people*, while "the tower" on that house symbolized the temple, which was not to be rebuilt in the future restoration of the people (cf. 1QS 5:5-7; 8:4-10; 9:3-6; 4QFlor 1:1-13 in which the Qumran community understood itself as the temple/house of God). Jesus' prophecy is evidently a declaration that God will destroy "the house of God" = the temple, but rebuild "the house of God" = the people.

Another prophecy of Jesus (Matt 23:37-38//Luke 13:34) is a lament over the impending destruction of the ruling house of Jerusalem because it had exploited rather than protected the "children" (a standing image for the villages subject to a ruling city, as in Isa 51:17-18; Deut 32:11).

These prophecies of condemnation of the high priestly rulers and the temple cannot be reduced to mere "criticism" of "corruption." As earlier in Israelite tradition, prophecies uttered in performative speech were tantamount to announcements of God's (imminent) action. That Judean rulers found them threatening and took repressive action is illustrated by their arrest of that other prophet named Jesus, the son of Hananiah, who similarly pronounced doom on Jerusalem (Josephus, *War* 6.300-309). An important aspect of the (at least temporary) power of these prophecies and especially of the (forcible) prophetic demonstration that blocked temple business, was the authority that Jesus, like John, had among the people who, in the volatile situation in Jerusalem, could generate more widespread resistance (Mark 11:27-33). The high priestly rulers could only take action against the prophet surreptitiously.

Finally, in recognizing the direct action and ominous prophetic statements in condemnation of the temple-state, we should recognize that Jesus' confrontation against the rulers also takes aim directly at Roman rule, specifically at Roman extraction of the tribute.[14] The Pharisees and the Herodians evidently recognize that his prophetic condemnation of the temple and high priests is also an attack on the Roman imperial order in Palestine. They shrewdly ask him the question that will entrap him: "Is it lawful to pay tribute to Caesar?" Pompey and Caesar had laid Judea under tribute (as discussed above). It was reinstated (certainly) by 6 CE, with the high priests responsible for its collection. Meanwhile, Caesar had come to be honored throughout the empire (including by Herod the Great) as divine Lord and Savior. The Judean scribal dissidents whom Josephus calls "the Fourth Philosophy," who (he says) agreed basically with the Pharisees and were led by a Pharisee and a scribal teacher, had organized serious resistance to the tribute in 6 CE. They argued that Israelites could not render tribute to Caesar since

---

14. Further analysis and discussion in Horsley, *Jesus and the Spiral of Violence*, 306-17.

they already had a Lord and Master, as noted above. Thus the Pharisees and everyone else listening to the confrontation knew that it was not lawful, forbidden by the first two commandments: "no other god" and "do not bow down and serve . . ." But the Romans viewed nonpayment as tantamount to insurrection—hence the entrapment of the question.

Jesus first tricked the Pharisees into "showing their hand" (they had a coin with Caesar's image). Then, avoiding saying "no" directly, he skillfully crafted a reply that everyone would have understood: "Give to Caesar the things that belong to Caesar, and to God the things that belong to God." For Israelites, all belonged to God and nothing to Caesar. In this cagy reply, Jesus had declared that Israelites did not owe tribute, although the Gospel stories give no indication that he called for active resistance to its payment. Surely Jesus and the loyalists who produced the Gospels knew that active public refusal to pay the tribute would have led the Romans to retaliate with brutal military suppression.

This cagy reply provides a significant indication of the overall political-economic-religious strategy of Jesus' mission and movement(s) as portrayed in the Gospel stories and speeches: the renewal of the people in recommitment to covenantal sharing and cooperation in their constituent village communities in opposition and resistance to their rulers, but without taking provocative collective action that would evoke brutally destructive Roman military action. Unlike other popular prophets who also led movements in mid-first century CE, Jesus did not summon followers out of their families and villages in anticipation of some fantastic divine act of deliverance like those of old. Contrary to modern interpretation—especially modern Christian individualistic interpretation—the teachings of Jesus were not statements of ideals or values for individual "discipleship." Rather Jesus' mission and movement focused on the renewal of the constituent village communities of the people that were beginning to disintegrate under the burdens of intensified extraction of their economic resources by their multiple layers of rulers. Jesus' mission and movement portrayed in the Gospels involved collective action in implementing what might well be called a concrete political-economic program of renewal of those village communities. In performative speech that enacted what it pronounced, the covenant-renewal speeches generated the people's (re-)commitment to mutual aid and cooperation in those village communities according to the Mosaic covenantal principles that had long governed local social-economic relations.

The assumptions of the Mosaic covenant were that the people, in their households/families and village communities had economic rights to a subsistence livelihood and that the community (people) as a whole had responsibility to ensure that they remained economically viable. The mutual aid and cooperation in the covenant renewal, people cancelling their needy neighbors' debts as they petitioned God for cancellation of their debts (in the Lord's Prayer) would have enabled the component families to regain and maintain a subsistence living in the face of the demands for tithes, taxes, and tribute from their rulers. And the renewal of mutual aid and cooperation would have enabled village communities to resist further deterioration due to the extractions of the Romans and their client rulers.

A further key assumption of the Mosaic covenantal tradition was that the people did not owe and should not really yield some of their produce that they needed for support of their families to human rulers, such as kings and high priests, much less to imperial rulers. And again as in the long Israelite tradition of prophets such as Elijah, Isaiah, and Jeremiah, a key aspect of the broader role of Jesus as the prophet of renewal was to pronounce God's judgment against rulers who exploited the people economically. Again, as in Israelite history and tradition, while rulers feared prophets because of their authority with and support by the people, they were all the more determined to silence them. In the first century CE, Roman governors sent out their military forces to suppress their movements and kill the prophets, and Herod Antipas arrested and killed John the Baptist. As indicated in Jesus' prophetic pronouncements against the Jerusalem rulers, he would have known the outcome of his direct confrontation with the rulers. And as clear from the rapid expansion of the Jesus-movements and the Gospels they produced, his execution by crucifixion ostensibly as a leader of insurrection ("king of the Judeans") became the martyrdom that motivated that expansion into villages in other areas and eventually cities as well.[15]

Jesus' mission and movement(s) evidently had no illusions about the continuing presence and power of the Roman imperial order. Their political-economic-religious strategy, moreover, seems to have had a sense of political realism that enabled them not only to survive and spread but also to continue the resistance to the Roman imperial order in Palestine and beyond.

The extensions of Jesus mission in the movements of loyalists continued to carry out renewal of covenantal community in cooperation and mutual sharing. In the case of the *koinon* in Jerusalem, this was sharing all goods in common (see Acts 2 and 4). These movements continued their resistance to the local rulers, refusing to cease their organizing. The Roman client rulers (such as the high priests and the Agrippas) and governors and

15. For discussion of Jesus' crucifixion as a "breakthrough" event for the movement(s), see Horsley, *Jesus and the Powers*, chap. 8; and Horsley, *Jesus and the Politics of Roman Palestine*, chap. 7.

other local officials periodically took repressive measures, and the Jesus-movements remained steadfast in their organizing and resistance (Mark 8:34–38; 13:9–11; Matt 10:17–20, 29–33; Luke 12:2–12). But they had sufficient communal solidarity and collective economic "staying power" to continue the community renewal and resistance to the Roman imperial order that the Gospel story of Jesus' mission exemplified. And they evidently did not engage in any direct collective opposition that would have evoked repressive Roman military action.

The Political Economic Project of Jesus

Consideration of the economic aspect of the Gospel stories of the interactive mission of Jesus in historical context forces us to move well beyond the domestication of Jesus into a mere "talking head" who uttered pithy sayings about love and justice that reinforce our liberal values. The Gospel stories present Jesus as having discerned concretely what was happening in the Roman imperial order in ancient Palestine, in Galilee and Judea in particular. As indicated in his covenant renewal speech and "the Lord's prayer," he discerned that families/households were being impoverished and village communities disintegrating from the economic extractions (exploitation) of their rulers: the Romans' demand for tribute after they brutally conquered Palestine and the Herodian "kings'" and the Jerusalem high priests' demand for taxes, tithes, and offerings. This political-economic-religious exploitation was exacerbated by the Herodian and high priestly elite manipulation of needy families into debt at high rates of interest. According to the Gospels' portrayal, Jesus focused his mission precisely in village communities, and commissioned his disciples to expand the mission in villages, first in Galilee and then in the villages of nearby areas. The core of the mission was the renewal of Mosaic covenantal community in mutual aid and cooperation that would restore community solidarity and enable families and village communities to resist their exploitation by the Herodian, high priestly, and Roman rulers. Jesus' mission thus drew deeply on and renewed covenantal community at the center of Israelite (popular) tradition that focused on collective responsibility for keeping each component family economically viable, for example, by ensuring their "daily bread" and the mutual cancellation of debts.

Jesus thus catalyzed a movement of the renewal of the people of Israel in their traditional village communities in opposition to and by their rulers appointed by the Romans. Whether in Jesus' own mission or in its expansion by the disciples and others, the movement(s) soon spread to other peoples subjected to the Roman imperial order. Throughout the Gospel stories, but especially in their climactic events, Jesus pronounced God's condemnation of the rulers' (political-religious) economic exploitation and insisted that the communities of the expanding movement(s) maintain their solidarity in resistance to the Roman imperial order whose face were the local political-economic-religious institutions.

Part 3
Paul and Political Economy
An Alternative Society of Local Communities among Peoples Subject to Rome

6

Political-Economy in the Early Roman Empire

Interpreters of Paul have been heavily dependent on scholars of the Hellenistic-Roman world for their understanding of the context of Paul's mission and letters. Nothing has been more bewildering than the variety of differing views on what is meant by "economics" or "the economy" and the different, often opposed, reconstructions of "the Roman economy."

A generation ago Moses Finley and others had laid out how ancient cities were economically dependent on the countryside, increasingly on land controlled by the wealthy living in the cities but farmed by tenants or slaves.[1] Informed by how Karl Polanyi was rethinking pre-modern economies, Finley also recognized that while trade was important particularly for luxury goods for the elite, the ancient economy was not dominated by "the market" and "trade," that is, it was not proto-capitalist. In the last few decades, however, as neoliberal economic theory and practice came to dominate not only in the West but in a globalized capitalist economy,[2] a new generation of Roman historians revived neoclassical economic theory, as exemplified in recent books on *The Roman Market Economy* and *The Ancient Middle Classes*.[3] In these neoclassical constructions, "the Roman economy" appears to have been proto-capitalist after all.

---

1. Finley, *The Ancient Economy*.

2. Recent criticism as it pertains to biblical studies in N. Elliott, "When Bridges Fail Us," 208–10.

3. Temin, *The Roman Market Economy*; and Mayer, *The Ancient Middle Classes*. While balanced by more critical articles, many of the essays in the synchronic *Cambridge Companion to the Roman Economy* work with the controlling concepts of "market," "money and prices," even "economic integration through the expansion of trade and markets." The reversion to neoclassical economic theory is interwoven with much more extensive and detailed research into economic matters, relying heavily on archaeological investigations. Much of the evidence available is from cities and pertains to local production, for example, of ceramics and trade. Many of these studies lack historical perspective, do not consider the overall Roman imperial political-economic

Neoclassical economics, however, abstracts "the economy" from society. Indeed it assumes that "the economy" is something in itself, an independent entity operating according to its own laws, such as that of "supply and demand."[4] In the early Roman Empire, however, as in any empire or society in any historical circumstances, *concrete economic realities were embedded in networks of social-political-religious power relations* that were often complex and full of conflict, whether in the Empire as a whole or in the particular cities where Paul and his co-workers generated new communities. The concepts and generalizations in which "economics" is discussed do more to hide than illuminate the conflictual relations. For example, to conclude from recently unearthed archaeological evidence of urban artisan production that economic structures and personnel were "complex, diverse, and vibrant" does not ask, much less investigate, the exploitative relations between those artisans and their "patrons" or "landlords." To discuss a "labor market" in which "free urban workers" found work stops short of inquiring about the masses of people who had been thrown off the land. In Italy, for example, large numbers of peasants were displaced by slave-labor on large estates during several decades of Roman conquests and enslavement of subjugated people (including in Judea and Galilee).[5] These displaced people joined the mass of "surplus" population in Rome.

The recent focus on Rome as having had a *market* economy that achieved a considerable degree of "integration" through "the expansion of trade" imagines "the economy" as somehow separate from "the state." But this analysis ignores the historical reality that the Roman imperial state stood not only at the apex but at the center of the Roman imperial economy.[6] It is puzzling to read an argument (based on a limited set of data) that Rome had a "unified wheat *market*"[7] when, according to extensive historical sources, the Roman imperial state was extracting huge quantities of grain from Egypt and other areas of the Empire that it had conquered. One of the central concerns of the imperial state was the food supply for the Roman populace and army, which would have been a significant part of the imperial economy.[8] More than one emperor fixed food prices and

---

structure, and revive neoclassical economics uncritically.

4. For the intellectual history that defined the economy as an independent entity, see now Boer and Petterson, *Idols of Nations*.

5. Hopkins, *Conquerors and Slaves*.

6. "The dominant force in the Roman economy," as explained by Morley, "Economy and Economic Theory, Roman," 12.

7. Temin, *Roman Market Economy*.

8. Garnsey and Saller, *The Roman Empire*, 2nd ed., chap. 5. This remains the most comprehensive critical analysis and presentation of the Roman imperial economy,

subsidized the shipping enterprises contracted to transport grain from Egypt and elsewhere, whether in the building of ships or in compensation for losses (Tacitus, *Annals* 2.59; 2.89; 15.18.2; 15.39.2; Suetonius, *Claudius* 18–19). Augustus had even established a grain dole for the citizens of the metropolis (*Res Gestae* 15).

Most of the grain supply for Rome, for the army, and for the urban elites and their underlings was expropriated in the form of taxes and tribute from previously conquered peoples. One effect of this drain on producers in the provinces such as Egypt was to make it more difficult for them to maintain a subsistence living.[9] There evidently was an expansion of long-distance "trade" (as well as of local trade) in "commodities" in the early Empire. Such trade, however, was primarily for the lifestyle of the wealthy in Rome and the other cities of the Empire (see the list in Rev 18:11–14). The economy of the Roman Empire was not a market economy but a *political economy* that was based not on "supply and demand" but on demand and supply, that is demand by the imperial state and its wealthy urban elites and supply coerced from subject peoples, tenants, and slaves.

Indeed, the percentage of goods needed to supply the Empire that was produced by slaves was so great, especially in Italy but also in the other areas, that some critical scholars have characterized the Roman imperial economy as a slave-economy.[10] Slavery was such a prominent reality in the Roman imperial political economy that slave relations affected every other aspect of the society and culture.[11] Ironically, the practice of emancipation was instrumental in the maintenance of the slave-system. It was frequent enough that masters' promise and slaves' hope for eventual emancipation helped motivate their obedience and acquiescence. Even when emancipated, slaves became "freedpersons" who were generally still dependent on their former owners, often continued as members of the larger household, and were socially despised as former slaves.

---

recognizing how economic structures and power relations were embedded with imperial political and cultural life.

9. Scheidel, "Real Wages in Early Economies."

10. Most important is the magisterial study of de Ste. Croix, *Class Struggle in the Ancient Greek World*.

11. Critical discussion in Boer and Petterson, *Times of Trouble*, chap. 4.

Analysis of Social-Economic Stratification Stops Short of Power-Relations

Until recently, the field of New Testament studies generally had largely ignored the economics as well as the politics of the Roman Empire in the focus on culture, Hellenistic culture. The tendency of New Testament scholars and interpreters of Paul in particular, like that of Roman historians, was to downplay or mystify the deep political-economic divisions and conflicts in the Hellenistic and Roman world, as well as to ignore the historical changes and regional differences. They concentrated on (textual) sources produced by the political-economic-cultural elite whose perspective they tended to share. New Testament scholars, moreover, tended to project schemes and models derived from study of modern or current economies onto ancient history and texts. In what quickly became a touchstone for further investigation of Paul and his mission, nearly forty years ago Wayne Meeks presented as a supposedly "new consensus" that Paul's congregations reflected "a fair cross-section of urban society."[12] He argued that free artisans and small traders were especially prominent, described several of Paul's converts as wealthy, and claimed that we hear nothing of those who lived at the subsistence level.

Meeks and others interested in "the social world" were following the structural-functional sociology that had dominated North American and, to a degree, Western European social science in the previous generation. This approach viewed society as a coherent system in which individuals of different social-economic locations, roles, occupations and interests all fit together into a cohesive whole. Focusing on social stratification enabled such sociologists to ignore or downplay historical change and political-economic conflict. Critical analysis from within the field of sociology itself explained that part of the agenda of structural functional sociology was to provide an alternative to Marxist analysis, which appeared all the more threatening to the Western academic establishment after the Russian Revolution in 1917.[13] Ironically, New Testament interpreters began borrowing the method only after structural-functionalism had been widely abandoned

---

12. Meeks, *First Urban Christians*, 51–73. Meeks ventures the generalization that the most active and prominent members of Paul's circle were individuals of "high status inconsistency" ("achieved status" higher than their "attributed status"), and suggests that the rise and success of early Christianity was due to their individual drive and abilities. Meeks relied heavily on Theissen, "Soziale Schichtung," see Theissen, "Social Stratification in the Corinthian Community."

13. See esp. the thorough criticism in Gouldner, *Coming Crisis in Western Sociology*, which was based on a self-study of the field led by Gouldner.

in sociology itself (by around 1970). Its influence spread in New Testament studies, despite some sharp criticism.[14]

The functionalist sociological focus on "stratification" and "social status" enabled New Testament scholars interested in "the social world" to continue to avoid recognizing economic conflict and economic exploitation, both then and now.[15] The functionalist approach also perpetuated the separation of religion from political-economic relations, assuming that differences in social-economic status could be mitigated or resolved by religion. In Theissen's construction the Pauline mission and congregations accepted and embodied differences in the political-economic order but ameliorated them by a "love-patriarchalism" that expected concern and responsibility from the wealthy and respect and subordination from the poorer members.[16]

As interest in economic issues developed in New Testament studies, analysis of social stratification was adapted for analysis of economic stratification. Important in the deepening criticism of Meeks' and others description of the "social world" of Paul, Steven Friesen developed his "poverty scale" of the population of the Roman Empire that found 3% extremely wealthy, 7% with a small cushion, and 90% living at or near subsistence.[17] This "poverty scale" in the Roman Empire calls attention to the vast "income gap" between the extremely wealthy and the vast majority of people who lived at or near subsistence, including the vast majority of women and men mentioned in Paul's letters or in Acts.[18] The recognition

14. See J. H. Elliott, "Social-Scientific Criticism"; Horsley, *Sociology and the Jesus Movement*, 1–64, 147–65; and, more recently, N. Elliott, "When Bridges Fail Us," 213–15; and N. Elliott, "Diagnosing an Allergic Reaction," 7–8.

15. The avoidance of recognizing economic division and exploitation ran deep in Pauline interpretation. As Friesen recounted, at a church conference early in the twentieth century, Adolf Deissmann and the distinguished liberal theologian Adolf von Harnack, responding to recent successes of the Marxist Social Democratic Party, had explained that social inequality and poverty were not serious problems since the Gospel could bring inner enlightenment and that by better caring for souls the church could win back the hearts and minds of the working class. Friesen, "Poverty in Pauline Studies," 330–31; cf. Deissmann, *St. Paul*, 216–17.

16. Theissen, *Social Setting of Pauline Christianity*, esp. 107–9. One suspects that bourgeois Christianity was being read back into Paul's letters and mission.

17. Friesen, "Poverty in Pauline Studies" (originally a presentation to a 2002 session of the SBL Paul and Politics Group). With access to fuller "economic data," Friesen produced a revised version of the "poverty scale" in collaboration with the Roman economic historian Walter Scheidel; see Scheidel and Friesen, "Distribution of Income in the Roman Empire."

18. This "poverty scale" evoked some push-back in the field, such as an attempt to relocate a greater percentage of the population of the Roman Empire and of the

of this yawning gulf between the few extremely wealthy families and the vast majority is surely relevant to the dawning awareness of the increasing "income gap" in today's world of global capitalism, the current context of our interpretation of Paul and his letters.

Estimating the scale of relative economic levels in the social stratification, however, does not yet move toward an analysis of *the historical power relations* between the tiny hyper-wealthy elite and the mass of people living near subsistence, that is, of *who had power over whom*.

Addressing these power relations will require a multifaceted analysis that can shed some light on the political-economic-religious structure and dynamics of the Roman imperial order. An obvious focus toward better understanding the historical context of Paul's mission would be recognition and analysis of the dramatic changes that Rome had imposed and evoked in the very cities into which Paul carried his mission.

Historical Developments and Regional Differences

Treatments of "the Roman economy" have often been presented synthetically and synchronically, as suggested in the titles of important and influential books, such as *The Ancient Economy* (M. I. Finley) and *The Roman Economy* (A. H. M. Jones). Such presentations seem somewhat analogous to the synthetic Hellenistic urban culture that previously provided the context of Paul's mission and letters in New Testament studies. Synthetic overviews do contribute much to our understanding. But ancient Rome had a long and changing history. Already in the second century BCE Roman warlords and their armies were building an empire around the eastern Mediterranean.

In the last few decades, moreover, Roman historians have become far more candid about the brutality of Roman conquest. The slaughter and enslavement of conquered people and the destruction of their villages and even cities were clearly major factors in the political economy, particularly in the devastated areas. Roman historians have also brought attention to the distinctive historical differences between the various cities and areas of the Empire, including in ancient Greece and Asia Minor. These initiatives help provide a more precise picture of political-economic-religious relations in the cities and areas in which Paul and his coworkers focused their

---

membership of the Pauline communities back up into the middle level of an "economic scale." See Longenecker, "Exposing the Economic Middle"; and Longenecker, *Remember the Poor*. Is this an attempt to revive the direct relevance of the Pauline mission and "churches" for "middle-class" churches today?

mission—and one that should replace the picture of the synthetic Hellenistic culture that was supposedly everywhere.[19]

In the same year, 146 BCE, that the Romans annihilated the city of Carthage, for example, they also utterly destroyed the classical city of Corinth and enslaved its populace. For a century it lay in ruins until Julius Caesar established a Roman colony on the site, sending army veterans, freed slaves, and other unwanted "surplus population" from the city of Rome that the patricians were finding difficult to control. As the principal hub of shipping and communications between Italy, the Aegean, and points eastward, Corinth grew in size, with displaced people from diverse backgrounds including people who had been enslaved. At Philippi two successive colonies of Roman army veterans were established in 42 and 30 BCE. The previously conquered indigenous Thracians (and/or "Greeks") were pushed off their lands by the Roman colonists and subordinated to the now predominantly Roman politics and political culture of the city. Slaves (or other dependents) were brought in to work the estates of the Roman veteran families.

Distinctive as they were in their origins as Roman colonies in the first century BCE, Philippi and Corinth shared many of the key developments of the political-religious-economy of Greece (and Asia) generally. While the Roman metropolis extracted huge quantities of grain from conquered peoples, particularly Egypt, other cities of the Empire depended largely on their own countryside (*chora*) for food.[20] Exploitation of both agricultural producers and urban populations by the wealthy urban elite was intensified and consolidated under Roman domination. The political economy of the Roman Empire was dominated by an alliance between the imperial court and the local and provincial wealthy elite.[21] The imperial court placed them in charge of tax collection and favored them in every way. By gaining control of more and more land, they steadily expanded their wealth and local power, and as land-tenure became less secure, small-scale cultivators disappeared.[22]

---

19. Laid out, in reliance on key works of Roman historians, in Horsley, ed., *Paul and Empire*.

20. "Agricultural production must always have constituted the lion's share of ancient activity" (Alcock, *Graecia Capta*, 109).

21. A common historical observation; see recently Alcock, *Graecia Capta*, 77.

22. For results from archaeological surface surveys that have confirmed textual indications, see Alcock, *Graecia Capta*, 71–72. For thorough analysis and discussion of the long-term process by which the magnates of Greek cities steadily increased their wealth and power by taking over people's land and forcing them into dependent tenancy and the continuation of this process in the alliance between the imperial court and the urban elite in the Roman imperial order, see de Ste. Croix, *Class Struggle in the Ancient Greek World*. Drawing on de Ste. Croix, Boer and Pettersen, in *Time of Troubles*,

In the generations preceding the Pauline mission in Macedonia and Achaia, many people were evidently being forced off their land and into the cities in hopes of eking out a living.[23] Some wound up far from their origins in search of a living. Some of the people in any of these cities, probably many in Corinth, would have been displaced people, uprooted from their ancestral homes and homelands, having lost supportive family and village community with their familiar customs. As noted, recent efforts to quantify and stratify the "income" of the (freeborn urban) population of the Empire (on the basis of limited evidence) draw sobering estimates of the huge gulf between the tiny percentage of extremely wealthy-and-powerful and the poverty of the vast majority, with nearly 90% living at or below subsistence and only 8–10% having a moderate surplus.[24] Also, some of the people on the land and certainly in the cities would have been slaves, although it is difficult to know what portion of the population (far less than in Rome and Italy), or freedmen/women (or their descendants), who remained dependent on their former owners.[25]

What held the Roman imperial economy together city by city, especially in the Greek East, was not an imperial bureaucracy or the army, but the elaborate honors to Caesar.[26] It may be difficult for comfortable people in modern Western countries to appreciate just how destructive and unsettling the chaos left in the wake of the Roman civil war fought for over a decade by rival Roman warlords and their armies was for the elite of the empire. Octavian's great victory over the "dark" forces of Marc Anthony at Actium thus evoked intense relief and gratitude among the elite of the cities in Greece and Asia over the *Peace and Security* that Caesar Augustus had brought them. In cities such as Ephesus, Philippi, Thessalonike, Athens, and Corinth, the wealthy magnates sponsored the building and funding of temples and monuments grouped around newly constructed temples to the emperor, the *Lord* and *Savior* of the world. Statues of the emperor were placed in those temples, and rituals to the emperor were performed

---

lay out a comprehensive critical overview of the long historical process by which the colonate emerged as the dominant political-economic form in late antiquity.

23. Many references in Apuleius, *Metamorphoses*; see further, Alcock, *Graecia Capta*, 107.

24. See especially Friesen, "Poverty in Pauline Studies"; Scheidel and Friesen, "Distribution of Income in the Roman Empire."

25. One of the effects of the recent debates about social-economic stratification of the population of the Empire has been to distract attention from the presence and situations of slaves and freedpersons in the cities, and the situations of slaves/slavery and other forms of non-free labor in the countryside, such as tenants on large estates.

26. See esp. Price, *Rituals and Power*; and Zanker, *The Power of Images*; both summarized and abridged in Horsley, *Paul and Empire*, chaps 3–5, 7.

in other public arenas such as the theaters. Festivals and (Caesarian) games were held in honor of the emperor. The presence of the emperor came to pervade public space, and honors to the emperor came to structure the annual calendar. People who lived in the religious-political-economy of these cities were literally surrounded by (embedded in) images and rituals of the divine Caesar, *son of god*, *Lord* and *Savior*, who had brought *Salvation* to the world. By participating in these honors and festivals the people were expressing their loyalty (*pistis*) to their Lord and Savior. There could not be a more vivid illustration of how religion was inseparable from political-economy and of how political-economic power-relations were legitimated and mediated through the central symbols and rituals exhibited in the built environment and the annual rhythm of public life.

These elaborate honors to the emperor were funded and led by the wealthy men of each city, who held not only the city priesthoods and civic offices but who also held the highly coveted imperial priesthoods in those cities.[27] Through these civil-religious offices, as well as by their wealth, they wielded political-economic power in the cities and provinces. The wealthy elite's sponsorship of such public buildings, services, festivals, and other acts of "beneficence" generated much of the work on which the populace hovering at subsistence had become increasingly dependent.[28] As a further antidote to the hunger of the poor, and probably with an eye to preventing social unrest, the wealthy also regularly sponsored public banquets or other distribution of food. Such actions, memorialized in decrees and inscriptions honoring local benefactors (*euergetai*), consolidated the rule of the wealthy in city life and contributed to the acceptance of the new political-economic-religious order.[29] The council (*boule*) of the elite in Greek cities now held effective control; having been left without a voice, with the decline of the city assembly (*ekklesia*), the people were effectively controlled by the local imperial order.

---

27. Alcock, *Graecia Capta*, 163; Gordon, "The Veil of Power," 132–37.

28. Alcock, *Graecia Capta*, 114.

29. While some of the urban poor may have been pulled into patronage networks of wealthy figures, thus increasing the latters' political-economic power, the extensive pyramids of patronage that developed in Rome, filled with people forced off the land or otherwise socially and economically adrift, were probably not duplicated in Corinth and other Greek cities. See Horsley, *Paul and Empire*, part II, esp. 94–95. For the extensive patronage networks in Rome see Saller, *Personal Patronage under the Early Empire*.

In but not of the Empire: Alternative Forms and Pockets of Resistance

Despite their political domination and economic vulnerability, the people in the cities of the Empire and in the countryside were remarkably resilient. As noted above, many had been displaced from their socio-economic origins in some way. Yet among those displaced, indigenous language and culture and even aspects of social structure persisted underneath the dominant Hellenistic-Roman political-economic-religious forms in some of the cities around the eastern Mediterranean. While also involving degrees of adjustment, the formation and persistence of religious-ethnic communities in the Greek cities (e.g., the "synagogues" of Judeans in the diaspora) was one possible form of resisting more complete assimilation into the local and wider imperial order.[30] In the narrative of Paul's and his coworkers' mission in the book of Acts, they habitually begin by speaking in the local assembly of Judeans in a given city or town; a conflict develops, and Paul's faction splits off. Despite this being a repeated scheme in the narrative, it is possible that the Pauline mission built on already existing networks and communities. In Philippi, on which Roman warlords had twice imposed colonies of Roman veterans, the Philippians pushed out of their homes and lands may well have had continuing indigenous networks and identity over against the dominant new Roman ethos of the city that Paul and his coworkers could mobilize into a community of Christ-loyalists.

In recent decades, interest has increased in "associations," variously called *collegia, familia, synodoi, thiasoi*, etc., as analogies or even models for the assemblies (communities) that developed from the mission of Paul and his coworkers.[31] Given the origins of this mission in a movement of renewal of Israel based in villages and in village and town *synagogai* it seems more likely that Paul and his coworkers were adapting the form of the Judean and Galilean synagogues/assemblies in which the movement(s) had originated during and after the mission of Jesus.[32] In the cities of the Empire, especially once the assemblies became viable and relatively stable communities over a period of decades, they may have resembled the "associations."

30. This possibility, exemplified perhaps by the Jewish/Judean communities/synagogues in Alexandria or Rome, has not been adequately investigated, perhaps largely because of the lack of sources.

31. A very helpful critical review of the "models" that scholars suggest for the communities Paul and coworkers catalyzed is Adams, "First-Century Models for Paul's Churches." On *collegia* etc., see the collection of source material in Ascough, Harland, and Kloppenborg, *Associations in the Greco-Roman World*; see also Harland, *Associations, Synagogues, and Congregations*.

32. Discussed in Horsley, "Paul's Assembly in Corinth."

Key aspects of such associations provided communal economic self-help, such as periodic feasts, funerals, and in times of need, possible low-interest loans. Membership in a *collegium*, however, was costly, involving expenditures including entrance fees, periodic dues, and ad hoc contributions. Such resource-pooling could help members alleviate poverty in difficult times. But such associations "had the effect of obstructing the poorest from accessing support networks, resources, and work opportunities."[33]

Considering how important slavery was in production in the Roman imperial order, including in households with only a few slaves, note should be taken of the steady and widespread *resistance by slaves*.[34] Earlier New Testament interpretation, following classical historians, underestimated slave resistance—in arguments that ancient slavery was generally benign and/or that slaves were acquiescent if not content with their lot. The sources on which they depended, of course, were from the elite, who were involved, directly or indirectly, in slave ownership. Slaves themselves, like peasants, left no written accounts that can be used to balance the slave-owners' views. Elite sources do, however, regularly indicate various forms of slave resistance and the measures slave-masters and imperial or local authorities took to suppress or retaliate against such resistance. And these indications open toward recognition of various "hidden" forms of resistance by slaves who knew that open defiance or revolt would be suicidal.

Pretense or (grudging) "performance" of acquiescence and obedience was one way slaves might lessen potential cruelty and brutality from their masters, even while they may have been slowing down or sabotaging production in the household. That slaves ran away was a direct "withholding" of their labor as well as a challenge to their authority for slave-masters. Literary sources are rich with references to *fugitivi* and to professional "slave-catchers," suggesting runaway slaves was a familiar phenomenon. Plays entitled *Fugitivi* and *Captivi* characterize slaves as likely to run away. City-states made treaties with the specific purpose of extraditing fugitive slaves. In his *Res Gestae* (25), Augustus boasts that following his victory in the Roman Civil War he had returned 30,000 slaves to their masters for punishment—but not mentioning that he had simply crucified another 6,000 for whom no master could be found (Dio 49.12.5). Fugitive slaves themselves formed bands of brigands in remote areas (e.g., Athenaeus 6.265d–266e). Given the conditions of their servitude, in which slaves were dispersed onto smaller or larger farms in Italy and Sicily (and elsewhere), it is amazing

33. See the broader survey and critical assessment by Liu, "Urban Poverty in the Roman Empire," esp. 44–49.

34. More fully discussed in Callahan and Horsley, "Slave Resistance in Classical Antiquity."

that they could organize widespread revolts. Best know are the massive revolts in the late Republic, in 135–134, 104, and 74–73 BCE, but revolts were more frequent than usually acknowledged. These revolts are also significant because of the social-political forms in which slaves organized themselves, such as copying indigenous forms of kingship derived from the areas of their origin, such as Syria. Extensive slavery in Rome, Italy, and the provinces and cities of the Empire, and continuing enslavement of tens of thousands, for example, in Judea and Galilee (in 52 and 4 BCE and 70 CE), who were sent to Roman slave markets, created pressures from below and motivation to participate in forms of resistance.

There were thus interstices in which minimal alternatives and/or resistance to the Roman imperial order could gain a tenuous foothold. It is in these that we find the historical link between the movement(s) that Jesus catalyzed in Galilee and the mission led by diaspora Judeans who led the expansion of a branch of that movement into the cities and towns of the eastern Empire. At first glance, this may seem unlikely as a link that would lead to a rapidly expanding movement of communities that posed an alternative to the local and wider Roman imperial order. The book of Acts has schematized and idealized the events in which the connecting link was made. But the cast of characters is clear, and underneath the idealizing narratives are some configurations that invite historical exploration and explanation.

The twelve disciples (including a replacement for Judas) and apparently other Jesus-loyalists who had come up to Jerusalem with Jesus where he confronted the high priestly rulers and was crucified (martyred) by the Romans had remained in or returned to Jerusalem. And before long, many Judeans from cities in the diaspora—including Stephen, Barnabas, and Saul—joined the movement of the renewal of Israel and became leaders in the further expansion of the movements.

7

The Economic Base of the Movement that Led to Paul's Mission

Finally exploring the economic dimension of Jesus and the Gospels and of Paul and his letters in the different regional contexts of the Roman imperial order leads to the realization of what we have not been dealing with in New Testament studies. This division of Christian theological education has historically limited itself mainly to culture, to ideas and doctrines expressed in sayings or pericopes or other text-fragments. Its focus has been mainly on Jesus as the unique individual (divine) revealer and Paul as the individual hero of faith. Having narrowed the reality it dealt with to culture (religion), New Testament studies assumed that the dominant division was between Judaism and Hellenism. Corresponding to that division was the dichotomy of Jews vs. Gentiles. And correspondingly, while Jesus still belonged to Judaism, Paul belonged to Hellenism as the principal apostle who formulated the more universal Gentile Christianity. It seemed clear from his letters that Paul knew very little about Jesus and his teachings, but focused on his crucifixion and resurrection. Jesus may have been preaching a reform of Judaism, but Paul's Gentile Christianity was a "Christ-cult." It was simply assumed that Paul's mission and assemblies had little connection with the movement(s) of Jesus-loyalists attested in the Gospels.

When we (finally) investigate the concrete political economy of the Roman imperial order in regions of the eastern Mediterranean, it is clear that the principal division was not the cultural one between two synthetic scholarly constructs of Judaism and Hellenism, but the political-economic one between the dominant Roman imperial order and the various subject peoples. Texts, leaders, and movements all need to be critically reread and reconsidered once this is recognized.

It is evident in the Gospel stories that the Roman crucifixion of Jesus as a leader of insurrection, rather than end the movement he generated, became the "breakthrough," the martyrdom that further inspired it. Jesus' movement of the renewal of Israel diversified as it expanded. Some branches of the movement eventually produced particular Gospels. In the Markan story, for example, Jesus tells the disciples to meet him back up in Galilee where presumably they will continue the movement he started in his mission there. In the book of Acts, on the other hand, the disciples stay in or return to Jerusalem, where they form a community and recruit people into the movement. The Jerusalem community then serves as the base from which the movement expands outward through Judea, Samaria, and Galilee, then to assemblies (*synagogai*) of Judeans living in towns and cities in Syria, finally leading to the mission of Paul that expands the movement into the cities of Asia Minor and Greece.

The only source for these "events" is the book of Acts. Presumably the sequel to the Gospel of Luke and the only account of what happened following the crucifixion and resurrection of Jesus, Acts has played contradictory roles in New Testament studies. On the one hand, Christian interpreters pressed the standard old scheme of the origin of "early Christianity" from "Judaism" onto Acts in uncritical readings. More recently, on the other hand, Acts was deemed late and schematic and unreliable for historical reconstruction, particularly on the conversion and mission of Paul. Now, however, we are in a position to exercise sharp criticism of the schematic and often idealizing narratives in Acts against the background of what we know of the historical contexts from other sources.

There is scholarly consensus that episodes of the narrative in Acts do not provide access to particular historical events, and narrative sequences do not indicate the particular sequence of the movement's expansion. But the broader narrative sequence does appear to provide a sense of how the movement spread. Particular episodes, moreover, may be representatives of characteristic issues of the movement's interaction in the locations into which it spread. It thus seems possible to discern the key steps by which a branch of the renewal of Israel begun by Jesus, establishing a base in Jerusalem, expanded into towns and cities in Syria and Asia Minor, and eventually into the mission of Paul. In the key intermediate steps, the movement of the renewal of Israel evidently established further bases in assemblies of diaspora Judeans in those places.

In the investigation of the steps of the movement of renewal that follows, it is important to recognize several significant aspects of the movement. First, far from being a new religion, the mission of Paul was indeed connected to the movement of renewal of Israel begun by Jesus through intermediate steps of expansion into communities of diaspora Judeans. Neither the letters of Paul nor the "book" of Acts are about the emergence of (early) Christianity from (early) Judaism.[1] These are anachronistic synthetic constructs that must be avoided if the narrative of Acts and the expansion of the movement of renewal of Israel are to be critically understood.[2] Second, Judeans in the towns of Syria and Asia Minor had formed communities that the Romans had allowed to be semi-independent, semi-self-governing according to their own ancestral traditions; and these seem to have been the economic bases of the movement of renewal of Israel as its expanded to include more and more diaspora Judeans, God-fearers, proselytes, and other subject peoples who were eager to join communities of the movement. Third, throughout its expansion the movement of renewal was opposed to and by the Roman imperial order in its local forms and officials. Yet despite periodic repressive measures by local officials the movement continued to expand, because those assemblies of diaspora Judeans in which it established footholds were some of the alternative communities in the interstices of the imperial order, as mentioned in chap. 6.

As we investigate the steps that led from the renewal-of-Israel movement generated by Jesus to the mission of Paul it is important to clear away misleading concepts and terms in official translations of Acts and other texts that survive from the old scheme of (Gentile) "Christianity" developing out of and breaking away from "Judaism." To continue translating *ethne* as "Gentiles" perpetuates that old scheme, suggesting that something different from the renewal-of-Israel movement is happening. The narrative in Acts focuses throughout on the expansion of the renewal of Israel that has come to a turning point in the crucifixion and vindication of Jesus. As Jerusalem priests and more and more diaspora Judeans and God-fearers join the movement, peoples (*ethne*) other than Israelites/Judeans are also eager to join. These (other) peoples have also, like the Judeans, been subjugated to the Roman imperial order. Whether this was their principal motivation or not, they are attracted into a movement opposed to the Roman imperial order that has been expanding among Judeans who live in their midst. In a few episodes of the narrative, when some of the Judeans reject his message, Paul declares that he is turning to "the (other) peoples." But this is by no means a general scheme that recurs throughout the narrative. In his reflection about

---

1. See, e.g., Becker and Reed, eds., *The Ways That Never Parted*.

2. In this regard in particular I find the lengthy "Introduction" to his massive commentary on Acts by Craig Keener to present judicious judgment about the text of Acts and previous secondary literature; see Keener, *Acts*, vol. 1, 469. Since Keener and many others provide extensive critical reviews of the voluminous secondary literature on Acts, and because this chapter is a critical survey of the overall narrative of Acts with only a closer focus on only a few passages, I will avoid the extensive debates between various viewpoints and "readings" on Acts.

his mission, Paul had observed that the gospel message of the fulfilment in Jesus Christ had gone first to the Judeans and then to the other peoples. Evident behind these retrospective statements both in Paul and in Acts are the steps by which the movement had expanded. And even after other peoples joined the movement, it remained a movement of the renewal of Israel, only now open to other subject peoples.

It will further enhance our historical understanding to find translations of several other key terms more appropriate to the historical context. In the context of the Roman Empire, *pistis* meant "loyalty," mainly to Caesar, rather than religious "faith" that has become reduced to mere "belief" in modern Western culture. That people became "believers in Christ" is far too weak a translation; they became rather Christ-loyalists, meaning they could no longer be loyal to Caesar. The English term "synagogue" suggests a building where a Jewish congregation meets. The Greek term *synagoge*, however, referred to the local congregation or assembly of Judeans, which was an often self-governing ethnic-religious community within a city or town. To translate *ekklesia* as "church" is utterly anachronistic and elides the parallel use of the term for the popular assembly in a Greek city that had become almost powerless or defunct as local oligarchies and imperial authorities had come to control the political economy. Perhaps more important, insofar as it was the standard translation of the Hebrew *yaḥad* in the Septuagint (the "Jewish" scriptures in Greek translation), *ekklesia* suggested that the local communities of the movement were the assembly of the people of Israel. The movement of the renewal of Israel was expanding along the interstitial lines in the Roman imperial order that allowed for communities that were "in but not of"—and even resistant to—the imperial system.

"All Things in Common" and Aiding the Needy in the Early Jerusalem Community

The first step was that the (leaders of the) movement remained in or returned to Jerusalem following Jesus' confrontation with the high priestly rulers and his crucifixion by the Romans. Not just in the overall scheme of Acts and particular episodes and speeches but also in the historical context of the structural divide between rulers and people, this was a continuation of Jesus' program of renewal of Israel in opposition to and by the rulers of Israel. Among New Testament scholars, a standard explanation for the views and behavior of the "early Christians" has been that they were caught up in an apocalyptic fervor, expecting that the end of the world was at hand. Such an expectation, however, does not appear anywhere in the narrative of Acts about Peter and other Jesus-loyalists in Jerusalem. Their orientation is indicated probably by the speeches (supposedly) given by Peter that led to his and others' arrest and imprisonment and the speech by Stephen that led to his martyrdom. As suggested in his speeches, Peter and the other disciples were evidently acting in the conviction that the renewal of Israel, begun in the mission of Jesus, the prophet like Moses, had climaxed in his crucifixion and his vindication by God as the messiah-designate, requiring the expansion of the renewal of Israel, in fulfilment of prophecies and of the promises to Abraham. Peter accuses the forefathers of having been repressive, but condemns the high priests for handing Jesus over and the Romans for having executed him. In the conclusion of the speeches, Peter calls the people to "repent" and participate in the fulfilment, the restoration of the people anticipated by the prophets.

The conflict throughout the episodes is between the disciples who are Galileans, uneducated common people (*agrammatoi kai idiotai*), on the one hand, and on the other hand the Jerusalem high priests and elders and the council who forbid them to speak to the people, whom the disciples address as "Israelites" and "brothers" (Acts 2:7, 22, 29; 3:12, 17). In a motif known from the Gospel of Mark and now again from Acts, the rulers do not "crack down" on the disciples and their recruits—thus allowing an interstitial opportunity—because they are afraid of the people who are responding positively. This motif has considerable credibility from what we know of the deteriorating relation between rulers and people in Jerusalem in the mid-first century (discussed in chap. 3 above).

The conflict, however, is not simply between the Jerusalem rulers and Peter and the other disciples whom the rulers of the temple-state forbid to speak, but involves their movement, and that movement is a renewal of the people of Israel. Again it has been the standard older Christian reading of the text of Acts that has blocked recognition of what this movement was about. In their conviction that religion was separate from political-economic life and reacting with remorse over Christian complicity the Jewish Holocaust, Christian scholars assumed that, like Jesus himself, his followers were faithful "Jews" for whom the temple was the holy place of worship (in their synthetic construct of "Judaism"). One of the key decontextualized proof-texts on which they relied was the historic mistranslation (in the KJV and still in the RSV) that the believers were "day by day attending the temple together" (Acts 2:46).[3]

The sense of the text, however, is not that the early Jesus-loyalists in Jerusalem were "attending the temple" (like attending church or synagogue today),

---

3. Discussed decades ago in Horsley, *Jesus and the Spiral*, 291–92.

but that they were spending much time together in the temple courtyard. After Herod's massive reconstruction of the temple this was the central public space in Jerusalem and the Jesus-loyalists were probably gathering there to attract attention and to recruit. Translators, moreover, appear to have missed the connotations of key Greek terms applied here to the (Jesus-)loyalists. They were "all together" (*epi to auto*) in the sense of *the assembly* of Israel (*yaḥad* in Hebrew, for which *epi to auto* is used in the Septuagint, the Greek translation of Judean scriptures [Acts 2:44]). Similarly, the term *homothumadon* in the phrase translated "they spent much time *together*" also suggests that the Acts account is representing them as the true *assembly* of Israel (*yaḥad*, for which *homothumadon* was also used in the Septuagint).

This movement of the renewal of Israel, moreover, had formed a community that embodied an economic alternative to the Roman imperial order in Judea headed by the high priests and elders (Acts 2:44–47; 4:32–37). The distinguishing aspect of the Jerusalem community from which the movement expanded was its common possession of goods and distribution according to need.[4] The main point in the immediate narrative context is: "All who had become loyal were together and had all things in common (*eichon hapanta koina*); they would sell their possessions and goods and distribute the proceeds to all, as any had need" (Acts 2:44–45). Then, following the observation about "spending time in the temple," comes the account that "they broke bread from house to house and ate their food with glad and generous hearts" (Acts 2:46; evidently eating communally in small groups, as houses were quite small). Several episodes later comes a fuller statement of the community's economic practice:

> The whole group of those who had become loyal were of one heart and soul, and no one said that any possessions/goods were his/her own (*idion einai*), but that all things were theirs in common (*autois panta koina*) ... There was not a needy person among them, for as many as possessed lands and houses sold them and brought the proceeds of what was sold. They laid it at the apostles feet, and it was distributed to each as any had need. (Acts 4:32–35)

Establishment New Testament scholars, who are generally socially and politically conservative, dismissed these accounts as romanticizing

---

4. Extensive review of the many "parallels" found in ancient texts to sharing of goods, etc., in Acts 4:41–45 in Keener, *Acts* 1.1013–23. For a more limited critical review of dismissive previous interpretation and an argument for trusting the historical core of the account of sharing of goods in the Jerusalem community, see Bartchy, "Community of Goods in Acts."

and utopian.⁵ The narratives of the origins of the movement in Jerusalem in Acts are idealizing, to be sure. Yet it is evident from the continuation of the distribution of goods in the ensuing narrative (Acts 6:1-6) that there was some such sharing of goods and distribution to the needy more or less from the outset.

To understand this "communism" of goods and distribution to the needy that is often dismissed as utopian and impractical we need to explore both why it was necessary and the background of the practice in Israelite tradition. Who comprised the community of Jesus-loyalists in Jerusalem? At the core were at least several of "the twelve" disciples, headed by Peter. There may also have been others who had come up to Jerusalem with Jesus in his prophetic confrontation with the high priests in the temple. These people had left behind whatever economic base they had previously in Galilean villages. In their excitement from the "breakthrough" constituted by Jesus' confrontation with the high priestly rulers in the temple and his ensuing martyrdom, they may well have recruited others right away, either Jerusalemites or others from outside, including some from Judean villages nearer to the city. Some of these may also have left their previous economic base, but others were still in possession of some resources. The Acts narrative mentions in particular the Levite Joseph (Barnabas), who sold a field he possessed and donated the proceeds, and the couple Ananias and Sapphira, who sold some property but donated only a portion of the proceeds (Acts 4:36-37; 5:1-11).

It may help interpreters to allow for some concrete practice indicated by the supposedly idealizing language to recognize that such sharing of goods was not unprecedented in Roman Palestine. As the Hasmonean military leaders maneuvered to assume the high priesthood in Judea, a group of priests and scribes, committed to the central exodus and Mosaic covenantal- traditions of Israel, withdrew into the wilderness of Judea at Qumran, near the Dead Sea. They established a new exodus and renewed covenant community, claiming that they were the faithful *yaḥad* (assembly) of Israel. As indicated in their Community Rule, the Qumran community/ *yaḥad* required that members share all things in common.⁶ Those who remained committed to the covenant were to go through major steps of trial and approval. Upon entry into the community, if they were accepted after a two-year trial period, they were to hand over their possessions and

---

5. Critical discussions of the language of the Hellenistic ideal and arguments for the economic practices of the Jerusalem community in Draper, "The Social Milieu and Motivation"; and Scott Bartchy, "Community of Goods in Acts."

6. This is thoroughly researched and discussed by Catherine Murphy, *Wealth in the Dead Sea Scrolls*.

earnings, which would then be merged with the common goods (1QS 5:1–3; 6:18–24). It is noteworthy that, like the Jesus-loyalists who formed the Jerusalem community, those who joined the Qumran community had left their previous economic base (which for priests and scribes was presumably in the Jerusalem temple-state).

In sharing their resources in common and aiding the needy, the members of the Jerusalem community were following, and dramatically intensifying, the Israelite tradition they were familiar with in their Galilean and Judean village communities. As known from the adaptations of early Israelite (village) customs (and practices) in the scribal collections of laws and customs in Exodus 21–23, the "Holiness Code" in Leviticus, and Deuteronomy, Israelite village communities had traditional ways of cooperation and mutual aid that enabled component families to remain economically viable.[7] These practices included customs such as gleaning and leaving fields fallow every seven years so the needy could harvest the produce, liberal lending to the needy at no interest, and cancellation of debts every seven years. The overarching "social-economic contract," the general Israelite "moral economy," was summarized and focused in the Mosaic covenant between God and the people and between the people. The "ten commandments" were in effect rules or principles that guided economic relations in agrarian communities.[8]

As explained in chapter 4, the center of Jesus' renewal of the people of Israel was his renewal of the Mosaic covenant. And the center of his covenant renewal was a restatement and intensification of the demands for mutual aid and community cooperation midst the difficult circumstances imposed by the Roman imperial order in Palestine. In extending the renewal movement into Jerusalem and forming a new community as a base for expanding the movement these Jesus-loyalists appear to have been adapting Jesus' demands for the mutual aid and community cooperation at the core of renewal of the Mosaic covenant. In the new circumstances of having left behind their previous economic bases in village communities the newly formed community in Jerusalem needed to improvise. In their communal sharing of resources and aiding the needy they were intensifying the traditional Israelite covenantal principles, demands, and customs in the new circumstances. The claim in the Acts narrative that "there was not a needy person among them" (4:34) suggests that they were (supposedly) realizing

---

7. Careful, critical examination of Israelite "Law in the Villages," in Knight, *Law, Power, and Justice in Ancient Israel*, chap. 5.

8. For an application of the cross-cultural study of the "moral economy" of peasantries, see Scott, *Moral Economy of the Peasant*; this is applied to the covenantal law tradition in ancient Israel in Horsley, *Covenant Economics*, esp. chaps 2–3.

THE ECONOMIC BASE OF THE MOVEMENT THAT LED TO PAUL'S MISSION   119

the ideal articulated in the torah of Deuteronomy (15:4) that in (the *yaḥad* of) Israel there should not be a needy person if the people were keeping the covenant. Sharing "all things in common" may have seemed like a later Lukan projection of a utopian ideal for a previous generation of bourgeois New Testament scholars and the (culturally elite) Greek philosophers they cited. But in historical context it was more likely a vivid memory of the very practical economic practice of the Jesus-loyalists from Galilean village communities who eagerly extended the renewal of Israel to the capital city from which they might expand the movement.

Expansion of the Sharing as Judeans from the Diaspora Join the Movement

The second (and third) step(s) in the expansion of this movement of Jesus-loyalists in the interstices of the Roman imperial order was that many Judeans from diaspora communities who had presumably become pilgrims to Jerusalem joined. Although the Acts narrative devotes only a few episodes to them, the many "Hellenists" (that is Greek-speaking Judeans in Jerusalem) who joined the movement at an early stage must have played a significant role in its expansion.

Why would there have been so many Greek-speaking Judeans in Jerusalem? Judeans had been deported (dispersed) by conquering imperial regimes. Some had emigrated in disgust over collusion between priestly aristocrats and an imperial regime. Others had become mercenaries for imperial regimes. In conquering and reconquering Judea and Galilee, Roman warlords had enslaved thousands, a few of whom were lucky enough to become "freed-persons." By the first century CE there were communities of Judeans in many towns and cities of Syria and Asia Minor and a large community in Alexandria, Egypt. In his apology for the Judeans and their tradition, the Judean historian Josephus boasts that the communities of Judeans in various cities and towns had been intensively cultivating their ancestral traditions and customs. From hearing them recited in their weekly assemblies (*synagogai*), the ancestral customs and laws had become "inscribed" in their memories. Many Judeans in the diaspora communities would have become deeply familiar with the Mosaic covenantal customs, including those that required aiding the poor and keeping members of their community economically viable.

Also, according to Josephus, Roman warlords such as Julius Caesar and evidently later imperial authorities had, at least at points, taken into account just how committed Judean diaspora communities were to their ancestral traditions and customs. Judean communities were permitted a degree of self-governance, according to their traditions and laws, thus allowing for at least some of these "ethnic" communities to continue their social-economic affairs in ways that did not conform to the dominant Roman imperial order. This may well have been one factor in the hostility and even attacks that diaspora Judeans experienced in the first century CE. Diaspora Judeans may well have been feeling defensive and under siege in the early Roman empire.

What may well have attracted such diaspora Judeans to Jerusalem was what Jerusalem had become under the Hasmoneans and especially Herod. In the power-vacuum left by the demise of the Seleucid imperial dynasty in the late second century BCE, the upstart Hasmonean high priests, with their mercenary troops, had expanded the area and people(s) they ruled from the tiny territory around Jerusalem to include Samaria, Idumea, Galilee, and even some of the Hellenistic "cities" in Palestine. The Jerusalem temple-state became a regional capital. After the Romans installed Herod as their client king, he rebuilt the temple on a massive scale in grand Hellenistic style. Herod's temple thus became one of the wonders of the Roman imperial world. Whether it was his intention or not, Herod had thus created the Judean temple in Jerusalem as a sub-set of the Roman imperial order—located just "up-country" from his other monuments to the Empire and emperor such as the newly built city of Caesarea with its harbor facing Rome, its huge statue of Roma, and its temple to Caesar. All of this Herodian program of honorific building, of course, became a central aspect of the sacred imperial political-economy.

Judeans of modest means from diaspora communities in eastern Mediterranean cities could become pilgrims to the massive sacred temple in the vastly expanded capital of Judea and the monuments and tombs that Herod had built in honor of the great ancestral figures such as Abraham and David. In coming to the temple-city of Jerusalem they were presumably excited about visiting a monumental symbol of their own Judean tradition. And under the overall canopy of a tolerant and multicultural imperial order, with the tacit permission of the Empire, they could proudly celebrate their own cultural tradition. By the time the community of Jesus-loyalists was recruiting at "Solomon's Portico" in the temple complex and "sharing all things in common," large numbers of Judeans from the diaspora had come to Jerusalem. Besides Saul having come from Tarsus in Cilicia and Stephen and the other "Hellenists" mentioned appointed as *diakonoi* (Acts 6), there were whole "assemblies" (*synagogai*) of Judeans from areas such as the provinces of Asia and Cilicia, the city of Alexandria, as well as an assembly of freed slaves (Acts 6:9).[9]

If we keep in mind Josephus' claim about diaspora Judeans having been intensively cultivating their traditions, then Saul from Tarsus may have been typical of such pilgrims. As he reflects on the dramatic "revelation of Christ" in which he received his calling as an apostle, he had been "advanced in Judean ideology (*ioudaismos*) . . . , zealous for the ancestral traditions" (Gal 2:13-16). The NRSV perpetuates the standard old mistranslation of *ioudaismos* as "Judaism." The appositional phrase "traditions of the ancestors" indicates that he meant Judean ideology, parallel to *hellenismos*, the "Hellenistic ideology" that had carried over from Hellenistic times as dominant in the (Greek-speaking) eastern Empire.

He was super-proud of being "a member of the people of Israel, of the tribe of Benjamin, a Hebrew born of Hebrews, and (as to his understanding of) the torah/law, a Pharisee" (Phil 3:5-6). Saul may also have been typical of most Judeans who came to Jerusalem as pilgrims in his hostile reaction to the movement of Jesus-loyalists. Besides being proud of his Judean heritage, he was proud of his urban (and urbane) Hellenistic culture such as being able to speak Greek. Thus when he and other "Hellenist" Judeans encountered the movement of uncultured Galilean villagers led by *idiotai* who spoke a crude dialect of Aramaic (see Acts 4:13) and locked in opposition to the high priestly heads of the temple and temple-state they understandably reacted with hostility. Saul's active persecution of the movement, however, may well have been a more fanatical reaction than that of other Judean pilgrims from the diaspora. But this movement of countrypeople was a serious threat not just to the traditions of the ancestors (as Saul understood them) but to the Judean people and its sacred temple allowed and tacitly understood as subordinate to the imperial order.

Other Judeans from the diaspora, however, also zealous for the ancestral traditions, joined the movement. For some, coming to Jerusalem may have been a disillusioning experience. Actions of Roman governors such as Pontius Pilate would have seemed hostile. In their behavior the high priestly aristocrats were hardly adhering to ancestral traditions and covenantal laws. And/or the community of Jesus-loyalists may have seemed to be practicing covenantal customs and attempting to realize the aspirations of ancestral traditions. Whatever their motivations, some and perhaps many diaspora Judeans joined the movement. Stephen became an example

9. The claim about Pentecost (Acts 2) that there were "devout Judeans from all peoples under heaven living in Jerusalem," Judeans and proselytes from Mesopotamia and Parthia, etc., as well as from Pontus and Egypt, etc. is a gross exaggeration. As long recognized by scholars, it may suggest the reversal of the Tower of Babel story.

not only of articulation of how the movement understood the renewal of the people as the fulfilment of Israelite tradition, but also of steadfast loyalty/commitment even to the point of becoming a martyr (Acts 6:7—7:60). Insofar as "Hellenist" Judeans would have been familiar with the Mosaic covenantal traditions that required aiding the needy, the episode of the continuation and expansion of the sharing and distribution of food is quite credible. As the movement had expanded in Jerusalem, including by an influx of "Hellenists," so had the sharing of goods (Acts 6:1–6). In the narrative of Acts, this episode had become the illustration of the movement developing more complex leadership and administration. In the episode, what required this was the expansion of the sharing of goods, especially food for the needy. Although the Acts narrative does not mention it, some of the "Hellenists" may well have held some economic resources to contribute insofar as it would have required some means to make the journey to Jerusalem and to support themselves during their stay.

The Movement Spreads in Diaspora Communities of Judeans in Syria and Beyond

The third step in the expansion of the movement in the interstices of the imperial order toward the mission of Paul came in diaspora communities of Judeans in Syria and Asia Minor. As discussed just above, people in diaspora assemblies (*synagogai*) were well-versed in their Judean/Israelite tradition. These semi-self-governing communities' common life and communal identity would have been rooted in Israelite social-economic tradition and Judean history and not in Roman imperial culture. Presumably they understood themselves as having been subjugated by the Romans who had come to (conquer and) rule the eastern Mediterranean lands and peoples little more than a century before. Thus it may not be surprising that these communities would have been receptive to a movement of the renewal of Israel that was opposed to the Roman imperial order in anticipation of some sort of restoration of Israel under the direct rule of God, an ideal deeply rooted in early Israelite tradition and some (late) Judean prophecies.

The broader scheme of the narrative in Acts has the movement spreading out from Jerusalem into the areas of Judea, Samaria, and Galilee and then to synagogues in cities and towns in Syria. The narrative has some of this expansion but not all as resulting from the persecution related to the martyrdom of Stephen (8:1; 9:31; 11:19). Especially important was the movement's establishing a substantial and expanding community in Antioch that became a base for further expansion. In addition to the Judeans in these places, "God-fearers" and "proselytes" (that is, "hangers-on" of the assemblies of Judeans) and soon other people of the "peoples" in these towns and cities were eager to join the movement of renewal of the Israelite people. An action taken by the community of the movement in Antioch suggests that the practice of sharing resources especially to aid the needy was being extended to relations between communities of Jesus-loyalists. In a time of severe famine under Claudius, the disciples in the community in Antioch "determined [that] according to their ability, each would send relief (*diakonia*) to the brothers and sisters living in Judea" (Acts 11:27–30).

In this section (Acts 11:27—12:23) comes the only explicit attention that the narrative of Acts gives to the way the political economy of the Roman imperial order was set up so that urban oligarchies and regional client rulers extracted agricultural produce from their subjects (or tenants) and funded ornamentation of cities and spectacles in honor of the emperor. The emperor Claudius appointed Agrippa, a descendant of Herod the great, to replace Antipas as Tetrarch (in Galilee) and then as king over Judea as well (41–44 CE). The ambitious Agrippa became a key player in the imperial system in the eastern Mediterranean. From the revenues he extracted from his subjects he lavished benefactions on Greek cities, among them Beirut, and sponsored spectacles in honor of Claudius. Josephus' extensive coverage compares him favorably to Herod the Great in his benefactions (see, e.g., *Ant.* 19.436–445). He also evidently fashioned himself as a champion of Jerusalem and the Herodian temple as a sub-set of the imperial order and took an active role in running the temple-state. The movement of Jesus-loyalists having evidently become a threat to the established order in Jerusalem, Agrippa executed James the brother of John, one of the principal leaders. When this pleased the Judeans (evidently those of rank and position), he arrested Peter as well. In contrast to the elaborate coverage by Josephus, the Acts narrative zeroes in on the impact of the imperial political-economy on the peasant villagers. The Tyrians and the Sidonians (the magnates, not "the people" [NRSV], which is not in the Greek) were lobbying Agrippa because they depended on Agrippa's territory (his countryside) for food. The Acts narrative takes some glee in the death of Agrippa, who had violently repressed the movement, during his final public spectacle in which he arrogantly posed as a god (Acts 12:21–23; cf. Josephus, *Ant.* 19.343–346).

Interpreters of the middle section of the Acts narrative have characterized the mission at this stage, which already involved Paul and other Judeans from the diaspora, as having a repeated pattern in successive places: Paul and Barnabas (or other co-workers) start by preaching in the synagogue; when "the Jews" become hostile and/or the synagogue splits, they then go to "the Gentiles" (so that "Christianity" is becoming "Gentile"). But the episodes do not consistently follow this pattern. The mission proceeds in more complex ways from town to town. Clear throughout is that the movement remains a renewal of Israel, with indications here and there that it is against or an alternative to the Roman imperial order. Even after the narrative has "the peoples" joining the movement (11:1), those scattered by the persecution who went to Phoenicia, Cyprus, and Antioch "spoke the word to no one except Judeans" (11:19). In Antioch in Pisidia, Paul and Barnabas joined the assembly, were invited to speak, and when the assembly broke up many Judeans and devout proselytes "followed" them (13:13–43).[10] In Iconium when Paul and Barnabas spoke in the assembly a great number of both Judeans and Greeks became loyalists (suggesting the assembly was open to Greeks as guests). Here the hostile reaction came from both "the peoples" and the Judeans who, with their rulers, were ready to stone them.

Among the clear indications that the movement was a renewal of Israel (that other peoples were now eager to join) is the decision of the supposed "apostolic council" that those of the peoples who were joining the movement would not be required to become circumcised. They would only be required to abstain from food offered to other gods (idols) and from *porneia* (various forms of sexual activity) and from whatever had been strangled and from blood (Acts 15:1–21). Because the Acts narrative does not dwell on specifics, we are left to speculate on the relation between the (other) peoples who had joined the movement of renewal and the local assemblies of the Judeans: were they, like the God-fearers and proselytes before them, welcomed into the assemblies while being required only to observe special food laws, etc. as well as (presumably) the traditional customs in community social-economic relations?[11] In some towns the assemblies of the Judeans split over the upstart new movement, so that there may well have emerged new assemblies (*ekklesiai*) consisting of both Judeans and other subject peoples. In any case, it is clear that some very basic issues remained unresolved, such as whether loyalists from the (other) peoples would have to become circumcised; at least for a while leaders and others in the movement "rolled with the punches." For example, when Paul wanted Timothy, whose mother was a Judean but father a Greek, to accompany him (evidently) as

10. It should be noted that the paraphrase in the NRSV "converts to Judaism" is *not* in the Greek text. Only after this does the narrative add that, after the (other) Judeans become jealous, the apostles announce God's scheme of speaking first to the Judeans and, when they reject the word, they then turn to the (other) peoples (13:44–46).

11. Narratives of the expansion of the movement, like Paul's letters, evidently simply assume the community members accepted standard customs of social-economic relations in the community, such as people not swindling or stealing from one another or manipulating another into debt and dependency. But what would the implications have been for a slave-holding household?

a co-worker he had him circumcised because of (expected) pressure from other Judeans. Thus as it expanded in the cities and towns of Asia Minor, the movement was based in communities that were rooted in ancestral Israelite/Judean tradition and customs, that is in communities that were "in but not of" in the interstices of the Roman imperial order.

The Pauline Mission as an Alternative to the Imperial Order in Greek Cities

Episodes in the Acts narrative portray Paul's mission in the cities of Greece as a continuation of the renewal of Israel that now includes other peoples, mainly Greeks, in opposition to the Roman order established in cities such as Philippi, Thessalonica, and Corinth (and Ephesus?). The city of Philippi, as a Roman colony, would likely have been particularly sensitive to a movement opposed to the imperial order. It may be significant that Paul and Silas find the prayer-house (*proseuche*) of the Judeans outside the gate of the city; the two successive colonies of Roman troops had pushed the previous Macedonians living in Philippi out of the city, and immigrants, such as Judeans, would have located outside the walls.

As an illustration of how the economics of the movement's expansion worked, Lydia, already a god-fearer who became a staunch loyalist, insisted that the apostles stay in her house. After Paul, inadvertently perhaps, interferes with the profits some slave-masters are making from their slave-girl with the skill of divination, he and Silas are dragged before the local officials in the public square. The slave-masters, joined by a crowd of (other) Roman colonists as well, charge that these Judeans "are advocating customs that are not lawful for us as Romans to adopt or observe" (Acts 16:19–22). The opposition of the movement of renewal of Israel is rooted in and based on Israelite/Judean ancestral tradition and customs that are not only different from but opposed to and, if observed, resistant to the Roman imperial order—not just the conquest and domination of peoples such as the Judeans but the planting of colonies of Roman veterans on conquered people's land.

In the city of Thessalonica, Paul and Silas manage to recruit some of the diaspora Judeans in the assembly as well as some God-fearing Greeks and "leading women." Paul and Silas and their host in the city are charged before the city authorities with "turning the *oikoumene* (that is the known, Roman world) upside down," with "carrying out actions contrary to the decrees of Caesar and claiming that there is another emperor named Jesus" (Acts 17:1–8). The apostles found a more accepting assembly of Judeans in the town of Beroea (17:10–15). The movement of renewal of Israel continued to spread on its base in communities of diaspora Judeans in opposition to the Roman order. Understandably, however, some Judeans concerned about their continuing peace and security in the cities of the Empire were concerned about this expansion that might seem threatening to the city authorities.

Again in the large commercial city of Corinth, which had also been a Roman colony after its earlier destruction a century earlier by the Romans, Paul supposedly found the assembly of the Judeans open to participation by Greeks as well as God-fearers. The God-fearer Titius Justus and his household became loyalists and hosted Paul's mission, and the assembly official Crispus and his household and many Corinthians became loyalists (18:1–11). Other Judeans, concerned about disruption, brought Paul before Gallio, the Roman proconsul of Achaia; but Gallio refused to hear the case as a dispute within the larger community of the Judeans (18:12–17). They had good reason to be concerned since Claudius had recently ordered all Judeans to leave Rome (which sent additional Judean coworkers, Prisc[ill]a and her husband Aquila for the expansion of the movement in Corinth and Ephesus). Again in Ephesus both Judeans and Greeks joined the movement (19:8–10).

To recapitulate, the movement of the renewal of Israel started by Jesus in Galilee expanded from the community established in Jerusalem though diaspora communities of Judeans in cities in Syria and Asia Minor to the mission of Paul in the cities of Greece. Every step of the way the movement was *based in communities* of Israelites/Judeans deeply rooted in Israelite customs as well as historical traditions. The Jerusalem community of people who had left their original economic base in Galilean villages drew on Mosaic covenantal customs of the sharing of resources to ensure that needy people could have subsistence support. Diaspora Judeans in Jerusalem as pilgrims joined the movement and expanded the sharing of resources. In its next step, the movement found a base in communities of diaspora Judeans in Syrian towns and cities and beyond that the Romans had allowed to continue in ethnic communities that were semi-self-governing through their local assemblies and traditional customs. These were thus enclaves or islands of social-economic communities and interrelations that were not integrated into the Roman imperial order of the cities of the Empire. As the movement spread into assemblies of Judeans in Syria, the sharing of resources extended to relations between communities when the assembly in Antioch sent aid to the Jerusalem community during a serious famine in Palestine.

Dramatically, in the mutual opposition and conflicts between the community of disciples and others in the Jerusalem community and the high priestly heads of the temple-state and then continuing in its expansion into the cities and towns of Syria and Asia Minor, the movement of renewal of Israel opposed the Roman imperial order. Its leaders were arrested and charged with subversion of the established order again and again. Understandably Judeans who were more dependent on the imperial order in various towns and cities were concerned about the (potential) disruption that the subversive movement might cause for their own security and livelihood. Despite the periodic repression by city and imperial officials, however, the movement continued to expand and finally flowed into the mission of Paul. It established beachheads in the communities of diaspora Judeans that were important enclaves of different social-economic relations living out of a tradition of recognition of people's economic rights and the responsibility of the community to supply aid to needy members.

Paul's letters offer a more complete picture, although still fragmentary, of the situation of the communities he and coworkers catalyzed in the Greek cities. The expansion of the movement evident underneath the schematic narrative of Acts, however, indicates what Paul and his co-workers were building on in their mission.

8

Paul's Agenda for the Assemblies of an Inter-People Alternative Society

Until recently, Paul was understood in New Testament studies as the great hero of individual faith in the emergence of Christianity as a more universal and spiritual religion from the more parochial Judaism that was focused on legalistic obedience to the Law. Trained in New Testament studies as a subdivision of Christian theology, scholars treated Paul's letters as theological treatises from which they could cite text-fragments to attest certain theological doctrines such as christology and soteriology. Deeply embedded in the modern Western separation of religion from political-economic life, Paul scholars imposed this separation onto the ancient world in general and onto Paul and his letters in particular. They believed that Paul had been converted from the religion of Judaism to the religion of Christianity and became the principal apostle who generated and shaped Christianity as Gentile in the Hellenistic world.

Because Paul has been understood in Christian theology and New Testament studies as the hero and paradigm of individual Christian faith for many generations, it will be important to move beyond the limiting and distorting assumptions and interpretation that remain resilient. About a generation ago, many interpreters realized that it was inappropriate to read Paul's letters, particularly Romans, as reflections in his personal individual struggle as *homo religiosus* to gain a feeling of acceptance by God. That helped some to recognize that in his letters Paul was not struggling with the legalism of Judaism and its requirement for "works-righteousness" to gain justification; that he had not undergone a "conversion" from "Judaism" to "Christianity." Only slowly did scholars recognize how different, often distinctive, each letter (or composite of letters) was and that their difference was related to the "church" to which they were addressed. Most interpretation, however,

THE ASSEMBLIES OF AN INTER-PEOPLE ALTERNATIVE SOCIETY

remained interested primarily in issues of theological doctrines.[1] Moreover, insofar as Pauline studies shared the general Western European idealization and admiration of Hellenic and Hellenistic culture as the origin of Western culture—and understood Paul was the key figure in Christianity having been shaped by Hellenistic culture that was (more) universalistic in contrast with particularistic Jewish culture—Pauline words and statements were interpreted in terms of a general synthetic Hellenistic culture.

Remarkably, it was only about twenty-five years ago that interpreters of Paul finally began to recognize that the broader historical context of both Paul's mission and the communities and tradition in which he was rooted was the Roman imperial order *and* that Paul was opposed not to Judaism but to the Roman imperial order.[2] Even this recognition, however, has not always entailed also the realization that religion was not separate and separable from political-economic life. In the last twenty years, interpreters of Paul and his letters have devoted more attention to the political(-religious) dimension of the Roman imperial world as the historical context Paul's mission and letters. But little attention has yet been given to the economic dimension that was not separable from the political and religious dimensions in a movement of fledgling local communities in cities of the eastern Empire.

Paul's Understanding of the Historical Situation of His Mission

Although Paul does not lay out his "gospel" anywhere systematically, it is possible to discern from statements and arguments in different letters what his fundamental orientation and perspective is on the circumstances of the mission that he and his coworkers had undertaken. He was oriented to history and the particular turning point in history in which he had been called to an important role as an apostle of Christ. In his understanding, history had been running through the history of Israel and had reached a crisis (note that the Greek word *krisis* means judgment) and turning point under Roman imperial rule. The crisis was the Roman crucifixion and God's vindication/resurrection of Jesus Christ. It is striking and significant that he borrowed some of the

---

1. This was still the agenda in the "Pauline Epistles" Section of the SBL into the 1990s, replaced by a program unit on "Pauline Soteriology" since then.
2. The case was laid out with extensive excerpts from books and articles by leading scholars of Roman imperial history and culture/religion and some unusual articles by Paul scholars in Horsley, *Paul and Empire*.

central concepts and symbols of his proclamation from the Roman imperial order under the rule of Caesar in order to oppose it.

The *gospel*, inscribed on massive monuments throughout the Empire, proclaimed Caesar as the *Lord* and *Savior* who had brought *Salvation* and *Peace and Security* to the world. Paul's proclamation of his alternative *gospel* that Christ was now *Lord and Savior* meant that Caesar's rule had been "over-ruled" by that of Christ. "The rulers of this age," who did not understand the secret plan of God in working precisely though their actions, had crucified Christ (1 Cor 2:6–8). But in the resurrection God had vindicated him, exalting him as the new, heavenly ruler, the true *Lord* (1 Cor 2:6–8; 15:1–28). At the "coming" (*parousia*) of Christ in "the day of the Lord," (which Paul evidently thought would happen soon) the Roman imperial world—in which the wealthy imperial and local elite exploited, impoverished, and enslaved subject peoples—would be terminated and the kingdom of God finally be realized. The time in between the crucifixion-resurrection and the *parousia* was the period of Paul's and others' urgent mission to expand the movement of the renewal of Israel into new communities among subject peoples in the Empire.

Paul's urging the communities of subject peoples to persist in their *loyalty* (*pistis/fides*) to Christ, meant that they could no longer maintain *loyalty* to Caesar.[3] It seems evident from Paul's letters that the assemblies of Christ-loyalists were forming communities that Paul, at least, understood as an alternative, inter-people society whose *politeuma* (social-political order), already established in heaven with/by their *Lord*, would descend with him from heaven in the final realization of the kingdom of God (Phil 3:18–21).

Paul's Mission and His Letters

Claiming a dramatic commissioning as an apostle from "a revelation of Jesus Christ" (Gal 1:15–20), Paul had pushed himself forward in the leadership of the rapidly expanding movement of the renewal of Israel in opposition to and by their Roman client rulers. Yielding to Cephas as the leading apostle to "the circumcised," Paul claimed leadership of the expansion of the movement among the other peoples in the cities of Asia Minor and Greece.[4]

---

3. The term *pistis/fides* is usually translated in English Bibles and in New Testament scholarship by "faith"/"belief." In the Roman imperial world in which Paul worked and formulated letters, however, *pistis/fides* meant loyalty, usually to a lord or a political regime, especially to Caesar and to Roman imperial rule. Thus the term "Christ-believers" should be replaced by "Christ-loyalists" or "Jesus-loyalists" (see p. 114 above).

4. As noted in chap. 6, The term "the Gentiles" in dichotomy or opposition to "the Jews" is historically misleading and carries a good deal of Christian ideological

In contrast with Jesus and his envoys, who had worked to revitalize existing village communities already embedded in Israelite tradition, Paul and his coworkers attempted to catalyze new communities of people in cities of the eastern Empire. The generation of these "assemblies" was an audacious project to establish new communities that embodied alternative social-economic relations in the hostile context of the Roman imperial order established in cities of the Greek East.

When Paul and his coworkers moved on after working for many months in a given city to begin catalyzing another fledgling community in another city, Paul sent letters to the newly established assemblies, responding to questions and conflicts and urging them to maintain their loyalty to their new Lord and their solidarity as a community. Far from being theological treatises, Paul's letters focus mainly on the affairs of particular communities and their relations with the larger cities in which they had formed. Interpreters have only begun to ask what the political-economic situation was in each city where an assembly had come together, whether and how Paul and his co-workers addressed that situation, what economic issues may have arisen in or for the assembly, and what Paul and his co-workers were urging the assembly to do in the context of the broader Roman imperial (dis)order.

The "Pauline" letters in the New Testament that scholars believe Paul himself produced (Romans, 1–2 Corinthians, Galatians, Philippians, 1 Thessalonians, and Philemon) will be the basis of analysis of the mission of Paul and his coworkers. The "deutero-Pauline" epistles (2 Thessalonians, Colossians, Ephesians, and what are called "the Pastorals," 1–2 Timothy and Titus) offer access to one of the ways in which the movement generated by Paul developed in the ensuing generations. But it will be important to note other ways in which the Pauline tradition was developed.

With regard to use of Paul's letters as sources, it has only been recently that scholars are learning not to lift particular terms and statements out of context. Since the letters consist of Paul's ad hoc arguments in response to issues (or what he sees as problems) in particular assemblies, then rhetorical criticism of the arguments is the appropriate first step.[5] In a crucial example

---

baggage. In Paul's letters, the Greek term *ta ethne* usually refers to the *other peoples* besides Israel. The translation "nations" is also misleading insofar as it carries modern and contemporary connotations back into Roman antiquity. Nations were created in modern Western Europe from the top down, in the nineteenth century (e.g., Germany and Italy). Critical discussion in Benedict Anderson, *Imagined Communities*.

5. Instructive rhetorical analyses of 1 Corinthians and Philippians respectively in Wire, *The Corinthian Women Prophets*; and Kittredge, *Community and Authority*. For a consideration of the role of rhetoric in power-relations in the Roman imperial order, particularly as it bears on rhetoric in 1 Corinthians, see Horsley, "Rhetoric and

for this investigation, much of the problematic discussion of social stratification in the "Pauline" communities is rooted in a literalistic misreading of 1 Cor 1:26 (and 4:8): "if Paul says that there were not many in the Corinthian congregation who were wise, powerful, and wellborn, then this much is certain: there were some."[6] Terms such as "wise, powerful, and wellborn," however, had long since become widely used metaphorically as standard discourse among philosophers, particularly the Stoics (a discourse shared by the Wisdom of Solomon and elaborated by Philo of Alexandria) that not the political-economic power-holders but (only) the wise person, the *sophos*, was truly "wise," "powerful," and "nobly born"—and, to go on to 1 Cor 4:8, also "rich," "king," and "honored." In an argument (from 1:10 to 4:21) laced with irony and/or sarcasm (e.g., 1:26–31; 4:8–13), Paul is addressing people of low social-economic status who were suddenly claiming exalted spiritual status.[7] As this case illustrates, rhetorical criticism must be informed by knowledge of culture and subcultures and their uses of language as well as by information about the particular historical contexts. References to particular passages in the discussion below presuppose previous efforts of rhetorical criticism of Paul's arguments in particular situations.[8]

Building on the exploration of the historical context in the Roman Empire in chap. 6 and of the steps in the expansion of the renewal of Israel launched by Jesus in chap. 7, the agenda of this chapter is to discern the concrete economic aspects of the struggles of the newly established communities in which Paul was attempting to generate an alternative society "in but not of" the Roman imperial order. Since the network of communities that Paul and his coworkers started continued, we can then trace the different lines of its development, on the one hand, in the deutero-Pauline letters but also, on the other hand, in what appears as a far less accommodationist way in other texts.

The Assemblies as Local Communities in an Alternative Society

In attempting to understand the political-economic-religious agenda laid out in Paul's letters, it is necessary to take into account a factor not usually

---

Empire—and 1 Corinthians."

6. Theissen, "Social Stratification," 72.

7. All investigated in a series of articles in the late-1970s (based on a 1971 dissertation), later collected in Horsley, *Wisdom and Spiritual Transcendence in Corinth.*

8. For example, on 1 Corinthians, Horsley, *1 Corinthian*; on Philippians, Kittredge, *Community and Authority.*

considered in investigation of historical economic relations. New social movements sometimes initiate innovative changes in local social-economic relations and challenge the dominant power relations, even though they may not make much of an impact on the overall political-economic system. These innovations may be responses to the intensification of dominant power relations, and may be driven by a vision of a dramatically different political-economic-religious life, an alternative to the dominant system.

In his letters, particularly those to the Galatians and Romans, Paul struggles to explain that the communities that have come together from among other peoples subjected to the Roman Empire are an extension of the people of Israel. They did not become "ethnically" Israelite/Judean, much less "convert" to Judaism (which did not exist yet). But in the crucifixion and resurrection of Jesus Christ these people had become heirs of the promise to Abraham that all peoples would receive blessing through his "seed" (Gal 3–4); they were now being "grafted into" the main trunk that was Israel as a historical people (Rom 11:17–24). The movement of the nascent assemblies that he had catalyzed was the fulfillment of the tradition and history of Israel. The implication was that in the context of the Roman Empire, where it was assumed that history was running through Rome, Paul was making the audacious claim that the nascent assemblies he and co-workers were catalyzing were extensions of history that had been running through the people of Israel.

To appreciate how Paul's "gospel" of Christ's crucifixion, resurrection, and parousia may have resonated with and motivated subject peoples in cities such as Philippi, Thessalonica, and Corinth to join and continue in fledgling counter-imperial communities, it may help to review how that gospel addressed their life-circumstances. These peoples who had been subjugated by Caesar were variously slaves or freed slaves and displaced people living around the subsistence level in an environment that was pervaded by the presence of the imperial *Lord* and *Savior*. These peoples were regularly reminded of their subjugation by the imperial ideology and rituals and images of power that established distinctions between citizen and non-citizen, conquerors and conquered, free and slave.[9]

The counter-imperial gospel Paul preached focused on the crucifixion of Jesus by "the rulers of this age" (Romans officials). The assemblies lived their personal and community lives under the symbol of the crucifixion. And that crucified figure of abject humiliation had become their Lord and was imminently to come, as the direct rule of God would finally be realized

9. These were also distinctions between who could and could not be tortured in the Roman Empire, in which the principal instrument of torture was public crucifixion, mainly of slaves and subject peoples (provincials) who resisted their subjugation.

(on earth) and the *politeuma* of the alternative society descend with their crucified Lord from heaven (1 Cor 15:12–28; Phil 3:19–21). These interrelated successive images are all juxtaposed in the early (pre-Pauline) hymnic "creed," presumably recited regularly in community gatherings (Phil 2:5–11). Christ had taken the form of a slave, obedient to the point of death, even death on a cross. It was the crucified Christ who had been exalted as Lord (1 Cor 2:6-8). In Galatians Paul appeals to what he hoped would be the performative effects of his (and others') preaching before the communities of the movement: "It was *before your eyes* that Jesus Christ was publicly exhibited as crucified!" Later, when Paul's letters became Scripture, the imperial images that Paul borrowed to oppose the imperial order could easily be coopted to again reinforce imperial political-economic-religious structures.[10] But Paul evidently hoped that the performative effect of his "gospel" could reverse or at least effectively oppose "the sedimented effects" of the imperial images of conquest, enslavement, and domination in the nascent communities of subjected peoples that could now embody just and caring social-economic relations as they awaited the final actualization/realization of their *politeuma*.[11]

We have rarely if at all inquired specifically into the economic circumstances and practice of the assemblies as evident in Paul's letters. It has recently become clearer that Paul, his coworkers, and fledgling assemblies encountered serious political opposition in Philippi, Thessalonica, and Corinth, judging from his discussions in letters to the assemblies there (1 Thess 1:2–3; Phil 1–2), and these would have had economic effects. His and his coworkers' "shameful mistreatment" in Philippi, for example, led Paul to anticipate that he might soon suffer martyrdom. Only in the context of these official and unofficial attacks on the communities and their members can the implications of some of Paul's statements and the economic dimension of the assemblies be understood.

---

10. Paul may have hoped that he and the nascent "assemblies" were breaking free of the structures of kyriarchal domination. But as Neil Elliott notes, from his reading of Fredric Jameson, *The Political Unconscious*, 17–102, "the liberating impulses arising from the collective imagination, or 'political unconscious,' are limited and channeled by the dominant ideology of the power structure." Neil Elliott, "Ideological Closure in the Christ-Event," esp. 151–54.

11. See Butler, *A Politics of the Performative*, 147. On how Paul attempts to reverse the effects of the imperial ideology, see now Nasrallah, "You Were Bought with a Price."

Thessalonians and Philippians

As Paul mentions at several points in 1 Thessalonians, the assembly had suffered and endured serious persecution that had persisted for some time (1:2–10; 3:1-5, 6-10), so that they became an example of loyal endurance to all the loyalists in Macedonia and Achaia. Paul and his associates had also encountered "great opposition" in Thessalonica (2:2). The account of their work in Thessalonica in the book of Acts (17:1–9) confirms that they evoked political repression. The report of jealous opposition from "the Judeans" is suspect as a standard theme in the book of Acts. But the report that the political authorities of Thessalonica were concerned that Paul and his coworkers were acting "against the decrees of Caesar" in saying that there is "another emperor named Jesus" (that is, instead of Caesar) fits what Paul said in several of his letters to other communities. Evidence of such "decrees" and of Thessalonian coins make it highly likely that Paul and the community he had generated were seriously attacked by the authorities for their apparent opposition to the imperial order. The city was unusually active in its honors to Caesar, including ceremonies at the temple to Caesar, and the "politarchs" of the city were evidently charged with enforcing loyalty to the emperor, which would have been important in ensuring the cities' continuing "Peace and Security" under Roman imperial rule.[12] As part of his closing exhortation to perseverance in 1 Thess (5:1–11), Paul suggests that the urban elite who are trusting in the (imperial ideology of) "Peace and Security" established by Caesar, including those who enforce it, are making war on the community, whom he exhorts to put on the protective armor of "the breastplate of loyalty and love and for a helmet the hope of (concrete) salvation/well-being."

Paul's immediately preceding reassurance to the community about "those who have fallen asleep" that he has "by the word of the Lord," that is, by a direct revelation from Christ, suggest that some members have been martyred in the officials' attacks. Following the paradigmatic martyrdom and vindication/resurrection of Christ, whom Paul refers to as "the first fruits of the resurrection," those who have fallen asleep will also be resurrected to join their Lord. The scenario featuring vindication/resurrection in "the clouds of heaven" derives from a long Judean ("apocalyptic") tradition that we recognize from Daniel 7 and 11–12. Paul's version in "the word of the Lord" is also patterned after, and is perhaps a mocking of, the visit (*parousia* "coming") of the emperor to a city in which all the residents poured forth from the city in a ceremonial precession to greet their "Lord" and "Savior."

---

12. Discussed in Donfried, "The Imperial Cults of Thessalonica," and the research of Holland Hendrix on which he relies.

It is difficult to imagine that the members of the Thessalonian assembly under severe persecution could maintain even a subsistence economic livelihood. Many if not most people in the cities were directly or indirectly dependent on the wealthy and/or powerful in some way. It seems that Paul's exhortations to "abound in love for one another" (3:12) and to love all the Christ-loyalists, clearly addressed to the whole community, suggest that they aid one another economically. The further exhortations "to live quietly and mind your own affairs" (4:9–10), suggest keeping some separation from others in the city. And the admonition "to work with your own hands . . . and be dependent on no one" (4:11–12) and especially the "do good to one another" (5:15) imply some sort of taking care of one another economically. This love and mutual aid, moreover, is not just a desirable "value" that Paul recommends. Given the persecutions they were undergoing, the "doing good to one another" and "abounding in love for one another" refer to measures of concrete mutual aid, practices in which they are already engaged and that he urges them to continue.[13]

His letter to the Philippians Paul sends from where he has been arrested and imprisoned, presumably for his activities that at least seemed to the authorities to be subversive of the Roman imperial order. In his keen anticipation of possibly becoming a martyr for his resistance to the imperial order (in the image of dying and being vindicated in exaltation to the heavens [Phil 1:19–23]), he stands in the tradition of the "Enoch" scribes and the *maskilim* two centuries earlier who were being martyred for their resistance to the Seleucid regime's enforcement of the Hellenizing imperial order (1 Enoch 90:6–19; 104:2–6; Dan 11:32–35; 12:3).[14]

Once we have a clearer sense of the context of Paul's mission in Philippi and elsewhere, it is important not to perpetuate the de-politicizing translations of this letter. The (N)RSV of Phil 1:27–29 (and other passages) has been easily construed as exhortation to apolitical Christian pietism. The language, however, is literally political-economic in this passage that presses the Philippians to collectively resist those who oppose them: "Operate politically (*politeuesthe*) in a way worthy of the gospel of Christ [their alternative to the gospel of Caesar as Lord] . . . striving side by side with one mind (in solidarity) for the loyalty (*pistis*) of/to the gospel, in no way intimidated by those who oppose you . . ." Paul further suggests that they have been granted the privilege of suffering for Christ, hinting at possible martyrdom like his own

---

13. While it seems unlikely that Paul knew much of the teaching of Jesus, such practices of mutual aid in communities ("love your enemies, do good, and lend") was the core of the covenant renewal in the mission of Jesus; see discussion in chap. 5 above.

14. Critical analysis of texts and discussion in Horsley, *Revolt of the Scribes*, chaps. 4 and 5.

(1:29; and 2:15–17). His and their commonwealth (*politeuma*, in the sense of shared governance for the common social-economic good) is in heaven, whence they are expecting a Savior, that is, their alternative Lord, who is in the process of subjecting the imperial order (3:20—4:1).

Does the conduct of their own separate politics in resistance to the imperial order in Philippi also include an economic dimension? The letter includes no reference to economic aid of one another. But Paul expresses appreciation that the Philippians have been sending aid to him again while he is imprisoned, as they had more than once during his mission in Thessalonica (4:15–19). That they were sending economic aid to Paul suggests that there had been at least some economic aid to one another in the community.

Corinthians

In discussion of 1 Corinthians, it is important to confront head-on the focus on social stratification that has dominated interpretation of the "social world" of Paul's assemblies and diverted attention from economic power-relations in the Roman Empire as noted above. Particularly influential has been a literalistic reading of 1 Cor 1:26: "if Paul says that there were not many in the Corinthian congregation who were wise, powerful, and wellborn, then this much is certain: there were some."[15] The logic of that statement, of course, is faulty. More important is the broader cultural context and a sense of the rhetoric of Paul's argument in 1 Cor 1:10—4:13. Terms such as "wise, powerful, and wellborn," had long since become widely used metaphorically to insist that only the *sophos* was truly "wise," "powerful," and "nobly born," that is, possessed of elite qualities. In his first argument (1:10—4:21) laced with irony and sarcasm (1:26–31; 4:8–13), Paul is mocking people who were suddenly claiming exalted spiritual status.[16] Indeed, most of Paul's long arguments that comprise 1 Corinthians are evidently addressed to several people whose boasting of their status as "spirituals" (*pneumatikoi*) Paul believes was disrupting the unity of the assembly. In 8:1—11:1 he counters their claim that their enlightened theology makes "all things permissible to them." In 12–14 he urges them to use their special spiritual gifts for the benefit of the whole community. And in 1 Cor 15 he insists on the collective resurrection of the body to counter their view of the immortality of the soul/spirit freed from the prison of the body. First Corinthians does not give evidence of different

---

15. Theissen, "Social Stratification," 72.
16. All investigated in a series of articles (based on a 1971 dissertation), later collected in Horsley, *Wisdom and Spiritual Transcendence in Corinth*. Laid out in commentary form in Horsley, *First Corinthians*.

social-economic statuses/strata, but of several people who are excited about attaining high *spiritual* status.

First Corinthians does, however, offer good evidence for what Paul was insisting on as the political-economic practices of the Corinthian assembly both within the community and in its relations to the larger imperial order in Corinth.[17] First, it is worth noticing that the overall *ekklesia* in Corinth was not a religious cult, but a nascent social movement consisting of several cells (centered in Corinth but extending into the surrounding Achaia), some of which were based in the households of persons who probably provided the leadership, such as Stephanas, Gaius, possibly Crispus, Chloe, and, in the suburb of Cenchreae, Phoebe. Some members of these households may have been slaves or freed slaves (e.g., "Cloe's people," 1 Cor 1:11; and "Lucky" and "the Greek," who accompanied Stephanas in traveling to see Paul in Ephesus [16:15–18]).

In 1 Corinthians 5–6, more explicitly than in other letters, Paul insisted that the assembly conduct its own affairs autonomously, in complete independence of "the world."[18] This did not mean cutting themselves off completely from contact with outsiders, including the immoral, the greedy, and those who might steal—presumably the insiders were attempting to recruit outsiders into an expanding movement. Not only were they to maintain group discipline, in contrast with the injustice of the dominant society, but they were to handle their own disputes in independence of the established courts, which were "unjust" (6:1). Courts in the Roman Empire were instruments of exploitation of the poor by the wealthy. That Paul's list of unjust outsiders features the economic injustices of coveting and theft suggests that the issue over which one member of the assembly had taken another to civil court was economic (perhaps "defrauding," which may have been via the court [6:7–8]). The rhetorical question, "Do you not know that the saints will judge the world," indicates that it was a standard teaching the Corinthians knew well.

Paul and his co-workers had evidently been teaching that the individual assemblies and the larger movement of assemblies were an alternative society, the beachheads of the new age, and were to act as such in handling their own affairs, including economic issues, in independence of

---

17. Some of the following points and arguments were first articulated in Horsley, "1 Corinthians: A Case Study of Paul's Assembly as an Alternative Society," in *Paul and Empire*, chap. 14 (pp. 242–52).

18. The previous projection of "church-state" relations (separation) on these arguments of Paul is anachronistic, and results in exegesis almost the diametric opposite of what Paul is arguing. See older commentaries, such as Hans Conzelmann, *First Corinthians*.

the established order. Although the immediate context concerns issues of marriage and sexual relations, the general statement in 7:29–31—"from now on let those who mourn be as though they were not mourning,... and those who buy as though they had no possessions, and those who deal with the world as though they had no dealings with it. For the present form of this world is passing away"—would have powerfully enforced the insistence on the political-economic independence of the assembly.

Paul's next argument, in 1 Cor 8:1—11:1, deals with how political-economic relations are inseparable from religious ceremonies. In the course of the argument he focuses on slogans of several "spiritual" or enlightened Corinthians, especially that "all things are lawful/permissible for me" (quoted in 6:12 and again in 10:23), as Paul moves to the conclusion of this argument. He begins with a "correction" (really a rejection) of their (Hellenistic Judean) enlightened theology that, since there is no God but one, the gods of the city and Empire have no real existence (but are mere "idols"). Religion in the ancient Roman world was not primarily a matter of personal belief. Religious ceremonies were the way social-political-economic relations were constituted. As noted above, statues, temples, and shrines to the emperor, located in the center of public space, and citywide festivals played important roles in the cohesion of the Empire as well as local urban society under the domination of the sponsoring elite. Sacrifices were integral to, in fact, constitutive of community life in the Roman world at every level, from households to guilds and associations to city-wide celebrations and imperial festivals.

Paul does not side with, but rebukes the *gnosis* of the enlightened Corinthian who have developed a "strong consciousness" that "idols (of gods) do not really exist" and hence, no longer obsessed with traditional Judean food codes, they have the authority/liberty (*exousia*) to eat meat offered to idols in temples. In an awkward aside to their slogan (8:5b), he insists that "in fact there are many gods and many lords" (in those temples and shrines and festivals and associations). His argument climaxes in 10:14–22, with 10:23—11:1 as a conciliatory afterthought and summary of the implications of his argument. This is not, as some modern theological interpreters suggested, a "sacramental realism," but a political-economic realism that Paul shared with both the unenlightened majority of ancient Greeks and Romans and the "biblical" tradition of unenlightened Israelites/Judeans. In 10:1–13 Paul insists that biblical traditions not be taken as symbols of spiritual realities (spiritual food/drink/rock), but as references to events that had happened to Israelites after their liberation from oppression in Egypt—hence a warning about collective discipline and solidarity. In 10:14–22 Paul insists on the exclusivity of the assembly of Christ-loyalists.

In the Lord's Supper the cup is "a sharing (*koinonia*) in the blood of Christ" and the bread is a "sharing (*koinonia*) in the body of Christ." The Corinthian addressees would already have known (as Paul reminds them in 1 Cor 12) that "body" was a well-established political-economic-religious metaphor for the "body-politic" of the citizen-body of a city-state, and by analogy the "body-politic" of their assembly. But Paul insists on exclusivity over against the dominant society in which many overlapping social bonds were established in sacrifices to multiple gods. It was simply impossible and forbidden for members of the body of the assembly established and perpetuated in the cup and table of the Lord to partake also in the cup and table of gods, that he now denigrates as "demons."

Paul insists that eating "food offered to idols" was not an issue of ethics, but of "building up" the assembly of saints over against the networks of power relations by which the imperial society was constituted. He insists on political-economic-religious solidarity over against the dominant society that was constituted precisely in such banquets and "sharing" with the gods. For members of the new alternative community in Corinth, this meant cutting themselves off from the very ceremonies by which their previous social economic relations in the established order were maintained.

Paul's discussion of his own example of *not* accepting economic support from the Corinthians (in 1 Cor 9) indicates one way in which the Corinthian and other assemblies were engaged in economic cooperation and collaboration: the support of the apostles and their co-workers who were organizing and teaching among them to build up the communities of the movement(s). As illustrated in the agrarian images that authorized the practice (not muzzling the ox, included in the authoritative torah of Moses, and the worker worthy of sharing in the harvest) that Paul cites, it had been the practice from the outset of the movement(s) that the envoys of Jesus who traveled and worked in local communities were supported economically by them. And as illustrated in Jesus' instructions to the envoys, "remain in the same house, eating and drinking whatever they provide; do not move from house to house" (Luke/Q 10:7), the support was modest—necessarily so since the communities, whether villages in Galilee or the assemblies in Thessalonica or Corinth, were comprised of people living near the subsistence level (like the vast majority of people in the Empire). As we know from the Didache (The Teaching of the Twelve Apostles) 11–12, in the decades after Paul's mission, traveling apostles and prophets became a serious burden on such communities of meager resources, and the movement had to establish criteria for such support.

Paul's motives for declining support in principle (or at least from the Corinthians) may have been several. He may have felt self-conscious or embarrassed as someone of previously adequate means who had joined a movement of marginal people. The reasons he gives in 1 Cor 9:15–23 are credible—he was defensive about his commissioning and his legitimacy as an apostle, as indicated again in 1 Cor 15:8–10—and/or he did not want to be a burden on people living mostly at a subsistence level. His acceptance of aid from the Philippians may have been a special case insofar as Paul's own situation there, like that of the Thessalonians themselves, was unusually precarious (Phil 4:15–16; 1 Thess 1–2; 2 Cor 8:1–2); but it makes him appear inconsistent.

Paul's Stance toward Slavery and Slaves' Status in the Assemblies

Slavery was central to the political-economy of the Roman Empire in which Paul and his coworkers conducted their mission. The "Pauline" letters later became part of the Holy Scriptures that carried divine authority for subsequent Western Christian history, including the history of slavery in European and American history. It is thus important to deal critically with slaves and slavery in Paul's letters, mission, and assemblies.

The "canonical Paul" has been understood as an advocate of slavery. If Paul himself was the "author" of Colossians and Ephesians and the Pastoral Epistles, he clearly accepted and supported the slave-holding patriarchal family that was a cornerstone of the Roman imperial order. Slaveholders and advocates of slavery in European and American history claimed the canonical Paul as scriptural authority for the institution, although abolitionists also appealed to Paul in arguing against the institution. It will be important to deal with the deutero-Pauline letters produced by some disciples of the apostle as a determinative influence on later interpretation of Paul in a subsequent step of this chapter. Perhaps under that influence, even many (perhaps most) interpreters of Paul who accept only the seven letters as "authentic" view him as a political-social conservative hesitant to challenge the established order. Interestingly, they base this view on one of the rare references to slaves/slavery in Paul's letters, focusing on an uncertain reading of 1 Cor 7:21 as their proof-text, along with a traditional reading of the brief letter to Philemon.

Once it is recognized that Paul and his coworkers were anticipating the termination of the Roman imperial order, the previous debates about whether Paul opposed or supported slavery seem beside the point. In the final fulfillment of the kingdom of God, slavery would be terminated along with less extreme forms of domination and exploitation. That slave relations were pervasive in Roman imperial society, however, was one of the key factors in the background to the intense expectation of freedom in Paul's letters: in the Christ-events people had been delivered from "slavery" and brought into the freedom of the children of God (Rom 8; Gal 3–5). The question is whether and in what way anticipation of the end of slavery may have affected slave-relations in the communities of the alternative society Paul and his coworkers were catalyzing, which were still living in the Roman imperial order in which slavery was central and slaves were under the coercive domination of their masters.

In his main argument in Galatians, Paul cites a "baptismal formula" that addresses three of the principal divisions and power-relations in the Roman world (including Hellenistic and Judean society):

> You are all children of God.
> For as many as were baptized into Christ
>   have put on Christ.
> There is neither Judean nor Greek
> There is neither slave nor free
> There is no "male and female"
> For you are all one in Christ Jesus.

In the slave-holding kyriarchal family that was foundational for the political-economy of the Roman world, women were subordinated to their husbands (*kyrioi*, "lords") and slaves lived and worked under the total domination of their masters (*kyrioi*, "lords"). In the eastern Empire where Hellenistic culture was still dominant, "Greeks" were privileged and often despised Judeans and Syrians and other subject peoples as suitable for little more than laboring or slavery. In the expansion of the movement of Christ-loyalists, however, in which history was understood as moving through Israelite tradition instead of Roman imperial dominance, this rank or precedence was reversed.

Standard older interpretation of Paul, still assuming the separation of religion from concrete political-economic life, understood the baptismal formula and Paul as referring only to spiritual life and/or the future in the final fulfillment of the kingdom of God following "the day of the Lord." Such interpretation had not yet discerned that this baptismal formula had been the pronouncement, in "performative speech" that effected what it pronounced, of the dramatic and powerful ritual drama (with the disrobing, immersion, reemergence, and re-robing) that (evidently) all members of the assemblies of Christ had undergone as the ceremony by which they

THE ASSEMBLIES OF AN INTER-PEOPLE ALTERNATIVE SOCIETY   143

had joined the community/movement of Christ. It is clear from Paul's adamant overall argument in Galatians (that continued with confused and confusing "rhetorical overkill"), however, that Paul understood, and was insisting that his addressees in Galatia recognize that the "no longer Judean or Greek" was concretely realized for those who were "in Christ," that is, in the communities of the movement.

But can we conclude that Paul also understood the other two social relations of domination to have been socially transcended in the assemblies of Christ? It should be noted that the formulation of the line pertaining to women and men is not symmetrical with the other two lines: it is "no longer 'male and female,'" clearly a reference to the creation of people in Gen 1, "male and female [God] created them." If this phrase was understood as a reference to patriarchal marriage, then the baptismal formula evidently meant that such patriarchal marriage has been significantly relativized in the communities of Christ-loyalists (although it is difficult to discern how marriage suddenly became egalitarian, given how people had been socialized). But what about "slave and free"?

Although the ideal of and exhortation to "freedom" is strong in Paul's letters, his references to slavery and slaves are very few.[19] This makes it all the more striking that the standard older view that Paul was a social conservative, standing solidly behind the established order politically-economically, is based primarily on a rare and highly debatable reference to

19. It may be important to recognize that the term *doulos/oi* has different meanings in Paul's letters and the Gospels and related texts that derive from the different political-economic-religious systems in the historical background. See the analysis and discussion in Horsley, "The Slave Systems"; Callender, "Servants of God(s) and Servants of Kings"; and Wright, "'Ebd/doulos." The one meaning, dominant in Greek texts of the Roman Empire, was the chattel slavery that became institutionalized in ancient Athenian and other Greek societies and expanded considerably in the Roman Empire. This is the meaning in the "baptismal formula" in Gal 3:28 and in Paul's statements in 1 Cor 7:21–24. On the other hand, in the ancient Near East in general and in Israelite/Judean society, all people were understood as "servants of God/the gods," and some had a special calling or rank or office as "servants of God." Kings, such as David, priests, and prophets were "servants" of God in this special sense. Ordinary people were then also "servants" of the king as well as of God, and depending on their relationship of debt or other subordination might be "servants" of their (land)lords, etc. (for which the term "debt-slave" is often used). Such relationships appear in several of the parables in the Gospels; considering the political-economic-cultural background, it is unclear why the NRSV opted to translate *doulos/oi* consistently with "slave(s)" and not according to the literary and social context and cultural tradition. When Paul refers to himself as "*doulos* of God/Christ" he evidently means "servant of God/Christ" commissioned as an apostle, just as the prophets had been specially commissioned. He does not regularly refer to Christ-loyalists in general as "*douloi* of God/Christ." The occurrence of the phrase in 1 Cor 7:21–24 must be determined from context. See the fuller analysis and discussion in Horsley, "Paul and Slavery."

slavery (1 Cor 7:21–23). The baptismal formula in Gal 3:28 indicates that some members of the assemblies were slaves or former slaves. Interpreters have also taken Paul's references to "Cloe's people" and "the household of Stephanas" in 1 Corinthians (1:11, 16; 16:15–17, in which "Lucky"/*Fortunatas*), and "the Greek"/*Achaicus* could have been typical slave names) as indications that those households included slaves. His brief exhortation in 1 Cor 7:21–24 assumes that some members of the Corinthian assembly had been slaves when they were brought into the community. Like women, who might have been wives of husbands who also joined the community or of husbands who did not, the slaves might have been enslaved to men or women who joined the community or to men or women who did not. If Cloe's people and "Lucky" and "the Greek" were slaves, we can only speculate whether they were emancipated when Cloe and Stephanas and they joined the assembly. It seems likely that, with no other options for a subsistence living, they would have remained in the household even if they were freed (and we can imagine that the dynamics in the household interaction may not have changed all that much).

The standard reading of the principal "proof-text" by which Paul was taken as a conservative supporter of the institution of slavery is highly questionable in a number of ways.[20] First, the conservative interpretation projected a peculiar translation and reading of Paul's argument when he comes to slaves. Paul's statement in 1 Cor 7:21 involves a rhetorical omission of an object in the last, imperative clause: "rather use [it]!" (*mallon chresai*). In the appropriate way of reading the Greek, the implied object for the slave to "use/make use of" would be supplied from the closest preceding clause that begins with a strong adversative to being a slave. "But indeed if you can gain your freedom . . ." This is what the RSV translation committee did, in a break with the traditional interpretation: "But if you can gain your freedom, avail yourself of the opportunity." Ironically, the NRSV committee reverted to the pro-slavery (mis-)reading of the Greek that filled in the missing object from three clauses before: "Were you a slave when called?"

Second, the standard conservative reading does not attend to the context of Paul's overall argument in 1 Cor 7. Paul begins this argument in the letter addressing an inquiry from the Corinthians about what the "spirituals" evidently took as an implication of their spiritual transcendence with regard to marriage and sexual practice (their slogan, "it is well for a man not to touch a woman," 7:1). With the threat of *porneia* in mind, he then gives advice or a "word of the Lord" to people in different kinds of situation or relationships

---

20. On these key points, see further the critical discussion of 1 Cor 7:21–24 in Horsley, *First Corinthians*.

(7:2–16). Then he states a general rule for all of the assemblies: "Let each of you lead the life that the Lord has assigned . . . ," and proceeds to apply the rule to the fundamental social relationships addressed by the baptismal formula (7:18–20). In further illustrating his rule, just as it seems to apply to variations on marriage and sexual relations, it applies well to Judeans and Greeks, the circumcised and the uncircumcised. When he comes to slave and free (slavery), however, he realizes that he must qualify the general rule in a major way (before restating the rule in 7:24). "Were you a slave when called? Do not be concerned about it. BUT IF indeed you are able to become free, rather use (it)." Seize the opportunity! He then follows up with a confirmation. "For whoever was called in the Lord as a slave is a freedperson of the Lord . . . You were bought with a price. Do not be(come) slaves of humans." Following Paul's argument carefully thus shows that Paul makes a significant exception to his general rule of remaining in one's situation for slaves who have an opportunity to become free.

Third, that Paul is making an exception to his general rule in 7:21–23 follows the pattern of his foregoing argument on marriage and sexual relations. In 1 Cor 7:5a, 9, 11a, 15, and again in 7:29, he makes exceptions to his main exhortations, advice, commands, or counsel in his respective treatments of different kinds of relationships.

Fourth, despite the efforts of those who produced the deutero-Pauline letters to represent Paul as supporting slavery, his statements in 1 Cor 7:21 continued to be understood to urge slaves to take the opportunity to become free. The fourth-century theologian John Chrysostom, whose influence contributed to the establishment of the proslavery interpretation, knew that this statement had been understood in the opposite sense.[21]

Given these and other considerations, there is thus no basis for the interpretation of 1 Cor 7:21 as an indication that Paul was advocating that slaves continue in their slavery. In 1 Corinthians Paul was advocating that the nascent assembly operate as independently as possible from the dominant order of "this world." That slaves should seize an opportunity to become free fits with other ways that the assembly should treat the conditions of the Roman imperial order, of which slavery was a foundational reality, "as if not" in attempting to be an alternative society.

21. Harrill, *The Manumission of Slaves*, 77–78. In his earlier, exegetical writing Martin Luther broke with the traditional interpretation, drawing the implications for the serfs of his day, reassuring them that they were not to interpret Paul to mean that they should remain in their servitude. But in his vociferous later reaction to the Twelve Articles of the Peasants in Swabia and the German peasant revolt, he reverted to the traditional interpretation. Luther, *Works*, 28:42–43; Luther, *Works*, 46:146–47; see Bartchy, "Paulus hat nicht gelehrt: 'Jeder soll in seinem Stand bleiben.'"

Interpretation of the brief letter to Philemon has been dominated by the assumption that Onesimus was a slave, evidently a runaway slave, and even a runaway slave who was a thief. Operating on the assumption that he was a slave, interpreters then find other characterizations of Onesimus in the letter that "fit" his slave role, such as being a "child" (v. 10), being "useful" (v. 11), and being "of service" (v. 13). Although none of these characterizations necessarily indicate that he was a slave, the net effect is to confirm the assumption. Some interpreters who follow along in this traditional assumption then find in Paul's subtle argument that he was an active advocate of emancipation of a slave in one of the communities he helped catalyze.[22]

In the ongoing debate over the interpretation of this letter, Allen Callahan has delivered the most telling criticism of the assumption that Onesimus was a slave and the interpretation based on that.[23] He argued that a careful, critical reading of the Greek text (as established by text-critics) reveals that it contains no clear indication that Onesimus was a slave, much less a runaway. The term "slave" (*doulos*) appears only in v. 16. There it is preceded by the term *hos*, "as (if)," which indicates a virtual not an actual state of affairs or relationship. The sense can be discerned in v. 17, where Paul asks Philemon "to receive him as (you would) me (*hos eme*)," and in v. 14, where Paul wants Philemon's good deed to be voluntary, and "not as though by constraint" (*hos kata anagken*). In the key clause Paul thus hopes that Philemon will have Onesimus back "no longer as if a slave, but more than a slave, a beloved brother." The letter could most easily be read on the assumption that Onesimus was an estranged brother of Philemon. (Had the latter been treating his brother "as if he were a slave"?) Callahan's further thorough investigation of the manuscript tradition and the reception-history of the letter finds that until the fourth century it was ignored or considered insignificant or even non-Pauline. Then in the late fourth century, primarily in the works of John Chrysostom appears the stereotyped runaway-slave-who-stole-his-master's-belongings reading stated explicitly against charges that Christianity was "the subversion" of the social order, specifically taking servants away from their masters. The debate continues; but after Callahan's critical reading of the text and survey of the reception-history, it would be difficult to revert to the assumption that Onesimus was a slave and the interpretation of the

---

22. Petersen, *Philemon and the Sociology*; Winter, "Paul's Letter to Philemon." For references to the numerous recent studies of slavery in the Greco-Roman world, of Paul and slavery, and of Paul's letter to Philemon, see the extensive notes in Marchal, "The Usefulness of an Onesimus." Many of these studies seem to assume that Paul's statements and relations would have fit into the slave-relations and slave-owning and slave-using culture attested in references from texts produced by the slave-owning elite.

23. Callahan, *Embassy of Onesimus*; and Callahan, "Paul's Epistle to Philemon."

letter as evidence that the assemblies were not concerned that some of their members were slaves.

It may be disappointing to some that Paul did not make some unequivocal statement of condemnation of the institution of slavery. We can assume, but cannot know for sure, that he had in mind that slavery would be terminated along with the whole dominant imperial "world that was passing away." It seems clear that in the performative speech of the ritual baptism by which people joined the assemblies the relations of "slave and free"—like the relations of "Judean and Greek" and the traditional patriarchal marriage understood as ordained in the "male and female" of the creation story—were transformed in the communities of Christ (at least in Paul's understanding). In the appropriate reading of 1 Cor 7:21, far from telling slaves to remain in their situation, Paul urged them to seize an opportunity to become free. The text of the brief letter to Philemon is sufficiently unclear and susceptible of different readings that it seems unreliable as a basis for conclusions about whether and when emancipation occurred in slave-relations in the assemblies that Paul and his coworkers catalyzed.

The Collection for the Poor in the Jerusalem Community

At the end of 1 Corinthians and at points in most other letters Paul focuses on the most striking economic aspect of the movement, one that is unprecedented and perhaps unique in antiquity: the collection for the poor among the saints in Jerusalem.[24] The collection was evidently connected with, indeed had its origin in, the practice of sharing goods in common in order to aid the needy in the early community of Jesus-loyalists in Jerusalem, as portrayed in the accounts in Acts (2:44–45; 4:32–37). Within a few years the practice had been extended to other communities. During a period of severe famine in Palestine, the community in Antioch had sent aid (*diakonia*) to the Jerusalem community for distribution to the poor, which was delivered by Saul and Barnabas, according to the account in Acts (11:27–29). This would have been the precedent behind what was extended in the agreement Paul and Barnabas had made with James, Peter and John (Gal 2:9–10) that they should "remember the poor" as they expanded the movement among other subjected peoples. This meant that, from the outset of Paul's mission, the newly-formed communities of "the (other) peoples" would be sharing some of their resources horizontally, in contrast with the usual vertical flow of resources in the Roman Empire to rulers, land-owners, and creditors.

---

24. Helpful summary of previous interpretation of the collection in Kloppenborg, "Paul's Collection for Jerusalem," 307–11.

Paul had evidently been giving instructions about the collection to the communities that he and coworkers catalyzed, from Galatia though Macedonia to Corinth. As he writes to the Corinthians: "you should follow the directions I gave to the assemblies of Galatia: On the first day of every week, each of you is to put aside and save whatever extra you gain (earn), so that the collections need not be taken when I come (back)" (1 Cor 16:1–2). The further instructions Paul gives the Corinthians indicates that he had developed an ambitious plan for how he would implement the collection (1 Cor 16:3–4; 2 Cor 8; 9). After the amount had accumulated week by week (for well over a year), then the Corinthian and other assemblies would choose delegates to accompany Paul in taking the gift to Jerusalem.

In two subsequent short letters to the Corinthians (1 Cor 8 and 9) he pressed them insistently about the collection. He first uses the Macedonians as an example to the Corinthians. Despite their "severe ordeal of affliction" and their "extreme poverty," they had been eager to "share in this service (*koinonia tes diakonias*) to the saints" (8:1–4). It seems clear that the people in these assemblies must have been living close to subsistence but nevertheless, with a good deal of persuasion, accepted the collection as an obligation. Not wanting to put pressure on the Corinthians to give what they did not have in relief of others, Paul suggested they seek a balance between their "present abundance" and the "need" of the folks in Jerusalem (2 Cor 8:9–14). He further grounded his appeal by quoting from the story of God's provision of manna to the desperately needy Israelites in the wilderness who shared among them, so that no one had too much and no one had too little. Paul urged that the Corinthians' contributions to the collection would be a further expression of their "love," which consistently in the letters means concrete care and sharing (e.g., 1 Cor 13). Again citing Israelite tradition in 2 Cor 9, Paul draws a homology between the justice of God, which means giving to the poor, and ("the harvest of") the justice of the Corinthians in giving to the collection. The service of the poor folks in the Jerusalem community by the Corinthians and other peoples, moreover, is a manifestation of "obedience to the confession of the gospel of Christ." That is, the concrete results of the gospel of Christ were the communities of the movement that had an economic dimension, and that included the sharing of resources with other communities in need.

As he heads toward Spain after completing his mission in the Greek cities and writes to the Romans, Paul continues to conceive of the collection in terms of what the peoples involved in the movement share in common. The other peoples now share in common "the spiritual things" that originated with the Israelites (Judeans), and are obligated to share in common "the material things" with the poor in the Jerusalem community.

For Paul at least, the economic and the spiritual dimensions of the movement that he was devoted to expanding were inseparable. In the collection for the poor in Jerusalem the local assemblies of the movement shared economic resources (albeit quite limited) across considerable distances. The movement of assemblies had an inter-people ("international") economic dimension that was virtually the opposite of the centralizing tributary political-economy of the Empire.

∽ ∽ ∽

In sum, although it was limited by the Christ-loyalists' own marginal existence, the counter-imperial, inter-people, alternative society that Paul thought he was building did indeed have an economic dimension with some distinctive features. The *ekklesiai* were still within the Roman imperial order. But in significant ways they opposed and resisted it in their own practices, although probably not to the degree that Paul wanted. In cases where they were under attack locally, some sort of cooperation and mutual aid would have been necessary in order to survive. Paul urged them to mind their own affairs in community solidarity and separation from the established political-economic-religious order. In what was the most striking aspect of the alternative society Paul hoped they might embody what would have been unique in the Roman or any other imperial order. The sharing of resources among marginal subject peoples in the collection for the poor in Jerusalem was the diametric opposite of the vertical flow of resources to the urban elite and the imperial Lord and Savior.

The Deutero-Pauline Letters— and Other Developments of the Pauline Legacy

The Deutero-Pauline letters produced by Pauline disciples display a dramatic difference from the "authentic" letters of Paul with regard to slavery as well as other issues. Critical analysis has determined that Colossians and Ephesians are probably at least a generation later and that the Pastoral Letters are two or three generations later than the letters that were integral in the mission of Paul and his coworkers. The communities addressed are now comprised of (at least some) slave-holding, kyriarchal families/ households that were basic to the overall Roman imperial order. Also, more families in these assemblies are relatively more comfortable than living close to the subsistence level. First Timothy even addresses some who are "rich," and accordingly instructs them to be "rich in good works, generous, and ready to share" (6:17–18). In the Pastorals there now appears a hierarchy in the communities, with deacons, elders, and bishops, who are to be honored and obeyed.

These deutero-Pauline letters include what have been called "household codes" that give admonitions for the basic component relations within families, for example, to wives to be subject and obedient to husbands, who are to love their wives. Slaves now come under constraint and obligation to masters that are above and beyond those of slaves in non-Christian households, insofar as their masters' authority is now also that of their heavenly Lord.

> Slaves, obey your earthly masters with fear and trembling . . . as you obey Christ . . . as slaves of Christ. Render service with enthusiasm, as to the Lord and not to men and women. (Eph 6:5–8)

Slavemasters are asked only to stop threatening their slaves, since they have the same Master in heaven (6:9).

It has been recognized in recent decades that the Pastoral and other deutero-Pauline letters were not the only continuation of Paul's legacy and at the time probably not the dominant line of development. Rooted in and descended from parallel and often rival "apostolic" missions, communities of Christ-loyalists developed in different ways contingent on different regions and influences. From the early second century (two generations after Paul's mission), there is considerable evidence from the former Pauline mission area ranging from Antioch in Syria, Smyrna in Asia Minor, Corinth in Greece, to Rome for the use of common funds of the communities to aid widows, orphans, the destitute, and to emancipate community members who were slaves.[25] A letter from the "Christian" community in Rome to that in Corinth, refers to voluntary enslavement as an example of noble self-sacrifice as if it were familiar as a frequent practice. "We know that many among ourselves have given themselves to bondage that they might ransom others; many have delivered themselves to slavery, and provided food for others with the price they have received for themselves" (*1 Clem.* 55:2). Another, somewhat later communication from the community at Rome exhorts (the better off?) members "to minister to widows, to look after orphans and the destitute, and to redeem from distress the servants of God" and "instead of lands, to purchase afflicted souls and to look after widows and orphans" (*Hermas, Mand.* 8:10; and *Hermas, Sim.* 1:8).[26] At mid-second century, Justin Martyr attests the same tradition

---

25. Callahan, *Embassy of Onesimus*, 89–90.
26. Osiek, *Shepherd of Hermas*, 371–73.

and practice among "Christian" assemblies: a fund supplied mainly by the better-off members was used to "support orphans and widows and those in want and those who are in chains..." (1 Apol. 67.6).

Further attestation of the same practices is supplied by its sharp prohibition. Ignatius, the bishop of Antioch (later martyred), expresses the standard concern to provide concrete aid to the widow, orphan, the distressed, and imprisoned (*Smyrn.* 6:2). But he also has some pointed instruction for his fellow bishop Polycarp regarding slaves that resembles that in the Pastorals.

> Do not be haughty to slaves, either men or women, yet do not let them be puffed up, but let them rather endure slavery to the glory of God, that they may obtain a better freedom from God. Let them not desire to be made free from the common fund, that they not be found the slaves of desire. (*Pol.* 4:3)

Further, the fourth-century *Apostolic Constitutions*, which contains much earlier material and is usually located in Antioch/Syria, attests the deliverance of slaves and captives by drawing on the common fund (4.9.2; cf. 5.1–2). It also comments that the only reason for Christians to be found at public meetings was "to purchase a slave and save a soul" (2.62.4). These references to the practice among "Christian" communities of buying members out of their slavery by drawing on a common fund are made all the more credible by evidence that Jewish congregations and some associations engaged in the same practice.[27]

It would appear that many of the communities descended from Paul's mission and other missions came to act on the fundamental principles of their loyalty to Christ, such as articulated in the baptismal declarations of social relations to be embodied in the assemblies. Common funds of the communities were established for the purpose of aiding the destitute, widows, orphans, and of purchasing members out of slavery. It may well be that the prohibition of this practice by a bishop such as Ignatius, who with fellow bishops such as Polycarp was trying to consolidate ecclesial power in the monarchic episcopate, was motivated by the concern to make the nascent "Christian" assemblies appear less subversive of the Roman imperial order based in the kyriarchal slave-holding households by sustaining rather than subverting social hierarchies!

---

27. P. Oxy. 1205 = *CPJ* 3.473; Harrill, *Manumission*, 167–68, 174–77.

The Alternative Political-Economic Practices of Communities of Christ-Loyalists

These letters of Paul and other texts provide indications of the political-economic situations and social-economic practices of the communities they address. This enables us to move beyond the artificial and anachronistic separation of the political-economic and religious aspects of the texts and those communities. And this enables us to move well beyond a reductionist reading of these texts as expressions of theological ideas and ethical exhortation for individual believers to recognition of the texts' purpose and function. They were about and were addressed to communities of movements of subjected people struggling to maintain themselves and make adjustments in difficult political-economic circumstances and what was often a hostile environment.

The exploration of the political-economic situations and social-economic practices of these texts (and communities) of Christ-loyalists in the Roman imperial context suggests that there were likely some links between the practices indicated in the different texts. There were at least two different "legacies" of Paul's mission and "Pauline" communities. The deutero-Pauline letters of two or more generations after Paul and his co-workers' mission indicate that some "Pauline" communities became solidly established in cities of the Greek East. They indicate the kinds of compromises one strand of the expanding movement made in the process. That they were incorporated in a Pauline collection of letters and included in the New Testament in late antiquity meant that they tended to determine the way "the canonical Paul" was read and used to legitimate and reinforce the kyriarchal family in a hierarchical political-economic order ordained of God, including the subordination of women and the institutionalization and later reinstitutionalization of slavery. However, that a different, more liberation-oriented line of Pauline communities, including their communal practices and authority figures, persisted into late antiquity suggests that the "authentic" letters of Paul should not necessarily be read as scriptural support for the subordination of women and the legitimation of slavery and other forms of political-economic subjugation.

Part 4
The Bible and the New Form of Empire

9

Biblical Studies and the New Form of Empire

Biblical studies is beginning to recognize that "biblical" texts understood in their contexts were about all aspects of life, political-economic as well as religious. Part 2 above was devoted to exploring how in the Gospels Jesus was not uttering sayings but taking action in a crisis situation. He was catalyzing a renewal of Israel in its constituent village communities in resistance to Roman rule through its client Herodian and high priestly rulers. Similarly, Part 3 was devoted mainly to exploring how in his letters Paul was not teaching doctrines but taking action in a crisis situation. He was catalyzing new communities in a movement that constituted an alternative to the Roman imperial order in Greek cities.

The contexts of the action and the movements of Jesus and Paul, the Roman imperial order in Palestine and the Greek cities, of course, were very different from our context today. So it would be inappropriate to attempt simply to plug them into our context. Our context today is also an empire, but a different one that is much more pervasive in numerous ways. It seems only appropriate to consider our context, global capitalism, which determines the conditions of biblical studies today in order then to discern how "biblical" texts in historical contexts may be pertinent to the new form of empire and how they may inform our action in response to the new empire.

The New Form of Empire

The shock of the national and global economic depression that began with the collapse of the mega-banks in 2008 led many people to realize just how completely their lives had become controlled and manipulated by uncontrollable economic forces. The hurried "bail-out" of those banks that were "too big to fail" was a further revelation about what those forces were. The US Secretary of the Treasury, who had come into the administration from Goldman-Sachs, one of the mega-banks, insisted it was essential that the US government bail out the huge banks. That is, in order to save the international economy it was mandatory for US taxpayers to give a huge infusion of capital to the very uncontrollable mega-institutions of finance capital that had caused the crash. Suddenly the usually passive news media were asking questions and sponsoring discussions of how the impoverishment of families who lost their homes and/or their jobs was the direct result of decades of unregulated predatory exploitation of people of the world by those banks and other transnational corporations.

Although the uncontrollable predatory power of finance capital has largely disappeared from the front page, its centralizing institutions have continued to "grow their wealth" and political-economic power. The "news media" of course are owned by multinational conglomerates. The "news" is designed as just another form of entertainment, the purpose of which in turn is to sell products. And nothing sells like sensational controversy and fear. The news media thus further enabled the manipulation of the electorate by the wealthy, which led to the continuing deregulation of industries and the legislation of large tax-cuts for corporations and their wealthy stockholders. Thus, during the Covid-19 pandemic, the stock market and the wealth of the wealthy has surged while the majority—and especially the vulnerable poor—have been even further impoverished.

Since at least the end of the twentieth century, the system of globalized consumer capitalism has controlled nearly every facet of personal, social, and political life. In 2000 the academic press at the university with by far the largest endowment in the world, which grew with every advance in the stock market, published the deeply critical and comprehensive historical, political economic, and even social-psychological analysis of how global capitalism had become the new form of a now global *Empire*.[1] Then, and still today, we are accustomed to think of empire and imperialism as the territorial and political economic control by a powerful nation over subject lands and peoples. In the ancient Near East, where the texts later included in the Bible originated, one after another imperial military regime killed and plundered nearby peoples and weaker regimes: the Egyptian Pharaoh, the Babylonian "great ones" (kings/emperors), the Assyrian warlords, the Persians, and then the Macedonian Alexander the Great and his successors. The Roman patrician warlords and legions conquered the cities and peoples around the Mediterranean Sea, subjected them to payment of tribute to Caesar, and dominated for several centuries. Because the "forces of

---

1. Hardt and Negri, *Empire*. Relatively few professional academics and politicians, and very few biblical scholars, have read the incisive analysis of Hardt and Negri.

production" were so limited in ancient agrarian societies, the only way for a regime to expand its wealth and manifest its own and its gods' glory in monumental architecture and display was to plunder additional lands and peoples (labor). To control markets as well as territory, Western European monarchies (and chartered companies) invaded African, American, Asian, and Australian lands, as well as many islands, both Pacific and Caribbean, enslaved and/or exterminated the peoples, and planted colonies of Europeans. After the intense competition of European powers to colonize the rest of the world, the most successful by far was Britain: "The sun never sets on the British Empire."

The modern captains of commerce and industry figured out how to accomplish similar results by different means. Building on military conquest, extermination or displacement of indigenous peoples from the land, and displacement of people from farms into factories, capitalism exploited the now "free" labor of people to generate profits that relentlessly expanded the wealth concentrated in corporations and the power of the owners of capital. By the late twentieth century, capitalism had gained global domination, only in a much more comprehensive way than possible in territorial empires. Transnational mega-corporations (literally!) worked overtime figuring out new devices by which to siphon off the resources that had previously been the basis of people's livelihood and bring them under the centralized ownership of their mega-stockholders under the centralized control of their CEOs and CFOs. Most of these devices aim/ed to get people and whole countries into various forms of debt that were/are then leveraged at high-interest payment and penalties, foreclosures, and forced bankruptcies. Debt was/is the broad general mechanism by which both increasingly centralized wealth and relentless impoverishment were/are generated. Only in mid-twentieth century did many people become aware that, in its relentless drive for profits and deployment of its power, capitalism was systematically destroying the planet, polluting the earth and waters, and poisoning its peoples.

Historically, people subjected by empires have resisted and rebelled. The "books" later included in the Hebrew Bible include many instances of resistance and rebellion. The mission of Jesus was framed by revolts against Roman domination by Judean and Galilean peasants (brutally suppressed by the Roman military). Anticolonial movements finally erupted in Africa, Asia, and Latin America after World War II. The Viet Nam war that tore society apart in the US in the 1960s and 1970s was a counterinsurgency by an imperial power. The attempts of the old imperial powers to suppress anti-colonial insurrections and the closely related "Cold War" are what gave the "military industrial complex" the opportunity to gain wealth and power as part of the process of globalization. In fact, political struggles in the US and elsewhere helped divert attention from the relentless development of the new form of Empire, global capitalism. After the collapse of the Soviet Union and "the fall of the Berlin wall," the US President G. H. W. Bush declared the establishment of "the New World Order." That new world order turned out to be the new form of empire.

Some significant signs and symbols confirmed that this new form of empire had become dominant. Exhibit A would have been the targets of the attack on 9/11 (2001). The World Trade Towers were *the* symbol of global capitalism (which was centered in NYC) and the Pentagon was *the* symbol of the enforcer of global capitalism, the US military. The "neocons" of the George W. Bush administration, of course, insisted that the United States was still the empire that mattered. But their disastrous military invasion of Iraq and the ensuing "forever war" exhausted the United States (government) economically, giving further opportunity for global capitalism to expand its economic and political power. And internal political divisions in the US further diverted attention from the growth of the new form of imperial domination. The global crash of 2008 was what finally began to wake up people to the new form of empire. Then Occupy Wall Street, with its subsidiary Occupy demonstrations in many cities, brought further discussion and protest into the public square of the extent to which global capitalism determines the lives of people around the world.

Steps in the Development of the New Form of Empire

It may be illuminating to look briefly at steps by which the increasing centralization of wealth and power in global capitalism has taken control of people's lives and impoverished people in the US and beyond.

Historically most peoples and societies have honored and observed customs that preserved the common good. Many have practiced a kind of "moral economy" in which all component families of the village or society have rights to a subsistence living that the collective is responsible for maintaining. Early in its development, capitalism began to manipulate the common good and goods into private property, starting with the enclosure of the village commons and extending through the present unrestrained privatization of public utilities, public works, and public education.[2]

---

2. To illustrate the extent of the imperial rule of global capital today, let me refer to struggles that have been in the news in Canada and the US in recent years. Having gained the power and permits to extract oil from tar-sands (that has made northern Alberta an utter wasteland) and natural gas by fracking (that poisons the ground water for towns in Pennsylvania), huge fossil fuel companies then maneuver to get permits to dig pipelines (that pollute the land and water) across the continent through reservations,

To control international capitalism so it would not spiral into another depression—and paranoid about the USSR and communism—the United States and other western powers, at the Bretton Woods conference toward the end of WW II, set up the International Monetary Fund and the World Bank. Preaching the gospel that capitalist "development" was the path to prosperity, the IMF and the World Bank and the United States Agency for International Development forced the governments of "underdeveloped" countries to take loans at interest. When these governments were unable to repay the loans, due to an utterly unlevel international capitalist playing field, the powerful IMF and World Bank forced them to make "structural adjustments," to cut the desperately needed services they provided their citizens, thus further impoverishing whole countries. The US government, moreover, usually without informing the public, acted as the enforcer of this centralization of wealth that increasingly impoverished the populations of other countries. The US undermined or overthrew democratic governments, set up and/or supported military dictators, and insisted on "development," regardless of the tragic consequences for the people.

After a series of mergers, huge mega-corporations designed new ways to siphon off resources from the poor to generate more wealth for the wealthy. Through increasingly sophisticated multimedia advertising mega-corporations reached right inside people's souls to stimulate and channel their desire. Marketing experts, with advanced degrees in psychology, created highly desirable images of gratification, fun, status, and power that could be attained only by buying certain products. The trick was to get people to identify desirable states and images with certain products: quenching "thirst" with Coke or Pepsi; satisfaction of "hunger" with fast-foods; "fun" with beer; family coherence and "happiness" with a plethora of gift-giving; "sex" with cars; "love" with diamonds.

And how could people afford all of this escalating consumption on their limited incomes? Spiraling debt. Banks sent multiple credit cards to everyone, including teenagers. Automatic "credit"—at 18–20% interest, plus penalties.[3] To see how all of this worked to siphon off people's livings, we need simply look at what happened and continues to happen during "the Holidays" in the

---

towns, and cities to seaports for export. International trade agreements and federal laws and contracts trump traditional tribal and local town and city rights to the use of their own land and streets. Cities and towns bring lawsuits but lose in federal courts. So local and state police are constrained to arrest and charge their fellow citizens and even mayors and city councilors who demonstrate to protect traditional local rights to land and infrastructure.

3. All of this, of course, was against the laws of many countries, as well as against biblical commandments and church teaching.

United States and Japan and elsewhere: the climax of the annual cycle of consumer capitalism when a huge percentage of retailing is done without which the economy would collapse.[4] The key devices in this climax of consumer capitalism were/are advertising and credit cards.[5]

The conglomerate corporations that devised means such as advertising and credit cards to siphon off people's income became transnational mega-corporations. Having acquired such great wealth and power, they could make or break small countries whose net worth they dwarfed. They could even dictate the policies (and obviously the economies) of the largest states/nations such as the United States and Germany.[6] For example, the CEOs of the largest fossil fuels mega-corporations were called together by Vice President Dick Cheney, the former CEO of the largest of all, Haliburton, to formulate the Bush administration's energy policy. Of course, such manipulations usually took place less publicly. Candidates for public office were funded by corporations and the very rich who then had access to presidents and senators. The same was true in other countries, only to a lesser extent.

The capstone of the centralization of wealth and ever widening debt and poverty was the consolidation of banking into mega-banks.[7] In the forty years of my life from the 1960s to 2000, the local bank in Harvard Square where I had my checking-and-savings account, was merged into BayBanks, that operated in the ring of suburbs around Boston itself, then into BankBoston, the largest bank in the metropolitan area, then into Fleet Bank, and finally into Bank of America. Meanwhile, the credit card set up for all unionized Massachusetts teachers and professors was bought out by bigger and bigger banks until that too was owned by Bank of America. And my mortgage from a local Jamaica Plain bank was bought up by one after another huge bank until it too was owned by Bank of America. By around

---

4. Contrary to what most Americans probably assume, Christmas in America never did have anything to do with Christ. Its celebration having been banned in the seventeenth century in New England, it developed from a solstice and New Year's festival exploited by local merchants into the extensive civil-religious and consumer-capitalist festival from Thanksgiving to New Years, and now from Halloween to "Super Sunday" (Nissenbaum, *The Battle for Christmas*; Horsley and Tracy, *Christmas Unwrapped*, esp. chaps 1, 5, 8).

5. In my seminar in the Honors Program at the University of Massachusetts on "Christmas and Consumer Capitalism," one of the largely working-class students explained how credit cards drove his family ever more deeply into poverty year after year by getting the family deeply in debt at Christmas. To buy the objects that advertising had induced the children to beg for at Christmastime, the parents used credit cards, building up charges plus interest that they could not pay off from the limited income before the next Holy Days.

6. Korten, *When Corporations Rule*.

7. Phillips, *Bad Money*; Sachs, *Common Wealth*; Korten, *Agenda for a New Economy*.

2000, much of my livelihood was owned, controlled, and manipulated by the Bank of America. All of us have experienced the same process of consolidation and centralization of wealth and power.

Meanwhile, the Reagan administration in the United States and satellite governments in Europe and Asia deregulated the conglomerate megacorporations, and under the Clinton administration Congress repealed the Glass–Steagal Act, thus removing the "firewall" between investment banking and the finance "industry." Along with all sorts of legal loopholes, these steps of consolidation and centralization set up all sorts of opportunities for these megacorporations, with their "best and brightest" officers and researchers, to devise new schemes by which to get people further into debt and drain off what little remained of their livelihood. The mega-banks and huge mortgage companies (such as the one significantly named Countrywide) targeted even the very poor whom they had not thought of before because they presumably had no resources left after having already been lured into buying fast-food and low-cost processed food harmful to their health. The most obvious example, which led into the bubble that finally burst in September, 2008, was the utterly deceptive and manipulative sub-prime mortgages actively pushed onto poor people who, as the mortgage brokers knew very well, could not repay and could easily be foreclosed upon. And, as we now know, the mega-banks, knowing these assets were toxic, not only sliced and diced them into triple-A securities and "derivatives." They also hedged their bets, setting up "credit-default swaps," taking out insurance against losses so that they would make huge profits either way.

We all know the widely devastating impoverishment that has resulted, as millions of people lost not only the minimal assets they had left, but their jobs. With abandoned houses and foreclosures, moreover, the housing values in whole neighborhoods, suburbs, and towns plummeted. Finally, if there had been any lingering doubt that the megacorporations and monster-banks were firmly in control of the US government, the bailout of the banks and continuing manipulation of the Treasury Department by Wall Street made it unavoidably evident. Internationally, what was a minor manipulation in banking or finance could undermine the relative value of a country's currency, ruining even a medium-sized nation and its people in an instant. As is now abundantly evident, the mega-banks can manipulate the economy even of the nations of the European Union and the United States government.

The result of all this centralization of wealth and power we now discuss as *globalization*, while often leaving unmentioned that it is the *globalization of consumer capitalism*. Ironically, globalization was described ten years ago as de-centralization, the spread of economic power to centers beyond the

United States, to London, Bonn, Paris, Amsterdam, Tokyo, and Beijing. But all was coordinated by superordinate agencies such as the World Trade Organization, to maintain order in the globalized capitalist system. The economic crash of 2008 made it evident to the world that wealth is centralized in many intricate ways, as the big European mega-banks had invested in the sliced and diced Wall Street securities based on the subprime mortgages. The banks of Iceland, for example, were ruined because they had invested so heavily in those securities. Finally, who pays (and thus moves further into debt, collectively and individually) to bail out the mega-banks/international finance? Who pays to make up for their mountains of debt based on those mortgages, those toxic assets? The taxpayers and the small debtors down the line who lose everything—while the CEOs retain their bonuses as well as exorbitant pay-packages. The process of centralization of wealth and power and impoverishment of the people continued unabated.

Another great irony is that the economic centralization of global capitalism thrives on multiculturalism (which, in a further irony, is pushed in university curricula as an antidote to racism and xenophobia). Globalized consumer capitalism touts and exploits multiculturalism, as it "divides and conquers," as it targets particular cultures and consumer-groups. This is true also of globalized information, which has been made into a commodity, like everything else. As we now know, Google and other search engines provide the information that they have determined particular subscribers want, tailored to their biases. This keeps consumers politically and culturally divided among themselves while subjected to targeting advertising.

Finally, to make sure we include the religious dimension, we should inquire about what is sacred in this now globalized system. The way we can tell what is sacred in a society is what is off-limits to criticism. Today we can call God into question, but we cannot criticize capitalism. And not only is capital above criticism, which is subject to severe social-cultural sanctions, but it is legally protected as private property and is accorded the rights of human persons (in the US Supreme Court case of "Citizens United"). In an earlier era, smaller corporations might have been considered to have a responsibility to the wider communities they were a part of. In the reigning ideology of global capitalism, however, huge corporations are now considered responsible only to their stockholders, that is, those who own the shares in the company and receive profits on their investments. Those who borrow and are in debt to the owners of private property are legally bound to repay the property to its owners, with interest—which, of course, is against biblical law and repeated biblical prophecy and teaching.

An Empire with Unprecedented Control
over People and Planet

Not only has global consumer capitalism devised ever more sophisticated devices to suck up ever more resources, further impoverishing ever larger percentages of the people and manipulated governments into cutting desperately needed services for their people. Global capitalism has gained extensive and intensive control over people's lives in ways far beyond what any previous empire has even dreamed of.

In the process of alienating people from their land, developing capitalism dissolved the communities (and often families) in which people's lives had been embedded. Ironically, *individualism* was central in the bourgeois ideology that accompanied and legitimated capitalism. But isolation of individuals was also the inevitable effect of capitalism's dissolution of supportive community. Advertising not only channeled people's desire into consumption of unnecessary goods, but acted as an effective solvent for communal and even personal values. Capital's ownership and use of mass media and centralized electronic communication, moreover, further disintegrated community and civil society. With the further evolution of electronic media and devices, the individualism that had already become atomization of people became more complete as the huge social media corporations manipulated individuals and the mass of atomized individuals for record profits. Already able to influence and even control government policies and decisions by funding previously democratic elections, extremely wealthy people and corporate bodies were now able to manipulate target "demographics" through Facebook and other burgeoning media companies.

Through ownership of the mass media and now social media, global consumer capitalism also transformed culture. As noted already, it transformed different particular (peoples') cultures into commodities and thus both expropriated and marketed multiculturalism. More ominous for its control of people's lives, global capitalism effectively dissolved and replaced (all) culture(s), including people's history and cultural/religious tradition that had bound them together in community or broader society. It effectively *replaced meaning*, which had been sought by bourgeois culture, *with non-meaning*. We might say that not only are people deprived of any meaningful cognitive orientation, but also that global capital depends and thrives on disorienting people, on creating the episodic virtual reality in which people live.

Finally, it is basic to recognize also how global capitalism, like previous empires (often thought of as "political"), displaces or destroys not just people's culture but the people themselves. For example, it relentlessly takes control of land that previously provided the means of livelihood for millions of people, making them into homeless refugees, then has states and their military repress dissent, suppress local resistance, and take larger-scale military action where deemed necessary to maintain (social-political-economic) order. For example, under NAFTA, agribusiness and other transnational corporations made it impossible for over a million independent Mexican small farmers to continue to make a living from their land. When many of them became refugees, the US military intensified violent control over border-crossing, while the flow of migrants provided very low-cost labor for agribusiness and other enterprises on both sides of the US–Mexico border. Meanwhile, the "behind the scenes" US support of Central American states' political repression (killings, jailings) further exacerbated(s) the flow of refugees. In addition to destroying people and their livelihood, moreover, global capitalism steadily escalated its historic exploitation of land, water, minerals, and forests that has brought the very survival of the planet into question. Global capitalism may have brought the earth it dominates to the tipping point of collapse from which it cannot recover.

Biblical Studies

The field of biblical studies, a division of (Christian) theology, was developed on the basis of and as an expression of western European bourgeois culture, whose assumptions, orientation, approaches, and interpretive concepts it shares. As part of the (often tacit) agreement between church and state following the French Revolution, theology (including biblical studies) agreed not to interfere in the business of the state and the expanding capitalism that it fostered. With the increasing dominance of individualism in bourgeois culture, religion was not only relegated to the margins of political economic life but increasingly reduced to individual belief.[8] Biblical studies functioned and was supported in the training of churches' clergy, who nurtured the faith of believers. Well before the proliferation of disciplines in the twentieth century (such as literature and sociology) in the academic division of labor into discrete "fields," biblical studies had developed its own methods ("criticisms") and theological schemes and conceptual apparatus. As it became further marginalized from political-economic life, it remained in its ghetto, accepting the definition of its subject matter, Scripture/sacred texts, as strictly religious.[9] What came to dominate biblical studies in many ways

---

8. See esp. Asad, *Genealogies*, chap. 1, focusing on a critique of Clifford Geertz's influential definition/theory.

9. Any suggestion that, for example, Jesus or the Gospels had a political dimension

was the Christian theological scheme of Christian origins: beginning with the revelatory teaching of Jesus, the spiritual and universal new religion of Christianity superseded the overly political and parochial old religion of Judaism. Much of the agenda of biblical studies, including the Program of the Annual Meeting of the Society of Biblical Literature is still conceptually structured in terms of "(early) Judaism" and "(early) Christianity."

Strongly reinforcing the separation of religion from political-economic life and the individualization of religion was the fragmentation of the sacred text into separate verses or paragraphs. Determined by the format in which it was printed (in the KJV, Lutherbibel, and other translations), the Bible was read, memorized, and quoted in isolated sayings or laws. Biblical scholarship focused narrowly on pericopes literally "cut out" for exegesis in preparation for preaching. Focus on "verses" and "lessons" effectively diverted attention from and blocked discernment of broad narratives and arguments and the groups, communities, or movements to which the texts were addressed.

In the modern scientific context, the historical critical approach came to prominence, with the "objective" observer establishing the supposed "historical" meaning of the religious text-fragment, with all the philological aids available. The text-fragment and its meaning, however, remained narrowly religious and/or confined to an ancient language abstracted into lexicons. In any case, it had nothing to say to the extra-exegetical world.

The Diversification of Biblical Studies

In reaction—or boredom—biblical studies began to diversify and splinter, in three different directions, in the 1980s and 1990s. Some interpreters imported analysis of rhetoric and modern literature. This led to the recognition of sustained arguments and sustained narratives. But the arguments and narratives remained (only) religious. Literary criticism discerned a "world"; but it was the world within the text. Others creatively adapted the social sciences. But what many adapted was mainly the conservative structural-functional social science concerned with social stability of the overall social system consisting of various social strata, an approach that had been abandoned by social scientists by around 1970. Both the various kinds of literary criticism and the some of the social-science criticism remained within the individualism of modern Western culture and its separation of religion from political-economic life.

(Reimarus) was quickly refuted or explained away.

A variety of perspectival "criticisms" that are often lumped together as "postmodern" biblical interpretation honed sharp criticism of the pretentious ideology of objectivity in establishing nuanced (mainly scholarly) racial, ethnic, gender, sexual, geopolitical, or "postcolonial" identities. These criticisms also remained largely within the confines of the dominant individualism and restriction of biblical studies to religion. As in other fields, they were the further extension of the bourgeois revolution. They limited the contextualization of the interpreters mainly to the social-cultural and eclipsed not only the historical context but also the political-economic concerns of the texts. As capitalism generated additional profits from "multiculturalism," it became increasingly evident that the establishment of these diverse identities, like "identity politics," were susceptible to being coopted by global capitalism.

The civil rights movement and the anti-Vietnam War movement during the 1960s both took political action in attempts to change concrete social-political reality. It has often been observed that when government suppression came crashing down in reaction to the anti-war movement, grad students and young faculty members shifted their focus to the academic disciplines in which they were being trained. This was certainly true of biblical studies. The surge of (various versions of) postmodernism amounted to a critique of academe from within academe. By a change in "institutional structures" they meant the institutionalized structures of academic disciplines and fields such as biblical scholarship. In New Testament/Biblical Studies post-modernism became far more influential than pursuit of Latin American, Black, or feminist liberation theologies, leading away from interest in concrete historical political-economic relations in historical contexts, then and now. Nothing really changed in the basic individualistic orientation of the field and its self-confinement to the cultural dimension.

Recognition that Biblical Texts Addressed a Succession of Imperial Contexts

For interpreters of the texts that were later included in the Hebrew Bible (Old Testament), of course, it was difficult to utterly ignore that the contexts in which those texts originated were the invasions and domination by one empire after another. In many cases, significant portions of the narratives or prophecies focused explicitly on the threats they posed and the devastation they caused. While some interpreters devoted attention to these historical contexts in the 1970s and 1980s, the focus of interpretation followed the "literary turn" taken in many fields in the humanities. A significant exception is attention given to researching and rethinking the historical context of the tiny territory under the Persian Empire, in many ways the crucial watershed of texts later included in the Hebrew Bible.

New Testament studies historically allowed only formal attention to Roman imperial rule as the context of Jesus, the Gospels, Paul's mission, and the "writings" of the New Testament. Yes, the Romans ruled Judea; yes, they had appointed Herod as king; yes, by building roads across the Empire the Romans had facilitated the mission of Paul. By its focus on how the new religion of Christianity was emerging from the old religion of Judaism, however, along with its projection of modern Western assumptions such as the separation of religion from politics and economics, New Testament studies blocked recognition of the concrete historical context. The high priestly heads of the temple were/are merely "Jewish religious leaders" (an identification still ubiquitous in the secondary literature); Jesus' demonstration in the temple was merely a "cleansing," given the assumed separation of religion and politics; Pontius Pilate was the political authority; and Jesus was not only non-resistant but utterly a-political.

A few scholars had been pressing for recognition that religion and politics were not separate in the ancient world and that an apolitical Jesus could not have been the historical Jesus, for recognition of the diversity and conflict in the historical context, and for no longer imposing modern individualism and the synthetic constructs of "Judaism" and "Christianity." It was not until the 1990s that there was a push to insist that the historical context of Judean rulers; of Judean and Galilean society; and of all Judean and Galilean groups, communities, movements and their leaders—including Jesus and Paul—was the Roman Empire. In his letters, it is clear that Paul was not opposed to "Judaism" but to the Roman imperial order. As portrayed in the Gospels, Jesus was not engaged in conflict with "Judaism" or "the Jews" but with the Roman imperial order and the Romans and their client high priestly rulers in Jerusalem. While more fully acknowledging the Roman imperial context, however, the focus of the field remains on religion/culture, individual faith, and more and more on the "location" and views of the interpreter.

The focus of the field continued mainly in literary criticism, and post-modernist interpretation prepared the way for postcolonial interpretation. In response to the confusing label "postcolonial" (imitating "post-modernist") by those who point out that political-economic and cultural power relations are rather neo-colonial or neo-imperial, apologists claim that "postcolonial" still includes colonial relations. Arif Dirlik and others have criticized postcolonialism for diverting attention from contemporary problems of social, political, and cultural domination and for obfuscating its own relationship to the conditions of its own emergence, that is, to the

168 PART 4: THE BIBLE AND THE NEW FORM OF EMPIRE

growth of global capitalism that structures global economic, political, and cultural relations.[10]

The Bible Had Become the Imperial Bible

While some Westerners and many non-Westerners were already sharply aware of this, postcolonial interpretation has increased the awareness that the Bible as we have it is an imperial Bible. This is not simply a matter of the Bible's rhetorical use in interpretation, but the text of the Bible as we know it and as it has functioned. Let me focus on the emergence and function of the imperial Bible in modern European and North American history.

The printing press made possible the mass production of relatively inexpensive Bibles that played a role in limited democratization in some European countries. The printing press, however, also led to the generation of "national" languages and literatures, beginning with translations of the Bible "authorized" by the ruling authorities, such as the KJV and the Lutherbibel. This, in turn, enabled the rise of Western nation-states and nationalisms that—thanks partly to the grand-narrative of the Bible as well as nascent capitalism—had a sense of destiny to expand.

The biblical underwriting of Western imperialism was sometimes blatant. Some of this happened in the translation of the Hebrew or Greek in authorized versions. A prime example that became extremely influential, even causative, in modern history was (and *is*) the Hebrew construct phrase *yosheve*-[of fortified cities in]-*Canaʾan* (literally, "those who sit" in the fortified cities of Canaan"), which stood parallel to "kings" and other rulers in Hebrew poetry (e.g., in the Song of the Sea in Exod 15). This would most obviously have been translated (paraphrased) as "rulers" in legends of peasant guerrilla attacks against local "kings" and their chariot forces who dominated territories from fortified cities such as Ai or Hazor (Josh 8:1–29; 11:1–15; cf. 10:1–27). In prose passages in "books" such as Joshua, however, this construct was translated, for example, in the King

---

10. See his "The Postcolonial Aura" and his 1997 book with the same title. In his puzzlement over the impossibility of explaining how it can be described, this native of Turkey who is professor of modern Chinese intellectual history suggests, somewhat caustically, that it is "third world" intellectuals teaching in "first world" institutions. For preliminary criticism of postcolonial literary and biblical interpretation's focus on colonial and post-colonial culture to the exclusion of the political-economic conditions of that culture and its criticism see Horsley, "Submerged Biblical Histories and Imperial Biblical Studies," and the more searching and "@home" criticism in Gerald O. West, "Doing Postcolonial Biblical Interpretation @home."

James Version (perpetuated in other translations) as "the inhabitants of the land/cities," that is "the Canaanites."

This translation in effect became a charter for extermination of indigenous peoples in the Americas by the English, French, Spanish, and European-Americans, and in what is now South Africa by the Dutch and then the English, and more recently the conquest and displacement of the Palestinians in "the Holy Land." To modern European Christians, self-designated successors of "the chosen people," moreover, collectively occupied land was by definition empty and open for settlement by "civilized" people who would divide it into privately owned and cultivated properties. And, of course, this paved the way for the global expansion of capitalism.

A central aspect of European colonization of Africa, India, and East Asia were the Christian missions that brought the Bible (in various national translations) to the colonized peoples. As peoples "converted" to Christianity, the Western scriptures, their stories, and grand narratives displaced or overlaid indigenous cultures and native traditions and customs.[11] This further paved the way for the acceptance of capitalist enterprise and products.

Biblical Studies Facilitating Empire

Moreover, biblical studies as it has been developed and practiced in Western Europe and North America was/is also imperial or at least helps facilitate empire. The innovative new criticisms in the later part of the twentieth century, while not offering direct support of Empire nevertheless facilitated Empire as it shifted form. The structural-functional treatment of the social world of Paul's mission in the Roman Empire gave a relatively positive picture of the Roman Empire as facilitating the life of the "first urban Christians," suggesting that an empire is, on balance, benign for people. The new literary criticisms' insistence that individual readers of the Gospel stories stay within the "story world" excluded attention to the historical context of the text in its origins and the social-political context of the reader in the present.

Meanwhile New Testament scholars who were following and developing standard mainstream scholarship pushed biblical studies further into the intensifying individualism of Western culture and the realm of religion and theology separate from broader social-political life which had long since become imperial. For example, further refining the criteria used to ascertain the "authentic" sayings of Jesus purposely isolated from the Gospel stories (which were basically ignored), the Jesus Seminar reduced and domesticated

11. See further Kwok Pui-lan, "Discovering the Bible in the Nonbiblical World."

the teaching of Jesus into pithy one-liners that called followers to withdraw from family and community into an individual spiritual "kingdom." This publicity-seeking enterprise even became complicit in the process by which global capitalism cannibalizes culture, disintegrating images and fragments from local people's movements, then exoticizing them into commodities for consumption in innocuous depoliticized form.[12]

How Might Biblical Studies Respond to Its Current Context?

One of the principal criticisms of postcolonial criticism as practiced in various fields is that it diverts attention from current political-economic domination and, in effect, ignores or obfuscates its relation to the conditions of its operations. This seems to be true also of biblical studies, both historically and after its literary turn. More ominously, by not recognizing the contemporary conditions in which it operates, will biblical studies continue to be oblivious to or even facilitate the Empire that has taken a dramatically different form from modern European and North American imperialism?

The "Bible and Culture Collective" observed in 1995 that power is invasive and pervasive, but they did not examine how this worked in the global political-economic system. Considering the pervasive power of global capitalism, it is almost impossible to be *in* the new Empire but not *of* it. It would be possible to lessen our individual and collective contribution to how it "grows wealth" for the corporations that wield the power of capital by not using credit cards, by shifting our mortgages and bank accounts from mega-banks to credit unions, and (for example) by not ordering purchases from and allowing shipments by the burgeoning Amazon division of Empire that has gobbled up Whole Foods and a whole variety of already large corporations that span diverse industries.

As participants in a field that is institutionalized in higher education, we could assume some professional as well as personal responsibility. As noted, the Bible as we have it is the Western imperial Bible, its Hebrew and Greek text "established," that is reconstructed by scholars from widely-varying manuscripts and translated into various European languages, then read and interpreted by theologically-trained biblical scholars. But it was assumed to be religious, about religion separate from concrete politics economic life, and addressed to individual Christian and/or Jewish believers (faith). It is not necessary, however, for biblical studies to continue in such contradictory assumptions. At least one sub-sub-field of biblical studies

---

12. Probably unwittingly, scholars of the Jesus Seminar thus aided and abetted the cultural production process of burgeoning global capitalism by its fragmentation and commodification of exoticized sayings of Jesus in books heavily marketed by a Rupert Murdock publishing house.

(studies of the process of canonization) investigates the processes by which the Bible, the TaNaK ("Old Testament") and the New Testament, were defined by rabbinic or ecclesial practice and decisions. There was no Bible in what has become standard to refer to as the "biblical" world. Why not recognize that the texts later included in TaNaK and the New Testament were originally produced (developed) in and addressed to historical contexts very different from how they were later read and interpreted? With the recent more comprehensive and precise investigations of the historical contexts of these texts, biblical scholars have available a much more comprehensive and precise understanding of the development of the texts (later included in the Bible) and of how they address their contexts.

The next step would seem to be to *reread the texts in their contexts to discern what they were/are about*. They are not about religion separate from political-economic life, but about political-economic-religious life more completely. The texts and the characters in the texts, God and people, are *concerned with all aspects of life*. Closely related to this recognition, little in these texts is concerned with meaning or ideas (or "doctrine" or "values"). No. *They are concerned with actions, commandments or prohibitions of actions, and social-economic-political interactions, and pronouncement of judgment for political-economic-religious actions or anticipated actions*. Moreover, *many of these texts are concerned with invasion and/or domination by empires and the people's struggles against invasion and domination by imperial rulers or by local/indigenous rulers under the domination of imperial rulers*.

The texts that were later included in the Hebrew Bible and New Testament were produced in and addressed to historical contexts and circumstances very different from those of later capitalism and especially global capitalism. They may be suggestive perhaps precisely because they derive from different historical contexts. They may be suggestive of unfulfilled possibilities because of developments in subsequent history. These texts understood and appreciated in their historical contexts could help challenge the universality of the categories of capitalism. Texts later included in the Bible might serve as part of "a reservoir for thinking in non-capitalist terms."

These texts tell the stories of people who were living in (the conditions of) imperial domination, but struggling against it and/or attempting to live in communities of opposition that could resist in some way. Although the imperial domination they were living under was nowhere near as pervasive as that of the complex system of global capitalism, some of these texts give indications of the processes, schemes, and mechanisms by which particular historical imperial systems gained and consolidated their power over subject peoples. Many of these texts also indicate the principles of alternative practices of political-economic-religious relations and the actions people took to resist the processes and mechanisms of domination. It would be naive to expect that "biblical" stories, statements, or laws could provide models or injunctions for action in the very different and far more complex and pervasive imperial domination of global capitalism. It would be naive to be looking for equivalent patterns or actions. Stimulated by historical cases, however, it might be possible to discern some corresponding patterns and actions.

At the very least "biblical" scholars could explore how biblical studies might at least *elucidate* the contemporary political-economic conditions in which it is currently working and the implications of those conditions. As noted, one of the primary features of global capitalism is its creation of a universal system of *non*-meaning. Ironically the Bible and Culture collective and other recent innovations in biblical interpretation were seeking a way that biblical texts could still become meaningful in the conditions of postmodernism. But biblical studies' (like literary studies') pursuit of meaning seems like a feature of modern bourgeois culture that global capitalism has displaced and made nearly impossible in its nearly pervasive effects.

Instead, "biblical" scholars could take a cue from the texts they study, which are not concerned about meaning but about life circumstances and actions. The people represented in most of these texts and/or sections of them, recognizing that they were unavoidably *in* an imperial system sought courses of action not to be *of* that system. While it is not possible in current circumstances not to be *in* the new Empire, might it be possible for biblical scholarship not to be *of* the Empire? Biblical scholars too could take oppositional action. At the very least we could explore how to stop facilitating global capitalism. Might it be possible for biblical scholarship to help in imagining alternatives to the new imperial order to help undermine its hold on people. While global capitalism is the determinative context of biblical studies and its previous individualistic focus on religion, biblical scholars can change their assumptions, goals, agenda, and approaches. And for sure, global capitalism does not determine the biblical texts in their historical contexts.

I would like to explore further how biblical scholarship might try to stop facilitating the growing power of global capitalism. While it is not possible in current circumstances not to be *in* the new Empire, might it be possible for biblical scholarship not to be *of* the Empire? To repeat, might it be possible for biblical scholarship to help in imagining alternatives to the new imperial order, even to undermine its hold on people through alliances with movements that are seeking to lessen the pervasive power of global capitalism? I suggest that attempting to take public responsibility in the current circumstances will be integrally related to further exploring more critical historical reading in historical context.

10

(Proto-) Hebrew Bible Texts and Global Capitalism

Because of its origins in modern Western culture, biblical studies has generally assumed that "biblical" texts are concerned with religion separate from political-economic life, as noted in the Introduction. Biblical texts, however, are concerned with all aspects of life, not just religion. Biblical scholars tend to focus on interpretation of the meaning of texts or the doctrines and values they articulate. The texts they interpret, however, tell about or condemn or call for actions and social-economic practice. Nearly all of the texts later included in the Hebrew Bible and New Testament, moreover, tell stories or pronounce prophecies or give injunctions about people living under domination by imperial and/or local rulers and struggling against it and attempting to live in communities of opposition that could resist in some way. The texts later included in the Hebrew Bible were addressed to historical contexts very different from those of the global capitalism that now determines the context and circumstances of biblical studies. Yet they may be suggestive perhaps precisely because they derive from different historical contexts. They may be suggestive of possibilities that remain unfulfilled because of developments in subsequent history.

The Torah

In biblical studies, the books that became the Torah or Pentateuch have traditionally been thought of as the Law, one of the principal "pillars" of Judaism. These books are far more than law and the collections of customs and laws that loom so prominently in them. A more appropriate translation of *torah* would be teaching, teaching about all aspects of life. Much of "the contents" of these "books," moreover, consists of historical legends of the archaic origins of the people of Israel and of their ancestors.

Before the literary turn and fascination with postmodernism, analysis by biblical scholars discerned that these books underwent a complex process of development as learned scribes serving in the Judean monarchy and the Judean temple-state adapted the archaic legends of the ancestors of the "twelve tribes" of Israel. They wove these legends together as episodes in a grand narrative scheme in which the descendants of the ancestors who fled from the imperial civilizations of Mesopotamia and Egypt were the people especially chosen to receive blessings: they would become a great people, inherit land, and through them other peoples would receive blessings (Gen 12; 15; 17). Beginning with a scheme by which the world was created by God, the narrative in a series of legends sketches the rise of an arrogant imperial civilization in Mesopotamia (symbolized by the tower of Babylon) that is condemned to destruction and dispersal. The ancestors flee Mesopotamia and, followed by their progeny, live in the hill country of Canaan where they must struggle to resist dominance by predatory local kings. In a period of drought and famine, the ancestors seek food in the imperial civilization of Egypt where they are impressed into hard bondage by the Pharaoh. In what became the central legend of origin of the people of Israel, "the Hebrews" and a "mixed multitude" flee their bondage in Egypt. They then make a covenant with their liberator-force/power and one another: they form a covenantal society committed to exclusive loyalty to their liberator-god and non-exploitative social-economic relations with one another. Much of the rest of the Torah/Pentateuch consists of the covenantal customs and laws intended to guide their life as a covenantal people, evidently eventually under the rule of a temple-state and its priesthood.

In the course of the overall narrative are two particular passages that are especially instructive about ancient imperial civilizations and Israel's attempt to establish and maintain an alternative society.

A remarkable section of the narrative of the ancestors' bondage in Egypt portrays how ancient Near Eastern empires worked and maintained power over their subject people(s). Without explicit reference to the (divinized) forces/powers of Egyptian imperial domination, the story of how the empire worked begins with (what we think of as) the religious practices of the imperial regime. The wisdom (knowledge) of how to consolidate the power and wealth of the regime was acquired through interpretation of dreams deemed ominous by the rulers (Pharaoh). The rulers maintained a large staff of interpreters of dreams and omens (not "magicians," which is the pejorative and mystifying translation of earlier biblical scholars). In a puzzling irony, the narrative has Joseph, the youngest son of Jacob/Israel, become a successful courtier as the brilliant dream interpreter whom Pharaoh appoints as the "viceroy" or "CEO/CFO" of the regime.

How the story has him manipulate the people would have been typical of empires in the ancient Near East. Following the wisdom gained from interpretation of the seven fat cows and the seven lean cows, he commands a heavy levy of grain during years of plentiful harvests be gathered into the regime's storehouses. This is ostensibly a surplus from which the whole land could be fed during years of bad harvests, to keep the regime's economic base, the peasantry, alive through a period of famine (Gen 41). But Joseph uses the surplus to manipulate the people as he ratchets up the demands of the imperial regime. When famine struck, he forced the people to hand over any and all goods they possessed (money had not been invented yet) as payment for food from the storehouses. When famine struck again, he forced them further to hand over their livestock in exchange for food, so that the regime then possessed all of the draft animals and flocks and herds. Finally, in the next famine when the people had nothing left but their land and labor, he extorted those as well, so that Pharaoh (the regime) controlled all of the land of Egypt and the seed for subsequent crops and the people had to promise to pay a fifth (had it started with a tenth/tithe?) of all their crops to the regime (Gen 47). They had become sharecroppers or serfs of the Pharaoh. In the legend at the beginning of the book of Exodus, the Hebrews became further subject to forced labor in the construction of "public buildings" (the pyramids, tombs of the divine Pharaohs). This is how ancient Near Eastern empires consolidated their wealth and power over their people(s): manipulate the people into spiraling debt that enabled the "creditor" regime to take control of their land and labor.

The second significant passage to consider portrays the people's action not just to escape their bondage but to form an alternative social-economic-religious order free of empire (Exod 1–23). The exodus narratives grew as a basic legend that summarized and represented the people's many actions of withdrawal from or revolt against domination by (would be) rulers, such as remembered in stories included in the "books" of Joshua and Judges. In the Exodus narrative, after escaping from their hard bondage, the people received the covenant mediated through Moses. In the covenant, they formed themselves into a people committed to maintaining their independence and to avoiding slipping back into domination by human rulers. The importance of "the Mosaic covenant" for the texts later included in the Hebrew Bible and for the people of Israel is indicated by its prominence in being presented in schematic form twice (Exod 20 //Deut 5) and in ceremonies of covenant renewal (e.g., Josh 24).

By limiting texts to a religious sphere, biblical studies misses that *the Mosaic covenant required certain collective political-economic action and interaction.*[1] This should have been clear from the ten "words." All of these commandments concern social-economic relations and interactions that made it possible for each household in a village community to maintain a viable economic subsistence. As an interrelated set of principles, these "words" protected economic rights of families. With the prohibitions against coveting and stealing others' crops and goods or making false dealings, families' subsistence livings were protected. Parents were to be fed even when they become elderly and non-productive. The prohibition of adultery protected the basic family economic unit of production and consumption. All of those commandments pertained to economic action and interaction in the community.

The first two commandments protected the political-economic independence of the people as a whole. The first "word" commanded exclusive loyalty to the transcendent force Yhwh who had liberated them from subjection to the human rulers and the fearsome forces of an imperial civilization. The force/power that had liberated them was their ruler, their "king," which meant they could not yield to another ruler, whether the personified divine forces of a civilization or their human regents, such as Pharaoh. The seriousness with which the people took this commandment is vividly illustrated by the story of Gideon refusing the people's desire to make him their king: "you already have a king" (i.e., Yhwh). The second commandment has been reductively misunderstood and mistranslated as merely prohibiting the "worship" of "idols" and the making of images. The complete text of the commandment goes on to indicate the point: "You shall *not bow down and serve*" the (divinized) forces of human rulers in an imperial civilization. That is, the people are prohibited from *serving* human rulers and their "gods" with tithes and offerings from their crops that they need for their own subsistence.

The covenant, moreover, was a collective action with a particular structure or pattern in which the people committed themselves to their divine ruler and to one another. The three steps of covenant making and covenant renewal started with a declaration of deliverance: "I am Yhwh your god who delivered you from bondage in Egypt." The people were thus obligated to the divine liberating force with exclusive loyalty, and thus also obligated to obey the commandments. The third component of the covenant (renewal) was sanctions, calling down blessings and curses on themselves for obedience or disobedience of the commandments. It seems evident from repeated references that the people regularly engaged collectively in a renewal of the covenant. The collections of customs and laws included in the books of the

---

1. For a fuller discussion, see Horsley, *Covenant Economics*, chaps 2–4.

Torah/Pentateuch, many of which evidently derive from agrarian village life,[2] are understood in the texts as "applications" or illustrations of cases that fall under one or another of the covenant commandments. These include customary mechanisms such as leaving a remainder of the harvest in the fields for gleaners or giving survival loans at no interest that would have enabled needy families to remain economically viable.[3] Not surprisingly one of the collections of customs and laws became labeled as the "Covenant Code" (a law "code" is an inapplicable concept). The book of Deuteronomy, ostensibly a restatement of the Mosaic covenant, is a charter for centralization of political-economic-religious power in Jerusalem that adapts what appear to have been popular customs and measures.

These two passages—the first about Joseph's manipulation of the people into deeper servitude to the imperial regime and the second the covenant that "constituted" the counter-imperial society of Israel—may yield a more comprehensive and deeper understanding of how ancient Near Eastern imperial civilizations worked and how early Israel attempted to resist. The end-result of Joseph's manipulation of the people was that they had become the servants, share-croppers if not slaves, of the Pharaoh's regime. In fact, in the Enuma Elish drama of the origin of civilization at the annual Akitu festival in Babylon, people were created as the slaves/servants of the system. The people's status and role was more or less the same in Egypt, as illustrated in the story about Joseph's systematic extortion that made them the servants of Pharaoh's imperial civilization. In the exodus, the Hebrews escaped from this servitude and then in the Mosaic covenant were commanded to have no gods other than YHWH who had liberated them and were commanded not to "bow down and serve (them)."

Because biblical scholars and scholars of the ancient Near East alike have been imposing the modern Western separation of religion from political-economic life they have a somewhat superficial understanding

2. As noted above, the constraints, customary laws, and measures against exploitation of the poor in the (early) Israelite village communities also included injunctions to make loans at no interest and cancellation of debts and release of debt slaves, as noted above. While not confident that they can distinguish village customs and practices from the form of laws and measures as adapted in the legal collections in the Torah/Pentateuch (Covenant Code; Deuteronomy; Holiness Code), some scholars nevertheless conclude that just such measures were observed in Israelite village economic life. See Knight, *Law, Power, and Justice*.

3. Historians and anthropologists of comparative material (for example, medieval English; the "articles" of Southwest German peasants in 1524–25; modern Southeast Asian peoples) have found that many, perhaps most, peasant peoples have measures by which the villagers attempt to keep each village family/lineage viable economically. Laid out in Scott, *Moral Economy of the Peasant*. Applied to the "covenantal" society of (early and village) Israel in Horsley, *Covenant Economics*, chap. 3.

of who/what the "gods" were that the peoples of Egypt or Mesopotamia were serving. The key to understanding the political economy of the ancient Near Eastern imperial civilizations is to hear the complete second commandment in its historical context. The commandment prohibits the making of an image or statue of "anything that is in heaven above or that is on the earth beneath or that is in the water under the earth." Those phrases are references to the personified and divinized forces/powers on which ancient civilizations depended. These were what the Israelites were forbidden to bow down and serve.

In the well-attested case of Mesopotamia, the Enuma Elish ritual-drama of origins of the irrigation system of production depended on the divine forces River and Sky (= Authority) and Irrigation (= Wisdom/Technology) and Storm/Kingship, once there were kings with military forces to enforce order. As illustrated by the divine forces Irrigation/Wisdom and Storm/Kingship, these were not "natural" or "supernatural" forces but divinized and personified civilizational forces. These were the forces/powers on which the people /civilization depended. They were fearsome, at times overwhelming, powers that had the people terrified, for example, that Storm would destroy the irrigation system and crops. So the rulers had to appease them with an elaborate apparatus of ceremonies and offerings, funded by the tithes and offerings of the people, so that the civilization could survive. Yes, the people were manipulated into servitude through the mechanism of debts and they were subject to enforcement by kings and their military. But the ancient civilizations were unified political-economic-religious imperial systems in which the subject peoples were serving the fearsome divinized civilizational forces on which the system was dependent, that determined the people's lives and life-conditions. If we follow the narratives and covenantal commandments in "de-mythologizing," "de-divinizing," and "secularizing" these fearsome forces of imperial civilizations, we would stop referring to them as "gods." They would then appear more as what they were: the people were serving the powers/forces of a particular imperial civilization that determined their lives.[4]

☙ ☙ ☙

These texts may also be suggestive for our situation in the empire of global capitalism. In the simpler system of an ancient agrarian empire almost all production controlled by an imperial regime was agricultural. What

---

4. See further the fuller discussion in Horsley, *Jesus and the Powers*, 10–22; and Horsley, "Christmas: The Religion of Consumer Capitalism," 174–84.

corresponds to that today is virtually all production, most of which is controlled by global capital. What corresponds to serving the powers that determine lives by yielding up the produce of one's labor in an ancient agrarian empire would today be serving the power(s) of global capital by (producing and) consuming the products of corporations. As many are increasingly aware, capitalist production and consumption have become exceedingly problematic. Industrial and agricultural corporations have been allowed to pollute the air and water. Fossil fuel and mining companies have been allowed to exploit common resources and relentlessly ruin the land, water, and atmosphere. The consumption of fossil fuels in increasingly large vehicles and convenient air travel and tourism and the increasing production and use of electric power has spewed carbon into the atmosphere at a rate that may have already pushed the earth beyond the tipping point of global warming.[5] Industrial farming and processing has produced generally unhealthy food, ruined the land, and resulted in dead rivers and oceans.[6]

What if people today were to take seriously the covenantal commandment *not to serve* the powers of the empire that are determining our lives? It is probably impossible to completely avoid serving global capital insofar as its control is so pervasive. But it is essential if the earth and its people are to survive to reduce consumption to a more sustainable level, particularly in the consumption of fossil fuels.[7]

The Prophets

The second set of "books" in the Hebrew Bible are the Prophets. These are divided into the books of the Deuteronomistic History (Joshua, Judges, 1–2

---

5. Biblical interpreters paid virtually no attention to the incisive analysis of how capitalism was driving the climate crisis by Joel Kovel, *The End of Nature*; more seem to be aware of the recent bestseller that makes the case again: Naomi Klein, *This Changes Everything*.

6. The predatory practices of the Monsanto corporation provide an instructive window onto the manipulative devices by which capitalism has taken ever more extensive control over the production of food. Monsanto figured out how to make immense profits by combining genetic engineering, political influence and connections, and gangs of intimidators and lawyers to coerce small and large farmers into buying GMO seed (rather than use their own seed saved over from previous years' crops).

7. Given the extensive recent attention to food in widely-read books, TV cooking shows, pronouncements from the health-care industry, and new government warnings (ironically all embedded in global capitalism), however, there is increasing attention to food as a possible area in which at least some people might be able to gain some leverage on one aspect of global capital's control, through the industrial agriculture that produced most of the food consumed.

Samuel and 1–2 Kings) and the books of collections of prophecies (Isaiah, Jeremiah, Ezekiel, and the book of the Twelve: Amos, Micah, etc.).

The Deuteronomic History is a lengthy narrative of the rise, decline, and fall of the regional empire in ancient Palestine headed by "the Davidic monarchy." The sustained narrative that covers five centuries of obscure history draws on a rich array of historical legends and memories of the struggles of the people against local kings (Joshua and Judges), then the struggles of the Israelites to maintain their independence against the Philistine infantry made possible by the invention of iron weapons (1 Samuel), then the struggles of the people against the consolidation of wealth and power by David and Solomon (2 Samuel and 1–2 Kings), and finally the declining ability of the people and their prophets to mount effective resistance to the Jerusalem monarchy and its subordination to rival ancient Near Eastern empires (Second Kings). Critical scholars doubt that the narrative is a credible representation of historical events. It is rather an "historical" narrative composed to legitimate the Davidic monarchy in Jerusalem during its decline and/or the Jerusalem temple-state that became the Judean representative of the Persian imperial regime. Even at its most powerful in the historical fiction of its portrayal under Solomon, the Davidic monarchy did not measure up to the major ancient Near Eastern empires in Egypt and Mesopotamia. And as a narrative about an agrarian political economy headed by a monarch, it does not offer a very complete analogy to the complex political economic empire of global capitalism. Its importance in the legitimation/ideology of the rise of Western colonial/imperial capitalism (the basis upon which global capitalism built its empire), however, and its inclusion of stories of people's active resistance to its domination call for a critical review.

As presented in the narratives, the Jerusalem/Davidic monarchy was an outright contradiction of the Mosaic covenant (1 Sam 8). The scribes of the Jerusalem monarchy and/or the temple-state ostensibly apply criteria of the Mosaic covenant to the monarchy's treatment of the people, but selectively. At many points, they glorify its power with a blind eye to its oppression of the people, yet at other points they condemn its injustices. Closely related to the narrative's application of covenantal criteria to the actions of the monarchy is its inclusion of the rich array of stories and memories of the people's active resistance and revolt against the monarchy. This sustained resistance, moreover, arose from the people's roots in the Mosaic covenant. This resistance calls for a critical review as a potential resource for biblical studies' response to its situation under global capitalism.

Both in "biblical" texts and under capitalism, the wealthy and powerful (rulers) take control of peoples' land (or other bases of livelihood) by forcible seizure and by manipulation of people into debt. Far more often than not, biblical texts condemn both practices (although there are egregious examples of land seizure) and the Bible includes many short and sustained narratives and prophetic statements of the people's resistance and outright revolts.

The "book" of Joshua is a decidedly "mixed bag." In the first half of the book some stories and memories from earlier times have been edited from an elite perspective of later rulers and the second half is an idealizing scheme of the distribution of land as the promised inheritance of the twelve tribes of Israel. In the first half, two editorial "paragraphs" (Josh 10:40-43; 11:16-20) frame the narrative as a rapid conquest or blitzkrieg of the land of Canaan by the Israelites. In accordance with this framing of the narrative as a conquest of the land, the Western imperial Bible translates the Hebrew construct *yosheve-* (of fortified cities in) *Cana'an* as the inhabitants of the land, which parallels the statement in the summaries that Joshua "utterly destroyed all that breathed" (10:40). Modern European powers appear to have taken the "biblical" master narrative as a charter for their invasion and slaughter of the indigenous peoples of America and Africa and expropriation of their land (see chap. 9 above). Some of the episodes, however, are stories of guerrilla attacks by (proto-Israelite) peasants against fortified cities and their kings with chariot forces, and some episodes are attacks by Israelites against the many kings who ruled the land and were expropriating villagers' produce (Josh 8; 10:1-39; 11:1-15). These stories are examples and reminders that the (proto-)Israelite people regularly mounted collective action against rulers' domination.

Second Samuel tells of the popularly acclaimed ("messiahed") king David manipulating the people to consolidate his power, then claiming an unconditional right to rule with no check on his power (2 Samuel 7). The middle section of the "book," however, often ignored by biblical scholars, offers a narrative of a revolt by all of the tribes of Israel, who were not fooled by the royal ideology that was an outright contradiction and violation of the Mosaic covenant. David then sent his mercenary army to conquer his own people (2 Samuel 15-19). But the people of Israel (except for the tribe of Judah) mounted a second revolt, and again David sent out the mercenaries to conquer them (2 Samuel 20). The official narrative that insists that, despite his blatant violation of the covenant commandments and conquest of his own people, "Yhwh loved David" and had blessed him with unconditional power to rule. But it also includes the stories of the people's collective revolt against their "messiah," which was also an adamant rejection of the ideology of unconditional (right to) power.

First Kings presents the Davidic monarchy at the apex of imperial power in the reign of Solomon. According to the narrative, he possessed the power to transform the society from a confederation of "tribes" into the economic base of his glorious absolute monarchy. In what was surely his most onerous move, in order to mobilize the labor he needed for massive buildings to embody his glorious rule—including the temple, which was an accoutrement to his own power, not a sanctuary for the people—he imposed forced labor not only on Canaanites but on Israelites as well. For the people this was a return to bondage in Egypt. The monarchy had overriding claims on the people's land and labor and disdain for communal customs. The imperial regime even had unchallengeable power to override the covenantal economic rights of the people: to pay for the materiel he needed for his palaces and his royal temple, Solomon simply "ceded" twenty villages in Galilee along with their residents to Hiram king of Tyre. Following Solomon's death, however, the ten northern tribes mounted a successful revolt against unconditional power (1 Kgs 11–12). Despite the official narrative focusing on the unconditional blessing of the Davidic kingship, the history of the people of Israel was of persistent resistance and rebellion against domination and power.

After the revolt of the ten northern tribes, 1–2 Kings continued to include narratives of the northern Israelites' struggles against the kings who attempt to consolidate monarchic power over them. The deep conflict that led to the last successful revolt, led by Jehu, receives considerable attention in the substantial narratives of the prophets Elijah and Elisha in 1 Kgs 17–22 and 2 Kgs 1–9—probably because these prophets were working against the (northern) kingdom of Israel, the rival of the Davidic monarchy in Judah. The episodes are not in chronological order but their interrelationship in the crisis they portray is evident.[8]

Regardless of the extent to which the Elijah–Elisha cycle represents historical events, the Israelites in the narrative were struggling against the consolidation of monarchic power by the first king of Israel who had gained the power to bequeath the kingship to his son. Ahab's consolidation of political-economic power went hand in hand with the sacralizing ideology and rituals already developed in the Canaanite/Phoenician city-states. The monarchy's claim to general authority over people and land, including its claim on a portion of the people's produce, was mystified as part of the people's obligation to appease the divinized personified (natural-) civilizational forces that determined the productivity of the land (Baʻal/Lord Storm and Asherah/Mother Earth, that is the forces of fertility and productivity, the rain desperately needed by people who practiced "rain agriculture").

---

8. The latter stand out from the broader narrative of "the acts of kings" in their orientation to the subordinated people who are resisting the rulers. See Coote, ed., *Elijah and Elisha*.

King Ahab and his Canaanite queen Jezebel had brought large numbers of the "prophets" of Baal and Asherah into the court to bolster the new mystification of the regime. They were also killing the prophets of Yhwh, knowing that loyalty to Yhwh entailed observance of the covenantal commandments. The prophets of Yhwh were dispersed in the countryside (hiding in caves), suggesting that some communication and mutual support was happening among the people. The major contest between Elijah and the prophets of Baal and Asherah on Mt Carmel may be a summary symbol suggestive of many acts of local commitment (covenant renewal) that were happening in the countryside.

The story of Naboth's Vineyard (1 Kgs 21) condemns Ahab and Jezebel and other rulers who used their power to expropriate people's land. Ahab asks Naboth to trade his vineyard for another vineyard. Naboth refuses to yield up his vineyard, appealing to the traditional Israelite understanding of the land as parceled out as (unalienable) family inheritance (not the same as private ownership). But Jezebel, representing the newly established sacred political economy, uses monarchic power to subvert the customary village self-governance. The manipulation violates the Mosaic covenantal commandments against coveting and false witness, as well as murder and theft, which had been instituted to protect people's relation to the land, the basis of their livelihood, against the centralization of power by a would-be monarch. The prophet Elijah's pronouncement of judgment against Ahab and Jezebel is an appeal to the God of Israel as the transcendent guarantor of the household and communal relation to the land. The rest of the Elijah–Elisha cycle tells of the people's persistent resistance: Yahweh commissions Elijah to foment revolt (by anointing a people's king, 1 Kgs 19) and his protégé Elisha finally carries out the anointing of Jehu as God's agent, who leads a bloody revolt (2 Kgs 9).

Most of the "books" of the Prophets later included in the Hebrew Bible are collections of prophecies and stories of prophets. In some of these books there appear to be at least three layers of prophecies, in most of which the prophets speak words of Yhwh they have heard in the divine court of justice.[9] The presumably earliest layer consist of incisive *indictments* of rulers (kings) and their officers for particular actions of exploitation and/or oppression of (often poor) people, often in violation of particular covenantal commandments, and pronouncement of *sentences/ punishments* that are irrevocable, in which often "the punishment fits the crime." Evidently presupposing the first layer of irrevocable punishment are prophecies that exhort (evidently) the rulers to reform their ways and

---

9. See Coote, *Amos among the Prophets*.

practice justice (i.e., according to the demands of the covenant commandments) in a second layer. In a third layer, delivered evidently at a later time in which the punishments pronounced in prophecies in the first layer have happened historically (in the conquests of the monarchies of Israel or Judah by the Assyrian or Babylonian armies), come prophecies of divine mercy and restoration, some in rather fantastic terms.

It appears, even from the narratives of the kings of the eighth and seventh centuries in Second Kings, that the monarchies had further consolidated their political-economic power so that they were no longer seriously challenged by collective popular revolts led by prophets or popular "kings." From the earliest layer of prophecies in the books of Amos, Micah, and Isaiah, it seems evident that the kings and their officers were ratcheting up their demands on the people, manipulating them into debt, and taking control of their lands.

In dealing with the situation of the monarchies in Judah and Israel in the eighth century BCE, "biblical" scholars, perhaps imitating their colleagues in economics, often write euphemistically as if economic development just happened, naturally: a region's economic goals "evolve"; economic advances "unfold." In the eighth century, for example, "Judah experienced an economic transformation that involved a heightened production of goods to serve trade." By contrast, biblical texts, historical narratives and prophecies alike, are specific. During a period of Assyrian imperial withdrawal in the early to mid-eighth century, King Uzziah deliberately and systematically expanded cattle raising into the often-arid Negev, with fortresses and cisterns, and he expanded oil and wine production in the Shephelah and hill country, deploying "farmers and vinedressers" (2 Chr 26:9–10). As indicted in many prophecies, the Judean monarchy (king and officers), like their counterparts in the kingdom of Israel (under Jeroboam II) were also manipulating villagers into debts, on the basis of which they would take control of their land. Archaeological and other evidence suggests that they were then trading the oil and wine produced to the Phoenicians for luxury goods and materiel for monumental construction and military equipment.[10] The "Judean rulers" were not only the beneficiaries but also the agents of further economic development in the late eighth century through manipulation of debts. By then, in addition to expropriating produce to trade for luxury items, they had come under pressure for tribute from the Assyrians—or were building up their military fortresses and armaments to rebel against or resist the Assyrian imperial regime.

---

10. Chaney, *Peasants, Prophets, and Political Economy*.

The prophecies of Micah and Isaiah, like the Naboth vineyard story, address the conflict between the people's communally-based relation to the land (in which each household had use of a family inheritance) and the monarchy's overriding claims on the people's land and labor (and its utter disdain for the communal customs). The prophecies condemn the powerful and wealthy living in the "great/beautiful houses" who have the leisure to "lie on their beds" scheming (the meaning of "covet") how to "steal" people's houses and fields.

> Because it is in their power,
>> they covet fields, and seize them,
>> houses, and take them away;
> they oppress householder and house,
>> people and their inheritance. (Mic 2:1–2)

As Marvin Chaney explained, kings and their officers schemed to get people into debt and, when they could not pay up, to seize their houses (households) and lands.

> Yhwh enters into judgment
>> with the rulers and officers of his people:
> It is you who have devoured the vineyard;
>> the spoil of the poor is in your houses.
> What do you mean by crushing my people,
>> by grinding the face of the poor?
>> says Yhwh, God of the heavenly armies. (Isa 3:14–15)

> Ah, you who join house to house,
>> who add field to field . . .
> Yhwh of hosts has sworn in my hearing:
> Surely many houses shall be desolate,
>> large and beautiful houses without inhabitant. (Isa 5:8–10)

But these houses and fields were understood in the Mosaic covenant and the "moral economy" in which it was rooted as inheritances of the component lineages (families) of the village commune. The wealthy and powerful seizing land for debts was a blatant violation of the commandments against coveting (scheming to take control) and stealing (seizure) that were meant to protect the economic viability of households in their village community. With the people no longer able to generate effective collective revolt, as Elijah and Elisha had touched off, individual prophets now appealed to the divine court of justice, whose condemnation they pronounced against the wealthy in their "great houses."

∾ ∾ ∾

European and European-American imperial conquests took the imperial Bible's grand narrative of the ancient Israelites conquest of the "promised land" and of the "inhabitants of the land" as their charter. They slaughtered or enslaved the indigenous peoples and took over their land. The conquered land and slave labor were the "forces of production" that generated profits for nascent capitalist enterprises, profits that, for example, provided the endowment of elite universities and theological schools. Building on the wealth that grew from this base, global capitalism, an imperial system quite different from the simpler agrarian monarchies of ancient Judah and Israel, expanded into more systematic expropriation in whole countries in Africa and Latin America by manipulating them into debt. As noted in the previous chapter the International Monetary Fund, the World Bank, and other huge banks induced these countries to take development loans at interest, then when they were unable to repay on schedule, forced them to cut back on services to their people.

By working on individual households but affecting whole neighborhoods and poor communities, mega-banks devised ingenious new schemes (scams!) to systematically manipulate people into debt. As noted in the previous chapter, the banks and huge mortgage companies designed "sub-prime mortgages" to target some of the only resources that economically marginal families had left. The economic crash in 2008 revealed that the sliced and diced "securities" based on the collateral of those properties were "toxic" and, as foreclosures on millions who were "underwater" from plummeting housing values, millions of families and whole neighborhoods were financially ruined.

Debt as the impossible difficulty that threatens the life of families and communities and debt as the means of generating wealthy by impoverishing people are recurrent and continuing issues in "biblical" texts. Debt is one of the most prominent themes in the history of the people of Israel that the texts address. The collections of laws in Exodus, Leviticus, and Deuteronomy include laws and customs supposedly designed to deal with debt, such as cancellation every seven years and the release of debt-slaves and, if all else fails, the Jubilee in which families could return to their ancestral inheritance after fifty years of debt and poverty. Reminiscent of what the eighth-century prophets addressed, the wealthy elite's use of debt to generate more wealth by impoverishing their fellow *Yehudim* seriously undermined the establishment of a viable temple-state in *Yehud* in the fifth century. Only the insistence by the Persian-sent governor Nehemiah that the wealthy elite restore the land and other social-economic rights supposedly protected by the covenantal commandments and customs overcame the crisis (Neh 5:1–13). The learned Jerusalem scribe Jesus ben Sira knows that "the poor are the feeding ground of the wealthy" (Sir 13:19). While Herodian and high priestly families in Jerusalem and Herod Antipas in Sepphoris and Tiberias were building up their wealth, the prophet Jesus of Nazareth was teaching communities of people to pray for the direct rule of God that focused on cancellation of their debts (Matt 6:9–13).

The economic crash in 2008, as noted in chap. 8, with the ensuing millions of foreclosures on sub-prime mortgages and others left "underwater" from plummeting housing values and similar impoverishing effects everywhere, was a rude awakening for many. In retrospect, the more critically aware could see that debt as the means of generating wealth by impoverishing people had long been a serious problem in capitalist society. Seeking a longer-range perspective, David Graeber, an eager academic participant in Occupy, produced a magisterial anthropological and historical survey in *Debt: The First Five Thousand Years* (2014). Some of the few biblical scholars who read the book found the coverage of the ancient Near Eastern civilizations and biblical texts inadequate. But this may be because he did not have sufficient previous studies to work with. Biblical scholars have carried out critical studies of particular prophecies and laws and sets of laws and other texts in ancient Near Eastern context, so solid ground-work has been done.[11] But there has been no recent comprehensive wider-ranging analysis of debt and the generation of wealth by manipulating the poor into debt in the historical contexts addressed by various texts. Thus one of the most obvious tasks biblical scholars could undertake, living as they are under the relentlessly impoverishing global capitalism, would be to carry out more comprehensive and wider-ranging study of debt in biblical texts—preferably in a cooperative collective endeavor.[12]

---

11. A generation ago, however, there did not seem to be the desired critical studies available for those of us wanting to deal people in debt and exploitation by their wealthy creditors in prophetic and Gospel texts in our courses and first publications—in my case, for example, in *Bandits, Prophets, and Messiahs*, and *Sociology and the Jesus Movement*; in Chaney's case, his earliest articles on the prophets, reprinted in *Peasants, Prophets, and Political Economy*; and also see Premnath, *Eighth Century Prophets*.

12. Shortly before the crash in 2008, a few of us started two new program units in the Society of Biblical Literature, on "Economics in the Biblical World" and "Poverty in the Biblical World," which sponsored sessions on debt and related issues, such as "Debt

In his *Debt*, David Graeber suggested that a blanket cancellation of debts would go far toward alleviating the global crisis of widespread debt, in imitation of the Jubilee cancellation of debts and return to the ancestral lands in the Holiness Code (Lev 25).[13] Critical biblical scholars suspect that this was a utopian ideal. According to some inscriptions, Assyrian kings (upon their accession/coronation) promised cancellation of debts in royal decrees that evidently appealed for popular support against officers of the previous regime or local "bigmen" who had manipulated villagers into debt. Judean scribes would appear to have adapted this ideal in the account in Lev 25.[14] Whether or not any such Jubilee was ever implemented historically, there does not appear on the horizon any global agency that could pronounce and implement a global cancellation of debts—which would lead to the complete collapse of global capitalism. On the other hand, the Jubilee has become a keen expectation in African-American churches and communities, whose enslaved ancestors would have heard such biblical passages eagerly. Also, a generation ago, Jesus' preaching of the good news of the kingdom of God was interpreted as a proclamation of the imminence of the Jubilee, e.g., in fulfilment of the prophecy in Isa 61.

Those understandings of the Jubilee suggest a more likely scenario for drawing on the stories of the people's resistance to exploitation led by Elijah and Elisha and the later prophecies that condemn exploitation and debt mechanisms lies in the active cultivation of collective memory by communities of subordinated people. These persistent movements of resistance to domination and expropriation, these prophecies, and the traditional rights and customs they defend offer models of political economic arrangements that is diametrically opposed to the effects of global capitalism. And there have been widespread similar protests and movements of resistance to imperial and other rulers' domination, exploitation, and expropriation in late-medieval European history and in anticolonial resistance and revolts in the Americas and Africa. As global capital thrives from crisis to crisis, the cracks in the system appear ever more evident and steady resistance seems more evident, at least locally. Some of the pockets of that resistance—in Africa, in Latin America, in certain communities in North America—have previously cultivated and could again cultivate memories of the Israelites' collective resistance to, and the prophets' condemnation of, exploitation by monarchic power. They might well draw on these memories in their own

---

and the Generation of Wealth and Poverty." Since economics and poverty have not previously been subjects of interest in biblical studies, however, the learning goes slowly.

13. Graeber, *Debt*, 390–91.

14. See Chaney on debt easement in *Peasants, Prophets, and Political Economy*, 106–20.

collective action and communal solidarity in resistance to European and North American imperial domination. In relearning or imagining alternative historical political-economic arrangements that protect the common good and people's economic rights that global capitalism is relentlessly wiping out, pockets of resistance to global capitalism could also draw upon the memory of communal-based social-economic forms among indigenous peoples in Africa or Asia in generating collective local resistance.

11

(Proto-) New Testament Texts and Global Capitalism

New Testament studies may not be the handmaid of global capitalism in the same way that biblical studies more generally was for earlier Western imperialism. Yet ironically, perhaps, in its diversification during the late twentieth century it was congruent with neo-liberal ideology and in effect helped facilitate the new form of empire. Throughout the diversification, the assumption prevailed that the texts included in the New Testament are religious and are about religion, separate from political economic life. The rise of various "liberation theologies" did not lead to questioning the controlling constructs of (early) Judaism and (early) Christianity that hide the structural division and conflict and the diversity of movements in the historical situation of early Roman Palestine. The "literary turn" in New Testament studies, while it facilitated recognition that the Gospels were sustained narratives/stories, further distracted attention from the historical situation by focusing instead on "the world of the text." The field's persistent individualism makes it passively complicit in the neoliberal ideology of global capitalism, preventing readers and interpreters from discerning that the texts address communities and movements and are about movements and their collective actions. The narrow focus on text-fragments and pericopes (without attention to broader narratives or arguments) prevents readers and interpreters from recognizing the political-economic-religious conflicts that the texts as complete stories or arguments portray.

It would help the field to become less congruent with the new form of empire to recognize that the texts are about all aspects of life, particularly about the division and conflict between rulers and ruled, and call for practice and resistance. Avoiding the standard controlling synthetic constructs of Judaism and Christianity (and apocalypticism and dichotomies such as "Jews" vs. "Gentiles") would better enable readers and interpreters to discern the historical contexts of texts. Reading and considering whole texts and arguments, moreover, would keep interpreters from domesticating text-fragments in ways congruent with neoliberal ideology. The people represented in most of the texts later included in the New Testament, recognizing that they were unavoidably *in* an imperial system sought courses of action not to be *of* that system.

Those courses of action and/or those communities and movements of resistance might be suggestive for people today who unavoidably must live *in* the new empire but may be seeking courses of action to avoid being *of* the empire.

The Gospels: The Prophet Jesus Catalyzing a Movement of Renewal vs. the Rulers

Neoliberal ideology became the hegemonic discourse in the culture of global capitalism. The ground for neoliberalism was well prepared by the culture of bourgeois capitalism. Individual freedom was central to bourgeois culture and individualism became central in Western culture generally (particularly in North American culture). Biblical studies as a subfield of theology, developed on the basis of this culture, fully shares its individualism. And nowhere has this individualism been more persistent than in recent American liberal interpretation of Jesus.

Although its motivating concerns were often social discontent, the development of sociology and of the social sciences generally in Western Europe and North America served to support and protect individualism. As noted in chap. 9, what was called structural-functionalism in particular was developed as a way of avoiding issues of power-relations (who had power over whom), especially with regard to the control of resources. People understood as individuals were found to belong to particular strata in society, social complexity being mainly a matter of "social stratification."[1] Whatever deviance, dissidence, or social conflict might emerge was explained as somehow functional for the overall social system. As social and political conflict became more widespread and intense in the 1960s, however, social scientists began abandoning structural-functionalism.

Ironically, when some biblical scholars began to ask social questions in the 1970s, they borrowed the structural-functional social science that had

---

1. Americans in particular took pride in the social mobility available to individuals. But there is less mobility today in the US than in other well developed countries *and* in Central and South American countries that North Americans previously viewed as dominated by a wealthy elite who wielded power over the rest of the people.

just been abandoned. One of the most influential efforts was Gerd Theissen's "sociology of literature" applied to the early tradition of Jesus' teaching. Focusing on selected individual sayings of Jesus (still standard procedure especially in study of Jesus) taken out of literary context and taken more or less literally, he constructed Jesus and his "first followers" as "wandering charismatics" who had purposely abandoned their homes and families for an itinerant lifestyle as vagabonds.[2] This "itinerant radicalism" was functional for the larger social system, of course, since it supposedly siphoned off discontent into harmless individual asceticism. Despite sharp criticism of Theissen's construction as conservative sociology that explained away serious social conflict,[3] the burgeoning enterprise of liberal interpretation of Jesus (the Jesus Seminar) seized upon "itinerant radicalism." Fusing Jesus' aphorisms with fragments from the ancient Cynic philosophers that reject the dominant Greco-Roman culture, the most widely marketed Jesus-book even reduced Jesus' sayings about "the kingdom of God" to an individual "kingdom."[4] Liberal scholarly interpreters could thus relish some of the pithy "countercultural" aphorisms of Jesus, while avoiding taking too seriously "the hard sayings" of Jesus, which were safely pushed to the margins as having pertained only to the radical itinerants, and the judgmental prophetic sayings, which were dismissed as secondary. This romanticization of Jesus' itinerant ministry in Gospel interpretation reinforces the dominant neo-liberal ideology that views homelessness today as an individual choice, and not a result of unemployment, housing shortage, and other effects of the dominance of global capitalism.[5]

Despite the trenchant criticism of the hypothesis, along with the assumptions and method that led to it, and the critical dismantling of the Cynic parallel, this individualistic liberal interpretation of the individual sayings of Jesus persists and has spilled over into "readings" of the Gospels. Its complicity with the neoliberal ideology of global capitalism is reinforced by being combined with the borrowings from structural-functional social science and/or the adoption of recent "criticisms" borrowed by Gospel interpreters from literary critics of modern fiction. Since texts of modern fiction have taken on a life of their own, so the theory goes, interpretation must stay "within the text."[6] The borrowing of literary criticism of modern fiction also

2. Theissen, *Sociology of Early Palestinian Christianity*.

3. J. H. Elliott, "Social Scientific Criticism"; Horsley, *Sociology and the Jesus Movement*.

4. Crossan, *Historical Jesus*.

5. Crossley, *Jesus in an Age of Neoliberalism*; Myles, "Homelessness," 217–21.

6. This makes a certain amount of sense, since the Gospels became texts of Christian scripture and professional interpreters are trained in the biblical studies division

smuggles some postmodernist discourse into interpretation of the Gospels alongside the continuation of Christian theological categories and standard old procedures such as word-study and dividing up the Gospels into pericopes that fragment the overall story.

Not surprisingly, the result is a projection of modern interpreters' experience of the world, postmodernist discourse, and social-science models onto the world of the text and its characters. The Jesus portrayed in the Gospel stories as a prophet like Moses (and Elijah) engaged in a renewal of (the people of) Israel becomes a lone itinerant who calls followers to leave home and family and become itinerants. This suggests the phenomenon of homelessness in contemporary capitalist society that is then projected into the Gospel stories. Homelessness is then further imagined in terms of social stratification and "marginality." These "readings" do not find homelessness "in the text" of the Gospels (because it is not there), but in their colleagues' borrowings from social science and read it into the text. From a survey of previous studies of many societies historical sociologists such as Gerhard Lenski, in their scheme of social stratification, labeled as "expendables" the people at the very bottom of the social hierarchy for whom "society" had no need and no place. These homeless people had been displaced by population pressures, were landless and itinerant, and had no normal family life. They did not fit in "society," which had no need of them and no place for them.[7] Recent scholarly "readings" of the Gospel texts imagine that Jesus became "downwardly mobile," having descended the "social ladder" to the "symbolic space" of an expendable. Closely related are the (other) spatial sociological metaphors of marginality and periphery. The itinerant Jesus and his disciples became "voluntarily marginal" and moved further to the periphery of society, as they "withdrew from full participation" in the dominant sociopolitical order.[8] In these readings of the Gospel texts, Jesus' preaching of the kingdom would have "unsettled the sensibilities of the normalized population." But his and his disciples' and other followers' itinerant withdrawal to the periphery would ultimately have been functional for "the smooth functioning of the wider sociopolitical order."[9]

In a "political exegesis" of a particular pericope in the Gospel of Matthew (4:12–25) that moves mainly from one key Greek word to another, as defined in New Testament handbooks, Robert Myles argues that the

---

of Christian theology. But the Gospel stories have thus become something like modern fiction, free-floating decontextualized Christian culture-texts dependent for their meaning on interpreters' "readings."

7. Lenski, *Power and Privilege*, 180–84; Saldarini, *Pharisees, Scribes*, 2nd ed., 44.
8. Carter, *Matthew and the Margins*; Duling, *A Marginal Scribe*.
9. Myles, "Homelessness," 242; cf. Myles, *The Homeless Jesus*.

Matthean Jesus' "itinerant ministry" cannot be romanticized. It is rather a response to "the intrusion of external political realities."[10] Yet, while he criticizes the social-stratification model, it persists in his reading. Jesus and his disciples withdrew from their "already marginal social statuses," places that secured their social identity in "normalized" "first-century Palestinian society," to a "deviant" place further to the margins. His withdrawal earned him fame among masses of others "located on the margins of Palestinian society." Ultimately, however, he concludes that the Matthean text "gestures towards external sociopolitical realities that become internalized in Jesus as an experience of perpetual uprooting and displacement."[11] But this seems like a psychological reading rooted in the problematic individualism of the neoliberal ideology he aimed to counter.

These "readings" of the texts, however, are not attested in the Gospels' portrayals of Jesus, his disciples, and the crowds he addresses that fit well with what we know of Galilean and Judean society from other (contemporary) sources such as the Judean historian Josephus.[12] It is difficult to find signs of homelessness or "expendables" in the Gospel stories and contemporary Judean texts and difficult to imagine what "marginal" might mean. The vast majority of people (Galileans, Judeans, Samaritans, etc.) lived in hundreds of villages where they lived cheek-by-jowl and grew crops in their nearby fields. The village communities were semi-self-governing through their assemblies (*synagogai* in Greek). Most families/households lived at subsistence or below, many were hungry and in debt (as in the petitions of "the Lord's Prayer" in Matthew 6). The villagers generally were evidently poor. These were the people among whom the Gospels portray Jesus and his disciples as working.

It would be difficult also to find in the Gospels and other sources anything like "a normal family life" or normal village life from which Jesus' or the disciples' itinerancy would have been deviant, from which they would have withdrawn to some hypothetical "margins." Galilean villagers had suffered invasion, destruction, slaughter, and enslavement. Roman conquest and reconquest in Palestine swept through Galilee first in successive invasions. On his way back from war on the Parthians, a Roman warlord had massacred large numbers in the town of Magdala (Josephus says 30,000, surely an exaggeration, but nevertheless . . .). Galileans had resisted Herod's conquest of his subjects for three years in 40–37 BCE. In

---

10. Myles, "Homelessness," 228.

11. Myles, "Homelessness," 243.

12. For a recent summary of the historical context attested by the Gospels and other sources such as Josephus, see Horsley, *Jesus and Politics of Roman Palestine*, esp. chap. 2.

suppression of the widespread popular revolt at Herod's death, the Romans destroyed and slaughtered people in Sepphoris (and/or its village environs?). Within twenty years, Herod Antipas built two capital cities in lower Galilee, Sepphoris (about three miles from Nazareth) and Tiberias ("across" the Lake from Capernaum), which would have required intensified extraction of revenues from his villager subjects.[13] The system always needed cheap labor; indebted hungry villagers supplemented their living with day-labor. Life in Judean villages was similarly disrupted by Roman conquests and the intensification of economic exploitation by multiple layers of rulers, Roman and high priestly. In northwest Judea and in the Great Plain just south of Galilee, indebted villagers who lost control of their land to wealthy creditors became tenants on estates controlled by wealthy creditors, often the Herodians or high priestly rulers. While seriously disrupted and at points disintegrating, however, the village communities survived as the fundamental form of social-economic life.

In mid-first century, half-way between the widespread revolts in 4 BCE and the great revolt of 66–70 CE, villagers mounted several movements of renewal and resistance led by prophets like Moses/Joshua, and in Galilee an organized "strike" in which villagers refused to plant their crops so that the Romans would have no tribute at harvest time. By the time the Matthean and Lukan Gospels were composed, the Galilean and Judean villagers had engaged in massive prolonged revolt against the Roman imperial order and the Roman armies had slaughtered people and devastated their villages in retaliation. It is difficult to imagine that at any time during these generations there could have been a "smooth functioning of the wider sociopolitical order."

Where would there have been "normal" family or village life that would have provided a sense of identity? Were there some out-of-the-way places where Jesus and his disciples could have secured their social identity in some idyllic "normalized" "first-century Palestinian society"? When if ever did villagers engage in anything like "full participation in the reigning ideological-political order"[14] from which Jesus and his disciples would have "withdrawn"? Given the sharp division between the Romans and their client rulers in Jerusalem, Sepphoris, and Tiberias, on the one hand, and the Judean and

13. A form of extraction from the villagers directly pertinent to the disciples recruited by Jesus in the Gospel stories was the "fishing industry" run by Herod Antipas. For an incisive historical reconstruction that counters the previous anachronistic scholarly projection that Jesus and his fisherman followers had voluntarily left a secure "comfortable middle-class" life of artisans and small (fishing) businesses for a life of homelessness, see Hanson, "The Galilean Fishing Economy and the Jesus Tradition."

14. Myles, "Homelessness," 239.

Galilean peasants in their village communities (and assemblies) on the other, the people's identity would have been oppositional. This opposition is what the Gospel texts portray in the mission of Jesus and his disciples and in the movement he generates. And in the climax of the stories, not withdrawal to some sort of "margins," but direct confrontation with the rulers in the center of political-economic-religious power.

A political reading of the Gospels in the context of global capitalism, however, requires a more thorough-going criticism of the ways in which contemporary Gospel interpretation is complicit in the neoliberal ideology of the new form of Empire. The Gospel stories and Gospel pericopes and the sayings of Jesus as they have taken on a life of their own have been de-historicized and domesticated. They are not allowed to stand over against readers/interpreters as ostensibly historical stories in the context of a very different imperial political-economic-religious system. It has been recognized recently that the Gospels were (ostensibly) historical stories (almost certainly) orally performed or recited to communities of Jesus-loyalists involved in movement(s) opposed to and by the local and Roman imperial rulers in Palestine and nearby areas. Also, while they did not undergo a long process of cultivation and further composition in elite scribal circles, they had developed from Jesus tradition that was deeply rooted in Israelite popular tradition. Close critical examination of the Gospels over the last few generations has concluded that one or more of the Gospels developed from knowledge of one or more previously composed and performed. Moreover, the Gospels were sustained stories of interrelated episodes that "fit" well into the historical context of what is known about the political-economic-religious structure and dynamics and historical conflicts and events in early Roman Palestine.

In sharp contrast with the dehistoricizing and thus depoliticizing individualistic interpretation of Jesus as a homeless itinerant who withdraws from the dominant sociopolitical order, the Gospel of Matthew presents him as a prophet engaged in a renewal of Israel in its village and town communities in opposition to and by the rulers. The political conflict portrayed in the story is all the more striking when read in the historical contexts of Jesus' mission and of the communities of Jesus-loyalists addressed by the Gospel. Besides being schematic, the story is told with a retrospective reflection on the dynamics of the fundamental political-economic conflict that is known from other sources, such as the Judean historian Josephus.

In its very beginning, the Gospel story has Jesus born into a leading role in Israelite history in the context of the people's subjugation to the Roman Empire. Jesus is the Messiah, the son of David, born as the alternative "king of the Judeans." But of course this makes him a threat to Herod, whom the Romans had appointed "king of the Judeans," who sends out the military to suppress any potential rebellion against Herod's rule and the Roman imperial order. The hearers of the story would have remembered vividly the economic oppression and political repression by Herod that continued under his son Herod Antipas in Galilee and the high priesthood in Judea. From the beginning Jesus and his family are forced to become political refugees. After recapitulating Israel's exodus from Egypt, Jesus' family settles ("under the radar") in the Galilean village of Nazareth. Nazareth, however, was hardly a village in a "normalized society" in which Jesus or others would have enjoyed "strong kinship ties, family, and (other) roots." The accounts of the Judean historian Josephus indicate that the villagers of Nazareth and other villages near Sepphoris had experienced periodic disruption, even devastation. Most recently, after villagers in the area, led by their "king" Judas, son of a brigand-chieftain, had raided Herod's fortress and taken back the goods that had been taken there, the Romans destroyed (the area of?) Sepphoris and enslaved people in retaliation. These episodes are clearly legendary. But they represent vividly the considerable collective trauma that Jesus and others may well have experienced from repeated invasion, loss of kin, heavy taxation, and Antipas' rebuilding the fortress city of Sepphoris and of Tiberias as his capital cities.

The Matthean story then presents Jesus as engaged in a deliberate mission of healing and teaching in the villages and towns of Galilee. Village communities and their component households were the principal social forms in which people's lives were embedded in any traditional agrarian society. As his first step after his announcement of the theme of the mission (and the Gospel story), he recruits disciples to assist. Then after a summary statement of his teaching in the local village assemblies (*synagogai*) throughout Galilee and a summary of his extensive healings, he enacts (in performative speech) a renewal of the Mosaic covenant as a charter for community life in the renewal of Israel (the first of five major speeches). After narrative of particular healings, Jesus then commissions the twelve disciples to extend the mission of proclaiming the kingdom and performing healings and exorcisms in the villages and towns of Israel.

In Matthew's Gospel, far from a "disengagement in the everyday life in Galilee" or a withdrawal "further to the margins" of first-century Palestinian society, Jesus and the disciples are engaged in a renewal of the people in their village communities, which were disintegrating from the economic drain of their resources by the rulers, leaving them hungry and in debt (addressed in the Lord's Prayer). Far from calling for an abandonment of family for an alternative community constituted by the disciples, Jesus is engaged in a renewal of family as part of community life. This could not be clearer in the sharpening of the covenantal commandments in "the Sermon on the Mount" (Matt 5:20–48). In perhaps the best-known case of this sharpening, Jesus demands that people come to the aid of their economically desperate neighbors with survival loans even though they may also be barely clinging to subsistence. These covenantal demands are further reinforced in the set of covenantal dialogues about divorce and remarriage, membership in the community, and non-exploitative economic relations in the community (Matt 19). Indeed, in the completion of the latter dialogue (19:27–30), Jesus declares that in the renewal (*palingenesia*) of Israel[15] the disciples who have left everything to follow Jesus will be playing the role of the representative twelve who are "establishing justice for" (*not* "judging") the twelve tribes.

Insofar as it alludes to the destruction of Jerusalem and the temple, the Gospel of Matthew reached its contours as the story we know from early manuscripts in the aftermath of the great revolt of Judeans and Galileans against Rome and its client high priestly rulers in Jerusalem. Insofar as the Gospel has Jesus born as the Messiah, the story may well have developed in the movement of Jesus-loyalists that had expanded from its early base in Jerusalem (as sketched in chap. 8 above). In contrast to the Markan story, which is hesitant about whether Jesus was the messiah, the speeches of Peter early in the book of Acts present Jesus as having become the Messiah-designate in his vindication and exaltation after he was crucified. The early development of the Matthean story would fit in the expansion of the movement beyond Jerusalem and Judea into diaspora communities of Judeans in towns of Palestine and Syria. Twice Jesus commands the disciples he commissions to go only to the lost sheep of the house of Israel. But the movement kept expanding and other subject peoples were eager to join. As indicated at the very end of the Matthean story, the destruction of Jerusalem had not slowed the momentum of this movement of covenantal communities. Judging from the attacks by governors, kings, and councils against them or at least their leaders, they were seen as a threat to the Roman imperial order in the towns in Syria-Palestine (10:16–18; 24:9). At some point, whether before or after the Roman destruction of Jerusalem, the movement was ready to expand to include other peoples in the renewal of Israel as an alternative to—while still under the power of—the Roman imperial order. As the concluding statement in the Gospel story, Jesus commands his envoys to "make disciples of all peoples," teaching them to obey everything he has taught in the Gospel (28:19).

---

15. Not the Stoic doctrine of the renewal of the universe. Josephus also uses *palingenesia* in reference to renewal of the people of Israel.

Far from the Matthean Gospel being about an itinerant who withdrew from the dominant sociopolitical order, it is about the Moses-like prophet who catalyzed the renewal of the people of Israel in opposition to their imperial rulers. Instead of escaping from the rulers, as in the paradigmatic exodus, however, the renewal movement expands rapidly in covenantal communities in the towns of Syria-Palestine, a movement that other subject peoples are eager to join as an alternative to the Roman imperial order even though they must remain subject to Roman imperial rule.

ೞ ೞ ೞ

The new form of Empire, global capitalism, however, is much more comprehensive and pervasive in its control of people's lives that it has effectively atomized in its destruction of local communities, church parishes, and the traditional forms of civil society (neighborhoods, towns, cities). The form in which it wields power has also changed dramatically. In ancient Galilee and Judea the Romans seized a portion of the people's crops as tribute; if the people did not pay up, the Romans killed or enslaved them and destroyed their villages and houses. Under the Empire of global capital, the people are forced to work and manipulated to desire and consume; the process by which capitalism produces the goods they consume, however, is gradually killing them by poisoning and ruining the environment as big corporations manipulate governments to subsidize and deregulate that process.

The extent to which mutually committed people might form an alternative to full participation in global capitalism is more limited than with ancient communities of Jesus-loyalists. Potential bases of covenanting communities that would support one another in withdrawing from serving global capital or more seriously resisting its operations already exist in churches, synagogues, mosques, certain community organizations, certain civil society groups, and of course labor unions and credit unions, and here and there local government. Groups striving to engage in partial alternatives and/or partial resistance would need to exercise critical analysis of the complex system and its local operations and imaginative strategies and tactics. The most important wide-ranging form of withdrawal from service of the new Empire would be drastic reduction of consumption, particularly of fossil fuels that are the principal driver of global warming (climate change) and of pollution of land, water, and air. To reduce collective consumption, it would help to withdraw from the electronic mass media and social media that channel our desire for consumption, mainly of unneeded goods the consumption of which only feeds the "growth of wealth/capital." For the increasing number of people who are poor or of moderate means, an important form of withdrawal from service of capitalism would be avoidance of debt to the mega-banks. This is possible through credit unions and certain local cooperatives and collectives (in by-gone eras churches used to include certain economic services and functions).

While global capitalism has become much more pervasively powerful than any historical empire, it is not (yet) all powerful. There is hope for possible partial alternative forms and lines building resistance. It is essential that the criticism that informs resistance be both comprehensive and probing, and not mistake the institutional form of power and its effects. Perhaps in some situations it might appear that "the task today is to resist state power by withdrawing from its scope."[16] While the United States government has recently exhibited pretenses of exercising imperial power, it was steadily being manipulated by global capitalism through coalitions of transnational corporations.[17] Moreover what needs to be resisted may be not just the scope of the new Empire's power but the forms in which it is exercised, such as through communications media, the channeling of desire, and the commodified culture of non-meaning. All this cannot be done by individual escape but might still be done by the collective action of covenanted communities—as modeled in the Gospel stories.

---

16. Žižek, *Violence*, 1–2. Žižek's suggestion here is almost exactly the opposite course of action compared with that taken by Jesus in Matthew and other gospels. Far from withdrawing, Jesus marches directly into the center of the temple-state backed by the Empire to confront its domination and exploitation, to "speak truth to power," in what today would be called nonviolent direct action.

17. The structures of the global capitalist system and its relation to states and to the people are complex so that resistance requires critical analysis and considerable knowledge of particular situations and concrete projects. Withdrawal only enables the system to grind on relentlessly, growing ever more powerful and pervasive and destroying more life and the environment itself. What is needed is for states, such as the United States, to summon the political will, for example, to rescind the permits for the building of massive pipelines (such as the KXL or Dakota Access pipelines) to move fossil fuels across continents, permits that overrode the express concerns of Native American peoples and the general public. In situations where national governments, state governments, and city and town governments use their military and police forces to enforce the permits for corporations and banks to generate further profits in projects that destroy life and the planet it seems necessary for the people, who previously had rights on the land and its resources, to physically oppose the projects in nonviolent direct action. Such actions have often been called "civil disobedience." But it is the powerful corporations, often with the complicity of the state at various levels, that are violating the civic order as previously understood and authorized by constitutions and laws. The actions of the prophet Jesus as portrayed in the Gospel stories offer vivid paradigms of nonviolent direct action against the temple-state as enforcer for the Roman Empire.

Expansion of the Movement among Other Peoples Subjected to the Empire

The book of Acts picks up where the Gospel story of Luke leaves off. In the heady days of Occupy Wall Street, it would have been tempting for those who wanted to tweak the exegetical noses of biblical interpreters who still reduced Acts to the story of the expansion and split of one religion, Christianity, from the religion in which it originated, Judaism. Peter, the twelve disciples, and others who were sharing goods in common, were not "attending (services in the) temple every day (as in earlier translations of Acts 2:46 such as the RSV), but an eclectic bunch of "militants" and "commune-ists" engaged in a political protest in their "occupation" of the very institutional center, symbolic as well as concrete, of an increasingly exploitative political-economy. Drawing such an analogy might well have scored some exegetical points, but would have been too simple and misleading. The community of Galileans expanded by diaspora Judeans in the provincial capital of Jerusalem was much less sensational than Occupy Wall Street at the very center of the new Empire of global capitalism but much more far reaching and ambitious in its project than the prolonged but unsustainable protest at Wall Street and at other centers of capital.

While Occupy became a crystalizing moment for already widespread opposition to global capitalism (by the "multitude"),[18] the Jerusalem "commune" was a key step in what began as a local movement among one people subjected to the Empire that then expanded steadily outwards among other subject peoples. While there was resistance to Roman conquest and domination elsewhere by other peoples, the resistance by Galileans and Judeans was sustained for nearly two hundred years, from three years of resistance to Herod's conquest of his subjects in 40–37 BCE and the widespread revolt after his death in 4 BCE to the great revolt in 66–70 and another in 132–135 CE, with many scribal protests and popular movements in between.[19]

It is only when we read the extended (historical) narrative of Acts, as sequel of the Lukan Gospel (historical) story, that we begin to get a sense of how it fits into the deeply conflictual politics and political-economy of Roman Palestine and how the local Jesus-movement and its first local expansion and then wider expansion began to have implications for the Roman

---

18. While the beginning of Occupy Wall Street was local in its locale, it was directed against the financial center of global capital and was also located not far from what had been the towers of the World Trade Center.

19. In its references to some of these movements, the narrative in Acts (5:33–39) indicates that the movement of Jesus-loyalists belongs among the many movements of resistance to the Roman imperial order.

imperial order and the subsequent history of the Roman Empire. The people who produced the historical narrative of (Luke–)Acts had the sense that they and the leaders of the movement in which they stood (the heroes of the story) were involved in events that constituted the turning point of world history. The Roman Empire was the broader context in which the decisive events were occurring. But history was moving not through (the history of) Rome, as the imperial ideology had it, but through (the history of) Israel, one of the peoples who had been subjugated by Rome, and now more particularly through the movement of fulfilment that had finally reached Rome (by the end of Acts).

The Christ-loyalists gathered in Jerusalem and recruiting in the temple courtyard were indeed a protest movement; but they were more. Their gathering in Jerusalem was a function of their drive to expand the movement generated in Jesus' mission, followed by his vindication by God after his ignominious execution, all in fulfillment of Israelite history as understood in terms of Israelite tradition. The movement expanded rapidly, with other peoples (*ethne*) also subject to the Roman order eager to join, they gradually became more broadly *inter-people*.[20] In the narrative of Acts the expansion started in Jerusalem, where the disciples' first act was to reconstitute the symbolic Twelve representatives of Israel. After being empowered, at Pentecost, to expand the movement, including speech in diverse languages, the disciples who had come with Jesus to "occupy" the temple at the Passover festival then used its courtyard and porticoes as the principal "public space" in which to recruit local and diaspora Judeans into the movement. In the idealizing retrospective narrative in Acts, Peter proclaimed in the temple courtyard that the long-anticipated prophet of the renewal of Israel had come in Jesus and had been killed by the Romans but vindicated by God as the Messiah who would return to complete the restoration of Israel. This proclamation induced Judean pilgrims from the diaspora as well as local Judeans to join the movement, to *become loyal* to the vindicated prophet/messiah. In the context of the Roman Empire *pistis/fides* meant (exclusive) *loyalty*, more specifically to a particular figure. When Judeans became loyal to Jesus/Christ, they could no longer be loyal to Caesar.[21] The high priestly rulers charged with maintaining the Roman imperial order in Judea as the heads of the central political-economic institution of the temple recognized that increasing numbers of people

20. Since nations and nationalism are modern developments (Anderson, *Imagined Communities*) it is inappropriate to translate *ethne* as "nations" and say that the movement became "international" as it spread "to the ends of the earth" (1:8).

21. The standard translation as "faith" or "belief in" depoliticizes the narratives in Acts and the references by Paul to people who had become loyal to Jesus/Christ.

becoming loyal to Jesus was a threat to the fragile social order in Palestine that periodically erupted into overt conflict.

Galilean country people now ninety miles from their home villages, however, in an expanding community that included diaspora Judeans much further from their hometowns, they had to arrange for their subsistence. Having come from Israelite village communities with covenantal traditions of cooperation and mutual aid and recent stays in other villages to heal and teach where local families had shared their food, they established a "commune" in which goods were shared in common. Lest we miss the symbolism as well as the concrete alternative economic arrangement, this is a telling juxtaposition. Herod's temple was one of the great wonders of the Roman imperial world. In charge of the temple were the wealthy high priestly families installed by the Romans; they took taxes, tithes, and offerings from the villagers and made high-interest loans to poor families in order to take even further control of their land and labor. In the shadow of the temple, on the other hand, somewhere in the alleyways of Jerusalem, was the fledgling commune of Galileans and others in which goods were shared in common while they were aggressively recruiting Judeans into their movement of renewal of Israel as an alternative society.

In the continuing narrative, the movement does not become merely religious or a new religion. Recent interpreters have suggested that as it blames the diaspora Judeans in some towns for attacking the movement in some episodes in Acts, the movement makes its peace with Roman officials. The continuing narrative in Acts, however, states that many Judeans as well as other peoples joined the movement, and that the apostles were proclaiming that there was another king other than Caesar and were teaching customs that it was illegal for Roman-loyalists to observe (Acts 16:21; 17:6). As the movement expanded among other peoples through Asia Minor and into Greece and, by the end of the story, to the very center of the Empire in Rome, it evidently did not become any less political or any less an alternative society to the Roman imperial order. And as the movement expanded beyond its base, the Jerusalem community, while experiencing repression, did not exhaust itself, but continued as the center of the movement, partly by receiving a "collection for the poor among the saints in Jerusalem" that Paul had contracted to organize (Gal 2). The interpeople, intercity association of "assemblies" thus also retained an economic dimension while persisting "in but not of" the Roman imperial order. Despite its confidence about being the vanguard of history, however, the movement that the Acts narrative portrays was still small and insignificant. It had not yet expanded to the point that it would become "successful" as a new religion, that is, coopted as the official religion of the Empire.

While the movement of renewal of Israel expanding from its base in the Jerusalem "commune" does not provide a good analogy for Occupy, which raised critical awareness of the control that global capitalism exerts on people's lives, it offers a model of effective resistance to centralized imperial political-economic domination. Building on deep Israelite tradition of communal responsibility for economic aid to the needy, it devised a sharing of resources to enable a movement of resistance to expand in the interstices of imperial control. As the movement of alternative communities spread, what began as local sharing of goods expanded to sharing of resources between communities, whether as support for organizers or new alternative communities or as support for the base community in which the members had left their earlier economic base. In the far more complex situation under the power of global capitalism sharing of resources would probably be more partial.

On Recognizing the Divine Power and the Religion of Empire

The Apocalypse to John confronts modern interpreters with a visionary text that they do not understand.[22] Interpreters inherit a long history of misunderstanding and misinterpretation of the Apocalypse as about the final destruction of the world. This is not only the meaning of the term "apocalypse/apocalyptic" in popular culture; it continues in biblical scholarship as well. The Apocalypse to John and a range of late second-temple Judean texts that became labeled "apocalyptic" were understood as about the End of the World. In the late nineteenth century, biblical scholars seized upon text-fragments and images taken literally to construct an "apocalyptic scenario": the End of the World in the Last Judgment, the Great Tribulation, and the Resurrection of the dead. Through most of the twentieth century, mainline biblical/New Testament scholarship believed that "(early) Judaism" and "(early) Christianity," including Jesus and Paul, were caught up in "apocalypticism," as articulated not only in "apocalyptic" texts but also in the Gospels and Paul's letters, focused supposedly on the imminent end of the world in a "cosmic catastrophe."[23]

The elaborate vision or series of visions in the Apocalypse was addressed to assemblies of Christ-loyalists in the province of Asia in the late first century CE, encouraging them to persist in their resistance to the

---

22. See esp. Rossing, *Rapture Exposed*.
23. Criticism in Horsley, *The Prophet Jesus and the Renewal of Israel*, chaps 1–5.

Roman imperial order despite sharp repression. The key to understanding so-called apocalyptic texts is to discern the relationship of the visionary imagery to the general political-economic-religious situation of the seer and addressees and to historical events (then, not now). The Apocalypse to John draws on a rich Judean tradition of visions in which sages/seers sought to understand violent imperial domination in visions of disruption in the divine/heavenly governance of earthly events (evident particularly in the Book of Watchers and Animal Vision included in 1 Enoch).[24] Despite appearances that historical events are utterly out of control, as imperial forces attack and even kill those loyal to God (or Christ/the Lamb that was slain), God remains ultimately in control, as the transcendent heavenly emperor on the glorious divine throne. But particularly powerful heavenly forces (the dragon) have rebelled against the divine governance, been cast out of heaven, and are wreaking violence in earthly affairs.

The visionary text of the Apocalypse unfolds in a series of (seven) sevens ("and I saw").

If the situation the vision addresses had not been evident before, the central fourth step in the unfolding revelation (Rev 12–14) is transparent in its reference to the general historical situation of those addressed in what appear to be the climactic events of history. The first beast to which the dragon has given his power is the Roman Empire that is seeking to devour the messiah (child) born from the people of Israel (the woman). And the second beast has devised the elaborate imperial cult in which people are forced to do obeisance in loyalty to the first beast (Rome/Caesar, 13:11–17). With the enthronement of the Son of Man, however, the time of judgment has come. Other heavenly and/or earthly events flow into or out of or respond to the imperial domination by the beast(s), with regular reassurance that Christ/the Lamb and the martyrs have been vindicated by God/saved in heaven.

While much of the visionary imagery *is* of destruction and some of it is downright misogynist, scholarly as well as popular interpreters have misunderstood much of it as "cosmic catastrophe." After the seven letters to the seven assemblies, the seer "in the spirit" is called up to the very height of heaven where God is enthroned in splendor across a "sea of glass." The latter is the sea of waters above held back by the firmament of the heaven (as in Gen 1) across which the Creator is enthroned. The opening of the seals prefigures what is about to be revealed about the current situation of those who are loyally serving God and resisting repressive

---

24. See further the analysis of sections of 1 Enoch and Daniel in Horsley, *Scribes, Visionaries*, chaps 8–9.

imperial rule. Conquest, war, famine, and death plague those who are being martyred for the word of God, but God appears in judgment, which is an utterly awesome "earth-shaking" event (symbolized by the sun darkening, etc.), as the sky (firmament of heaven) rolls up so that the kings and magnates and warlords and wealthy have nothing to shelter them from the terrifying day of divine wrath (Rev 6:1–16). This visionary imagery is rooted in an Israelite prophetic tradition of theophany (see, e.g., God's coming in judgment in Isa 13).[25] But earthly life is not to be damaged until the servants of God are sealed (Rev 7:1–17).

What is touched off by the blowing of the trumpets looks like further theophany, but the fire cast upon the earth from the heavenly altar is now indeed destructive, as a third of the earth, the sea, the waters, the heavenly bodies are all destroyed, and those who do not have God's seal are slaughtered by the brutal armies released from the underworld, headed by "Destruction" and "Destroyer" (Rev 8–9). As indicated in the ensuing hymn, the point of these manifestations of God's wrath is to "destroy those who destroy the earth."

It is possible to further zero in on what the Apocalypse is about by attending to the visionary description of the "second beast" and the description of "Babylon the Great" and "the kings of the earth."

The "second beast" is a symbol of the Roman emperor cult, as noted. The revelation does not offer much about its scale and workings, but it required far more than mere "idolatry," the "worship" of lifeless works of human hands. Biblical scholars were unable to discern this insofar as they were working with a narrow, reductionist view of religion as individual faith. Starting nearly forty years ago, Roman historians began to explain just how elaborate were the honors to Caesar and Rome institutionalized in the built environment of temples, shrines, rebuilt city-centers, and annual games/festivals in nearly every city of the Empire.[26] The presence of the emperor came to pervade public space; the built environment surrounded people with images and rituals of the divine power that determined their lives, Caesar.[27] Christian scholars could not discern this because they were working with an understanding of religion focused on individual "faith" or "belief" separate from politics and economics. The imperial cult, moreover,

---

25. For textual references of this prophetic tradition see Horsley, *Scribes, Visionaries*, 158–59.

26. See the abridgments of Price, *Rituals and Power*; and Zanker, *Power of Images*, in Horsley, *Paul and Empire*.

27. On Ephesus and the complete reconstruction of the agora/city center to focus on the temple to Caesar and other temples and shrines that also honored Caesar, see Friesen, *Imperial Cults and the Apocalypse*.

was produced ("owned and operated") by the imperial urban elite (the 1% or .1%); and those elites, in turn, legitimated themselves as the benefactors who "donated" the built environment that glorified and celebrated imperial power via the power of those images and rituals. They built up their wealth, of course, by draining resources and labor from their slaves and other dependents in the cities and on rural estates and manipulated and controlled them through the pervasive imperial temples, shrines, and cycle of celebrations and festivals in each city. The term "emperor cult" is surely too weak and misleading for these elaborate buildings and festivals including the calendar that structured space and time of life in the cities of the Empire. These institutions of honors to the emperor were *the central forms of the religious-political-economy* of the cities controlled by the wealthy political-religious elite who were *serving* the principal power that determined their lives, that is, the divine Caesar.

The description of Babylon the Great and the kings of the earth further reveals what was happening at the center of the political economy of the Roman Empire. The Babylonian conquest and devastation of Judea and Jerusalem had been deeply traumatic in Judean tradition, so that Babylon became the code name for imperial domination, here in the Apocalypse for the Roman Empire. Like earlier empires, the Roman Empire was a complex structure of city-states and client kings who controlled and exploited peoples and their resources locally. "Babylon" (the Roman metropolis) and "the kings of the earth" who were in close collaboration with the imperial court/metropolis, lived in luxury with costly goods shipped by merchants who had grown rich from the cargoes of luxury goods: fancy foods, spices, clothing, military equipment, and slaves and other victims of trafficking (Rev 18:2–4, 11–13, 16).

The purpose and principal message of the elaborate visionary sequence of the Apocalypse was to insist that the assemblies in cities of the province of Asia steadfastly adhere to their loyalty to Christ and continue to avoid participation in the honors to Caesar.[28] The "emperor cult" had become prominent as the central political-economic-religious institution(s) in each city as well as the form by which it participated in and served the overall Roman imperial order. The members of the assemblies were unavoidably in the Empire. But they were loyal to Christ, and not to Caesar. They had evidently withdrawn from participation, which must have been threatening to the local urban and imperial "priests." Their repressive measures included the killing of some members. In the midst of an elaborate vision that God was still ultimately in control of history, was vindicating martyrs, and would eventually execute

28. See further Hansen, "On Trying to Praise the Mutilated World," 305–12.

judgment on the Empire, "John" insisted that people in the assemblies stick together and continue their refusal to participate. Thus the cry of the visionary: "Come out of her my people!" (18:4). That is, extract yourselves as much as possible from the Roman imperial order at the apex of which was the lavish wealth and luxury of the dominant oligarchies.

The visionary narrative of the Apocalypse, however, is seriously problematic, and not just because of its previous misunderstanding in terms of the End of the world in cosmic catastrophe. That is what we can now realize will be happening unless governments of the world can summon the political courage and will to slow global warming. As noted briefly above, the vision of God's resolution of the historical crisis of attacks against Christ-loyalists is extremely violent not only in its misogyny and in its imagination of the destruction of those who are destroying the world, but in the deconstruction of creation. Also problematic, despite some compelling aspects, is the utopian vision of the New Jerusalem coming down to earth. As in earlier "revelations" midst violent imperial repression, the people are to be healed, renewed, empowered, and illuminated by the divine presence, with no need of a temple.[29] But the New Jerusalem is imagined as full of luxury and as yet another imperial center to which pilgrims will bring the glory and honor of other peoples (also prominent in late prophetic books, such as Isa 61).

The descriptions of Babylon the Great and the kings of the earth and of the second beast in the Apocalypse are (at least potentially) suggestive for people today living uncomfortably in the bowels of the current form of the first beast. This may not be surprising insofar as the composer(s) and addressees of the Apocalypse, like those of other texts later included in the New Testament, were living in the bowels of the Roman Empire that became the paradigmatic empire for the modern European and American empires that prepared the way and then "gave way" to the empire of global capitalism. These passages are all the more suggestive once we understand them more fully in their historical context of the Roman imperial political-economy and the institutions of the "emperor cult" that constituted the central political-economic-religious imperial order in the cities into which the movement of Christ-loyalists spread.

Babylon the Great and the kings of the earth, that is, the obscenely wealthy elite in Rome itself, the oligarchs in the cities of the empire, and the client kings in the provinces, were living in lavish wealth, with households staffed by scores of slaves. Merchants had grown rich transporting cargoes of luxury goods to them: fancy foods, spices, clothing, military equipment,

---

29. The temple was conveniently ignored in the visions of restoration of the people in Dan 7 and 10–12 and explicitly rejected in the Animal Vision in 1 Enoch 85–90.

and slaves and other victims of trafficking. A more complete picture of the political economy of the Roman Empire would have included the thousands of tons of grain that Rome extracted from the peasant farmers in Egypt and hired shipped to the imperial metropolis to buy off the plebeians with a dole, the "bread" that went with the "circus" of elaborate spectacles of combat in the arena. The wine and processed fish extracted from Syria-Palestine was probably for more "upscale" dining served by slaves in the great households.

∽ ∽ ∽

The broad analogy with the empire of global capitalism seems fairly obvious, with two major exceptions. In the Roman Empire the political economy was commanded by "the state," which contracted with merchants to bring (luxury) goods to the imperial metropolis and other cities. In the empire of global capital, the political economy is "privately" owned and operated by the transnational mega-corporations that manipulate states to deregulate and subsidize their operations in multiple ways. In the second major exception, the scale of consumption and wealth under global capitalism is utterly incomparable. In the imperial centers of consumer capitalism, not just the .1% or even the 1%, but a considerable percentage of people are living far above a level that is sustainable, as the resources of the earth are being exhausted (double sense intended) and the earth as a whole destroyed. In the dire circumstances of runaway climate change, the most obvious problem may be the consumption of fossil fuels being driven by giant corporations to sell oil and the super-powered monster-vehicles that burn it. But the food that people eat is now produced and processed by agribusiness. Mass produced food is grown by agribusiness on one continent (where people's land was seized), and trucked, then flown, then trucked again by burning oil to other continents. Similarly, clothes and computers and cellphones are manufactured in megacorporation-controlled sweat shops in Asia powered by burning coal and shipped and trucked to other continents by burning oil. It is a messenger from heaven whom the seer hears declare, "Fallen is Babylon the Great." Today it is scientists who have concluded that the earth, the climate, is about to be destroyed—unless, of course, capitalist growth can be stopped and reversed and people in the "developed" world move drastically toward a sustainable level of consumption.

Once we have learned more about how elaborate, political-economic-religious, and pervasive the "imperial cult" was that the Christ-loyalists were subjected to, then it too should be suggestive for people subjected to global consumer capitalism. The constantly "in-your-face" imperial presence in the built environment that replaced what had been the "civic center" of ancient "civil" society might well suggest a critical investigation of the much more massive and complex built environment and media environment of images and rituals of global capitalism that has replaced modern civil society. In the cities of the Roman Empire the images and rituals of Caesar, the divine power that had come to control their life, were constantly and everywhere "in your face." These concrete institutions participation in which was virtually unavoidable (literally built into the built environment) served to mystify and appease the (imperial) Power that had come to control their life as compelling/demanding, divine, and sacred (not to be questioned but celebrated). In global capitalist society, not just the massive high-rise megabuildings of the "downtown" of cities around the world but also the images and rituals and spectacles that channel desire and induce acquiescence are also pervasively "in your face" (that is, eyes, ears, nose, mouth/taste) but serve to veil as well as mystify the superhuman Power that has come to control our life and is sacred (that is, not to be questioned), and hedged about with laws and courts that protect its control.

There may be a major difference, however, between the function of images and rituals in the situations represented in "biblical" texts and the function of images and rituals in global capitalism. Images and pomp and circumstance produced by the wealthy and powerful in traditional societies were mainly for consumption (as well as performance) by the wealthy and powerful themselves. They were not particularly effective inducing support by the people, particularly the majority living in villages. In the development of consumer capitalism and its globalization, not only are the images consumed by the people generally, but the way they work is to induce people to believe that they can live (in) the images by spending some of their ever more scarce resources to buy the unneeded goods that the images represent.

Despite this contrast, it is conceivable that we might discern in the ubiquitous mystifying images and rituals of capitalism (not just of "marketing") the religious dimension of the controlling Power that corresponds to the Emperor honored/served in the emperor cult in the cities in which Christ-loyalists formed alternative communities. What "the second beast" was creating in the visionary narrative of the Apocalypse suggests that biblical studies as we know the field, and the larger field of Christian theology, might well learn from its texts and recent research into their historical contexts that our understanding of religion and its theology (understanding of the divine) are modern reductions.

The modern (Western) understanding of religion as individual faith or belief separate from political-economic life is severely limited and perhaps historically unique. In the Roman emperor cult and the urban temples and the village assemblies of most historical societies, religion was not separate but embedded with the political economy (and natural environment). As we might learn from the second commandment (discussed in chap. 8) and its historical context as well as from the Roman "emperor cult," moreover, in ancient imperial political-economic-religious systems the people were induced and/or forced to serve the powers that determined their lives (e.g., Storm-Kingship or Caesar) by yielding up their produce/resources and labor. It is clear that in the current historical context the Power that people are serving is global capital. The religious dimension of this political economy by which that Power is mystified are the pervasive and ubiquitous images and rituals of the culture of non-meaning that mystifies or simply hides global capital and its destructive exercise of power. These are the essential means by which global capitalism works, the cultural production by which it reproduces and "grows" itself. To state it clearly, the Power that people serve under the new form of Empire is global capital; the religion is consumer capitalism with its CEO high priests. The sacred is what cannot be questioned or seriously challenged. What cannot be questioned or seriously challenged today? Capital and capitalism.

Finally, it is not difficult to imagine what people today might feel compelled to do if they took seriously the call, "Come out of her, my people!" While we are unavoidably *in* the new form of empire, we can find ways of avoiding being completely defined and subservient to serving the Power of global capital that is determining our lives by acquiescing in the images and spectacles of the religion of global consumer capitalism. In his confrontation with the rulers in Jerusalem, Jesus declared carefully but clearly that the people did not owe tribute to Caesar, alluding to the first and second covenantal commandments. But he did not command the people to refuse payment, presumably since that would simply have led the Romans to kill or enslave the people. People in the assemblies addressed by the Apocalypse were being attacked for their refusal to participate in the emperor cult. The second beast of the empire of global capital, however, has far more subtle ways of inducing and seducing participation, ways that may include psychic and social-psychic violence but usually not outright killing. The capitalist system and even tacit participation in it, of course, are causing death and destruction. All the more reason for avoiding participation as much as possible. And critical and creative people can find or devise ways.

The Violent Exercise of Power

Interpretation of Rom 13:1–7, read as an abstract statement by the great apostle, has been shaped by and even remained within modern Western political thought. The issue has thus been the legitimacy of the modern state: whether rulers have their authority from God, and whether Christians must therefore be obedient to them. Now, however, we are living in and under the power of global capitalism. In this new situation, argues Bruce Worthington, the state is no longer relevant and the old debates divert attention from the dominance of global capital.[30] The interpretive question is no longer "how does Romans 13 fashion my disposition towards the state?" but "how does Romans 13 fashion my disposition towards the true seat of authority in the world, that of global capital?" With Worthington's indulgence, however, I would suggest a certain reformulation. This includes a critical assessment of the relation between global capitalism and the state (their interrelated power and lack of authority) and of Paul's stance toward Roman imperial rule.

It may help the analysis to make a distinction between (political-economic) power and authority. Authority is political power with legitimacy among the people over or among whom it is exercised. The legitimacy of the state might come from religion and/or propaganda and/or ideology and/or democratic election and/or some social contract/constitution and/or recognized service or benefit to the people. Too much exercise of arbitrary power and/or people's perception that power is being exercised against them or their interests might erode legitimacy. The capitalist economic system received some legitimacy through "liberal education" of professionals and the "middle class." But it is not clear that *global* capitalism ever had much legitimacy. And it is difficult to see any authority left in global capital after the crash in 2008 and the "bail-out" of banks whose use of power ruined so many people's lives. The states that bailed them out against the perceived interest of their people also lost legitimacy.

The state is not irrelevant but instrumental to global capitalism's expansion, consolidation, and exercise of economic power. Global(izing) capitalism's manipulation and control of states in North America became clear in NAFTA and before that in the manipulation of loans to smaller states by the IMF and the World Bank. Until recently, the US military, with assists from NATO, maintained sufficient international stability for investment and extraction and was global capitalism's military enforcer. States also deregulated corporations' actions, giving them free-reign, in keeping with neoliberal ideology, and further enabled global capital's

---

30. Worthington, "Romans 13:1–7: With an Eye to Global Capital."

manipulation of the political processes. The pretense of democracy is a key component in the ideology of global capitalism. Moreover, the media coverage of the (illusory) democratic political process, which forms part of the "entertainment" offered in the capital-owned and operated media, provides a smoke-screen that effectively diverts the public's attention from the actions and effects of capital. States, or the political parties "in power," still have considerable power (but less and less authority), and they exercise power on behalf of and for the benefit of capital.

Just as the power under which we interpret is no longer the modern state but global capitalism, to which the state is subordinate, so Roman imperial domination, under which Paul was catalyzing communities and communicating with them, was not comparable to the modern state. If anything, while different in form, it was comparable to global capitalism insofar as it exercised power over subject peoples, but had no authority. Classical historians have been far more candid in recent decades about how the Roman warlords at the head of the legions destroyed villages and cities and slaughtered or enslaved people as ways of terrorizing the remaining populations into submission and payment of tribute. They imposed rulers on their client states that had no authority. Not just the Gospel of Mark, but the wealthy Judean priest and historian Josephus as well, indicates that the high priestly "authorities" and their scribal representatives had no authority among the people. The imperial order was maintained in the cities by the local oligarchy (often politely termed "aristocracy") as clients of the emperor, who had long since consolidated political-economic power. The "citizen"-bodies of Philippi and Corinth at the time of Paul's mission were descended from the colonies of Latin-speaking army veterans or Roman urban riff-raff planted in the first century BCE by Roman warlords, displacing the local inhabitants.

As for Paul's own stance toward the Roman imperial order with its rulers, he was convinced it stood under God's condemnation and was "passing away," yet still wielding power and not well-disposed to the communities that were loyal to their own alternative "Lord." In his "revelation" he became convinced that the violence and domination of "the rulers of this era/time" had been exposed in the crucifixion of Jesus and that in his vindication by God he had displaced Caesar as the Lord and Savior who was reigning in heaven but at the imminent "day of the Lord" would establish God's direct rule on earth, having subjected every (Roman imperial) ruler and power. Meanwhile, he had been commissioned not just to proclaim the counter-imperial "gospel" of the crucified and vindicated Christ but to catalyze assemblies of loyalists whose politics were in (derived from) heaven, as they awaited the final step in the fulfillment of history that had begun with the crucifixion. This may sound delusional to us. But this is what he said in letter after letter. In ad hoc letters to somewhat different local situations in Philippi, Thessalonica, and Corinth, he urged the communities of Christ-loyalists to avoid attracting attention, even to avoid interaction with outsiders, while also recruiting others into the movement, as they awaited the judgment (destruction) of the elite who boasted of the "Peace and Security (Prosperity)" of the Roman imperial order. Precisely while he was building an inter-people alternative society based in local communities of peoples subjected to the Roman Empire, he wanted to avoid evoking reaction and repression.

Worthington's answer to the question he poses, "how does Romans 13 fashion my disposition towards the true seat of authority in the world, that of global capital?" is in effect that we do not allow Rom 13 or any other text to directly fashion our disposition toward global capital. Rome and Caesar never did have authority for Paul. We have already come to recognize that global capitalism is doing violence against both people and the planet. It has no authority, but exercises power, both subtly and not at all subtly. As biblical scholars, however, we can both learn from analyses of our own situation under global capital and do our own historical homework. Worthington has sharpened his insights into both our current situation and the text with the help of Althusser and others. This enables him to discern what Paul is saying in the text addressed to the assembly of Christ-loyalists in Rome because he knows the historical context from what Neil Elliott has laid out.[31] Knowing Nero's claim to have sheathed the sword was merely propaganda ("deceitful rhetoric"), he can see that in Rom 13:1–7 Paul is in fact (carefully) criticizing the violence of the Roman Empire. This insight into the text then leads us to further analysis and insight into our own situation. Worthington even draws an analogy. Rome's/the Emperor's violence is like the violence of global capital. This enables us to see that global capitalism is the new form of Empire, capital the new form of the Emperor (and we could add similarly divine/sacred and beyond/above criticism).

Far from doing nothing but continue to pay his taxes, however, Paul and his co-workers had devoted their lives to catalyzing fledgling local communities in an expanding movement in which they embodied an alternative society. Our situation under global capital is far more complex than the cities of the Roman Empire, including the ways in which our lives are embedded in society dominated by global capital, from our food and clothing to our mortgages, health care, and pensions. That Paul and his coworkers were driven to form communities that were at least

---

31. N. Elliott, *The Arrogance of Nations*.

semi-independent, "in but not of" the Roman imperial order, is at least suggestive—on which more just below.

Alternative Communities
in but not of the New Form of Empire

I have waited to comment on Roland Boer's explanation of the feasibility of subsistence economics[32] because several of the biblical texts discussed above are also suggestive for local responses to the domination of global capitalism. He focuses on evidence of subsistence agrarian communes in the southern Levant, the area marginal to the dominant empires where Israel arose. Exploited as the economic base of agrarian empires, peasant villages made a comeback when imperial regimes succumbed to the perpetual crises in which they operated. Communities of subsistence living persisted in various modes of production, with different functions in each. As noted above, James C. Scott found that the village communities he studied in Southeast Asia and those examined in historical and anthropological studies of different eras and areas shared some of the same features that Boer finds in subsistence communities in the ancient (and more recent) southern Levant. In addition to (biological) diversity of crops and herds that reduce risk to food production, village communities had traditional customs and cooperative measures by which they kept component households—and thus the whole community—economically viable (e.g., reallocation of land, gleaning, common pasturage, woodland, streams).

As mentioned above, something similar appears evident in the covenantal commandments and the traditional customs and measures of mutual aid that were adapted in the legal collections of the Pentateuch and mentioned in stories such as Naboth's vineyard and for the violation of which the prophets indicted the wealthy and powerful. That these had become strong as Israelite tradition seems evident in the measures Nehemiah takes (cancellation of debts, release of debt-slaves) to keep the subsistence communities viable as the economic base of the Persian regime. I have argued that the Gospels portray Jesus' mission as focused on the renewal of covenantal community in the villages of Galilee. The sharing of goods in the Jerusalem commune in Acts appears to be derived from the Israelite tradition of subsistence economics and the experience of the disciples on mission in village communities. One might argue that the idea of the collection for the poor among the saints in Jerusalem derives from this tradition and even that Paul and his coworkers' formation of new communities has

32. Boer, "On the Feasibility of Subsistence Economics."

similar derivation. These were not "churches," but *ekklesiai*, synonym (in Greek as well as Semitic derivation) of *synagogai*, that is, the local assemblies of semi-autonomous village communities.

It is important to emphasize, over against individualist biblical studies midst an individualist culture and individualist neoliberal ideology, that these texts are about communities, their subsistence and/or renewal or establishment and that collective responsibility and action are involved. Also collective action, including innovative action, is rooted in and draws (often quite creatively) on Israelite popular tradition (social memory), including customs that had proven their importance in generations of experience while being adapted to circumstances. As Boer points out, local self-governance was usually dominated by the male elders. In crises, however, women or marginal figures such as shepherds or bandits might emerge as leaders of collective action. It may be important to attend to these features of the rich tradition of (alternative) communities and collective action in "biblical" texts and history as suggestive for people seeking ways to resist or carve out some alternative forms of life while under the domination of global capital.

Many, mostly younger, people in my limited circle of acquaintance are becoming engaged collectively and often communally in initiatives aimed at fundamental social transformation. Most of them have little or no acquaintance with biblical texts, much less biblical studies. But I can imagine that there could be some suggestive conversations if biblical studies opened up in the way pioneered by this collection of essays. Let me summarize some of the initiatives of which I am aware, proceeding roughly according to their focus and/or breadth.

Most daring perhaps would be the move to subsistence that Boer explains is feasible—and probably necessary if we are to live sustainably! Indeed it would require desiring little, and many of those who are dedicating much or most of their time to political action against global warming have made exactly that move. Because the anti-culture of global capitalism has dissolved most historical memory of alternative forms of social-economic life, few are even aware of traditional subsistence community life, much less that it is feasible. Biblical studies can contribute by helping revive historical social memory that has previously informed community renewal and collective action.

Many recent initiatives are focused mainly on food production. Short of a group of people moving to establish a subsistence economic community, there are several initiatives of local food production in the US and Canada. These may not be motivated explicitly as resistance to domination by global capital, but have that effect by reducing the market for agribusiness. Individual families and small groups have moved back into farming, making a modest income supplying some or most of the needs of various numbers of people in nearby towns or small cities. They have also purposely trained others interested in moving back into farming. The flipside of this is local consumers, breaking their dependence on agribusiness, buying food from local farmers, thus keeping them economically viable. Farmers who produce sustainably also form cooperatives that sell locally and regionally, competing successfully with agribusiness. Individuals and small groups, sometimes cooperatives, have initiated urban gardening, in front or back yards, vacant lots or other city-land, and even on roof-tops. In the Community Supported Agriculture movement, groups—usually in cities—buy shares in the annual crop as an advance to the farmer(s) who can thus avoid borrowing from (now mega-)banks. In recent years, the organization of farmers' markets has expanded, some including city subsidies to low-income people (often in urban "food-deserts") so that they can afford fresh produce. Such farmers markets also become centers of community socializing that would otherwise not happen. All of these initiatives practice sustainable agriculture and reduce the burning of fossil fuels.

In addition to alternative food production, we see a number of moves toward local community cooperation motivated precisely by opposition to control by global capital. One is community solidarity in keeping fast-food chains or Wal-Marts out. Another is to support local banks and to revive or start credit unions in order to take at least some money back from the mega-banks and to harbor local resources. Not too many generations ago, some Roman Catholic churches in US cities also served as credit unions for largely immigrant worker members. Covenantal measures of local communal support included liberal lending at no interest to needy neighbors, as in Exod 22:24–25. An older initiative, now expanding, is workers forming cooperatives to continue local production where transnational corporations close factories or to generate local production of goods or services. Associations of such cooperatives have persuaded non-profit or civic institutions such as museums or symphony orchestras to contract for goods and services with them rather than with (subsidiaries of) large corporations.

In another form of community-based economic subsistence (and resistance) people with highly diversified training and skills are cooperating to form informal non-monetized networks of barter (good old village custom), with either a local form of currency or local form of credit (for hours of services or produce contributed), which strengthens the local community network and keeps scarce resources from being sucked up by transnational chains, megacorporations, agribusiness, and big banks. In the area of Boston where I live, a wider community network of considerable ethnic and educational diversity, led by young families, are beginning to implement a "community transitional economy" that includes urban agriculture, CSA shares, farmer's markets, a network of barter, support of small local businesses, withdrawal from and keeping out global capitalist corporations. Many of the participants are also engaged in collective action, organizing blockage of foreclosures on homes or continuing generation of energy from fossil fuels, and insisting that the city use whatever leverage it has to reestablish affordable housing. They have not yet figured out how to organize in sufficient numbers to gain minimal leverage on global capital, such as to negotiate with insurance companies or to get the "Commonwealth" to divest pension funds of state employees in fossil fuel companies.

It is difficult to know just how much the fissures and cracks in the global capitalist system are widening, as collective initiatives emerge from the multitude toward transitional community economy, including some experiments with subsistence economics. There are many movements of renewal of local social-economic community in resistance to different forms of empire in "biblical" texts, movements that were partly motivated and informed by a strong cultural tradition of cooperative communal economics. Through more comprehensive analysis of the texts, biblical interpreters can open access to these movements and the cultural tradition on which they drew, while also discerning the form of political-economic-religious domination that they were resisting. There are, of course, also many problematic texts and aspects of texts that have been easily used in support of forms of domination. These can be exposed, criticized, and critically learned from. Perhaps biblical interpreters can bring such resources into current political-economic-religious discussions wider than but including classrooms and churches.

One of the principal things that biblical interpreters can bring into the public discourse is greater historical awareness, including historical alternatives to thinking in capitalist terms. Integral to global capitalism's power is its dissolution or suppression of history and its commodification of people's culture, taking its edges off as it is transformed into mere entertainment that sells additional unneeded mass-produced commodities to consume for a price. One way to resist the global capitalist culture of ahistorical non-meaning consumed by atomized individuals would be for communities to cultivate and share and draw upon historical traditions, cultivating recognition of unfulfilled historical potential.[33] Individualism is simply impotent.

How to do this is yet another problem that biblical interpreters must face, as explored by Neil Elliott's incisive analysis of the interlocking constraints on professional academics that are becoming ever tighter in our

---

33. Taking seriously one of Alain Badiou's titles, *The Rebirth of History*.

current situation.[34] Since the technology of communications has passed me by, I must utterly defer to a younger generation adept in how to use the communications technology but also in how to counter its atomizing and non-meaning effects. Certainly, one matter that seems clear from the atomization that global capitalism has effected is that biblical interpreters, like other academics and intellectuals, must find ways of mutual support and of working cooperatively, even collectively. And that would also enable the attempt toward more comprehensive critical analysis and interpretation of biblical texts, tradition, and history.

34. N. Elliott, "Occupying My Desk."

Bibliography

Adams, Edward. "First-Century Models for Paul's Churches: Selected Scholarly Developments since Meeks." In *After the First Urban Christians: The Social Scientific Study of Pauline Christianity, Twenty-Five Years Later*, edited by Todd D. Still and David G. Horrell, 60–78. London: T. & T. Clark, 2007.
Alcock, Susan E. *Graecia Capta: The Landscapes of Roman Greece*. Cambridge: Cambridge University Press, 1993.
Allison, Dale C. *Jesus of Nazareth: Millenarian Prophet*. Minneapolis: Fortress, 1998.
Anderson, Benedict R. O'G. *Imagined Communities: Reflections on the Origin and Spread of Nationalism*. New York: Verso, 1983.
Asad, Talal. *Genealogies of Religion: Discipline and Reasons of Power in Christianity and Islam*. Baltimore: Johns Hopkins University Press, 1993.
Ascough, Richard A., Phillip A. Harland, and John S. Kloppenborg. *Associations in the Greco-Roman World: A Sourcebook*. Waco, TX: Baylor University Press, 2012.
Avigad, Nahman. *Discovering Jerusalem*. Nashville: Nelson, 1983.
Badiou, Alain. *The Rebirth of History: Times of Riots and Uprisings*. London: Verso, 2012.
Baltzer, Klaus. *The Covenant Formulary: In Old Testament, Jewish, and Early Christian Writings*. Translated by David E. Green. Philadelphia: Fortress, 1971.
Bartchy, S. Scott. "Community of Goods in Acts: Idealization or Social Reality?" In *The Future of Early Christianity: Essays in Honor of Helmut Koester*, edited by Birger A. Pearson et al., 309–18. Minneapolis: Fortress, 1991.
———. "Paulus hat nicht gelehrt: 'Jeder soll in seinem Stand bleiben': Luthers Fehlübersetzung von κλῆσις in 1 Korinther 7." In *Alte Texte in neuen Kontexte: Wo steht die sozialwissenschaftlich Bibelexegese?*, edited by Wolfgang Stegemann and Richard DeMaris, 222–41. Stuttgart: Kohlhammer, 2014.
Becker, Adam H., and Annette Yoshiko Reed, eds. *The Ways That Never Parted: Jews and Christians in Late Antiquity and the Early Middle Ages*. 2003. Reprinted, Minneapolis: Fortress, 2007.
Boer, Roland. "On the Feasibility of Subsistence Economics." In *Reading the Bible in an Age of Crisis: Political Exegesis for a New Day*, edited by Bruce Worthington, 109–30. Minneapolis: Fortress, 2015.
———. *The Sacred Economy of Ancient Israel*. LAI. Louisville: Westminster John Knox, 2015.

Boer, Roland, and Christina Petterson. *Idols of Nations: Biblical Myth at the Origins of Capitalism*. Minneapolis: Fortress, 2014.

———. *Time of Troubles: A New Economic Framework for Early Christianity*. Minneapolis: Fortress, 2017.

Broshi, Magen. "The Role of the Temple in the Herodian Economy." *JJS* 38 (1987) 31–37.

Butler, Judith. *Excitable Speech: A Politics of the Performative*. New York: Routledge, 1997.

Callahan, Allen Dwight. *Embassy of Onesimus*. Valley Forge, PA: Trinity, 1997.

———. "Paul's Epistle to Philemon: Toward an Alternative *Argumentum*." *HTR* 86 (1993) 357–76.

Callahan, Allen Dwight, and Richard A. Horsley. "Slave Resistance in Classical Antiquity." *Semeia* 83/84 (1998) 133–51.

Callahan, Allen Dwight, Richard Horsley, and Abraham Smith, eds. *Slavery in Text and Interpretation: Semeia* 83/84 (1998).

Callender, Dexter E., Jr. "Servants of God(s) and Servants of Kings in Israel and the Ancient Near East." *Semeia* 83/84 (1998) 67–81.

Carr, David M. *Writing on the Tablet of the Heart: Origins of Scripture and Literature*. Oxford: Oxford University Press, 2005.

Carter, Warren. *Matthew and the Margins: A Sociopolitical and Religious Reading*. Maryknoll, NY: Orbis, 2000.

Chakrabarty, Dipesh. "Subaltern Studies and Postcolonial Historiography." In *Handbook of Historical Sociology*, edited by Gerard Delanty and Engin F. Isin, 191–204. London: Sage, 2003.

Chaney, Marvin L. *Peasants, Prophets, and Political Economy*. Eugene, OR: Cascade Books, 2018.

Conzelmann, Hans. *First Corinthians: A Commentary on the First Epistle to the Corinthians*. Translated by James W. Leitch. Hermeneia. Philadelphia: Fortress, 1975.

Coote, Robert B. *Amos among the Prophets: Composition and Theology*. 1981. Reprint, Eugene, OR: Wipf & Stock, 2005.

———, ed. *Elijah and Elisha in Socio-literary Perspective*. Semeia Studies. Atlanta: Scholars, 1992.

Crossan, John Dominic. *The Historical Jesus: The Life of a Mediterranean Jewish Peasant*. San Francisco: HarperCollins, 1991.

Crossley, James G. *Jesus and the Chaos of History: Redirecting the Life of the Historical Jesus*. Bible Reconfigurations. Oxford: Oxford University Press, 2015.

———. *Jesus in an Age of Neoliberalism: Quests, Scholarship and Ideology*. Bible World. Sheffield: Equinox, 2012.

de Ste. Croix, G. E. M. *Class Struggle in the Ancient Greek World: From the Archaic Age to the Arab Conquests*. London: Duckworth, 1981.

Deissmann, Adolf. *St. Paul: A Study in Social and Religious History*. Translated by Lionel R. M. Strachan. 1912. Reprint, Eugene, OR: Wipf & Stock, 2004.

Dirlik, Arif. "The Postcolonial Aura: Third World Criticism and the Age of Global Capitalism." *Critical Inquiry* 20 (1994) 328–56.

———. *The Postcolonial Aura: Third World Criticism in the Age of Global Capitalism*. Boulder, CO: Westview, 1997.

Donfried, Karl P. "The Imperial Cults of Thessalonica and Paul's Conflict in 1 Thessalonians." In *Paul and Empire: Religion and Power in Roman Imperial Society*, edited by Richard Horsley, 215–23. Harrisburg, PA: Trinity, 1997.

Downs, David J. *The Offering of the Gentiles: Paul's Collection for Jerusalem in Its Chronological, Cultural, and Cultic Contexts*. WUNT 2/248. Tübingen: Mohr/Siebeck, 2008.

Draper, Jonathan A. "The Social Milieu and Motivation of the Community of Goods in the Jerusalem Church of Acts." In *Church in Context: Early Christianity in Social Context*, edited by Cilliers Breitenbach, 77–88. Pretoria: Kerkboekhandel, 1988.

Duling, Dennis C. *A Marginal Scribe: Studies in the Gospel of Matthew in a Social-Scientific Perspective*. Matrix 7. Eugene, OR: Cascade Books, 2011.

Ehrman, Bart D. *Jesus: Apocalyptic Prophet of the New Millennium*. Oxford: Oxford University Press, 1999.

Elliott, John H. "Social Scientific Criticism of the New Testament and Its Social World." *Semeia* 35 (1986) 1–33.

Elliott, Neil. *The Arrogance of Nations: Reading Romans in the Shadow of Empire*. Paul in Critical Contexts. Minneapolis: Fortress, 2008.

———. "Diagnosing an Allergic Reaction: The Avoidance of Marx in Pauline Scholarship." *Bible and Critical Theory* 8/2 (2012) 3–14.

———. "Ideological Closure in the Christ-Event: A Marxist Response to Alain Badiou." In *Paul, Philosophy, and the Theopolitical Vision: Critical Engagements with Agamben, Badiou, Žižek, and Others*, edited by Douglas Harink, 135–54. Theopolitical Visions 7. Eugene, OR: Cascade Books, 2010.

———. "Occupying My Desk." In *Reading the Bible in an Age of Crisis: Political Exegesis for a New Day*, edited by Bruce Worthington, 53–84. Minneapolis: Fortress, 2015.

———. "When Bridges Fail Us: Studying Economic Realities in the New Testament World." In *Bridges in New Testament Interpretation: Interdisciplinary Advances*, edited by Neil Elliott and Werner H. Kelber, 203–32. Lanham, MD: Fortress Academic, 2018.

Epp, Eldon Jay. "The Multivalence of the Term 'Original Text' in New Testament Text Criticism." *HTR* 92 (1999) 257–63.

Finley, Moses I. *The Ancient Economy*. Updated ed. Berkeley: University of California Press, 1999.

Freyne, Sean. *Galilee from Alexander the Great to Hadrian: A Study of Second Temple Judaism*. Wilmington, DE: Glazier, 1980.

Friesen, Steven J. *Imperial Cults and the Apocalypse of John: Reading Revelation in the Ruins*. Oxford: Oxford University Press, 2001.

———. "Poverty in Pauline Studies: Beyond the so-Called New Consensus." *JSNT* 26 (2004) 330–31.

Gager, John G. *Kingdom and Community: The Social World of Early Christianity*. Prentice-Hall Studies in Religion Series. Englewood Cliffs: Prentice-Hall, 1975.

Garnsey, Peter, and Richard Saller. *The Roman Empire: Economy, Society, and Culture*. Berkeley: University of California Press, 1987; 2nd ed., 2015.

Goodman, Martin. "The First Jewish Revolt: Social Conflict and the Problem of Debt." *JJS* 33 (1982) 422–34.

———. *The Ruling Class of Judea: The Origins of the Jewish Revolt against Rome. A.D. 566–70*. Cambridge: Cambridge University Press, 1987.

Gordon, Richard. "The Veil of Power." In *Paul and Empire: Religion and Power in Roman Imperial Society*, edited by Richard A. Horsley, 126–37. Harrisburg, PA: Trinity, 1997.

Gottwald, Norman K. "The Expropriated and the Expropriators in Nehemiah 5." In *The Hebrew Bible and Social Justice*, 3:35–53. Center and Library of the Bible and Social Justice Series. Eugene, OR: Cascade Books, 2018.

Gouldner, Alvin W. *Coming Crisis in Western Sociology*. Chapel Hill: University of North Carolina Press, 1970.

Guha, Ranajit. *Elementary Aspects of Peasant Insurgency in Colonial India*. Delhi: Oxford University Press, 1983.

Guha, Ranajit, and Gayatri Chakravorty Spivak, eds. *Selected Subaltern Studies*. New York: Oxford University Press, 1988.

Hansen, Ryan L. "On Trying to Praise the Mutilated World: Reading Revelation in the Midst of Ecological Crisis." in *Reading the Bible in an Age of Crisis: Political Exegesis for a New Day*, edited Bruce Worthington, 285–312. Minneapolis: Fortress, 2013.

Hanson, K. C. "The Galilean Fishing Economy and the Jesus Tradition." *Biblical Theology Bulletin* 27 (1997) 99–111.

———. "Transformed on the Mountain: Ritual Analysis and the Gospel of Matthew." *Semeia* 67 (1994/95) 147–70.

Hanson, K. C., and Douglas E. Oakman. *Palestine in the Time of Jesus: Social Structures and Social Conflicts*. 2nd ed. Minneapolis: Fortress, 2008.

Hardt, Michael, and Antonio Negri. *Empire*. Cambridge: Harvard University Press, 2000.

Harland, Philip A. *Associations, Synagogues, and Congregations: Claiming a Place in Ancient Mediterranean Society*. Minneapolis: Fortress, 2003.

Harnack, Adolf von. *What Is Christianity?* Translated by Thomas Bailey Saunders. 1901. Reprint, Fortress Texts in Modern Theology. Philadelphia: Fortress, 1986.

Harrill, J. Albert. *The Manumission of Slaves in Early Christianity*. Hermeneutische Untersuchungen zur Theologie 32. Tübingen: Mohr/Siebeck, 1995.

Harris, William V. *Ancient Literacy*. Cambridge: Harvard University Press, 1989.

Herzog, William R., II. *Jesus, Justice, and the Reign of God*. Louisville: Westminster John Knox, 2000.

———. *Parables as Subversive Speech: Jesus as Pedagogue of the Oppressed*. Louisville: Westminster John Knox, 1994.

Hezser, Catherine. *Jewish Literacy in Roman Palestine*. Texte und Studien zur Antiken Judentum 81. Tübingen: Mohr/Siebeck, 2001.

Hobsbawm, Eric J. *Primitive Rebels: Studies in Archaic Forms of Social Movements in the 19th and 20th Centuries*. New York: Norton, 1965.

Hopkins, Keith. *Conquerors and Slaves*. Sociological Studies in Roman History 1. Cambridge: Cambridge University Press, 1978.

Horsley, Richard A. "Ancient Jewish Banditry and the Revolt against Rome." *CBQ* 43 (1981) 409–32.

———. *Archaeology, History, and Society in Galilee: The Social Context of Jesus and the Rabbis*. Harrisburg, PA: Trinity, 1996.

———. "Can Study of the Historical Jesus Escape Its Typographical Captivity?" *Journal for the Study of the Historical Jesus* 19 (2021) 1–65.

———. "Christmas: The Religion of Consumer Capitalism." In *Christmas Unwrapped: Consumerism, Christ, and Culture*, edited by Richard A. Horsley and James Tracy, 165–87. Harrisburg, PA: Trinity, 2001.

———. "Contesting Authority: Popular vs. Scribal Tradition in Continuing Performance." In *Text and Tradition in Performance and Writing*, 99–122. BPCS 9. Eugene, OR: Cascade Books, 2013.

———. *Covenant Economics: A Biblical Vision of Justice for All*. Louisville: Westminster John Knox, 2009.

———. *Empowering the People: Jesus, Healing, and Exorcism*. Eugene, OR: Cascade Books, forthcoming.

———. *1 Corinthians*. Abingdon New Testament Commentaries. Nashville: Abingdon, 1997.

———. *Galilee: History, Politics, People*. Valley Forge, PA: Trinity, 1995.

———. *Hearing the Whole Story: The Politics of Plot in Mark's Gospel*. Louisville: Westminster John Knox, 2001.

———, ed. *Hidden Transcripts and the Arts of Resistance: Applying the Work of James C. Scott to Jesus and Paul*. Semeia Studies 48; Atlanta: Society of Biblical Literature, 2004.

———. "High Priests and the Politics of Roman Palestine." *JSJ* 17 (1986) 23–55.

———. "Imagining Mark's Story Composed in Oral Performance." In *Text and Tradition in Performance and Writing: Text and Tradition in Performance and Writing*, 246–78. BPCS 9. Eugene, OR: Cascade Books, 2013.

———. *Jesus and Empire: The Kingdom of God and the New World Disorder*. Minneapolis: Fortress, 2003.

———. *Jesus and Magic*. Eugene, OR: Cascade Books, 2014.

———. *Jesus and the Politics of Roman Palestine*. 2013. Revised with a new Preface. Center and Library for the Bible and Social Justice. Eugene, OR: Cascade Books, 2021.

———. *Jesus and the Powers: Conflict, Covenant, and the Hope of the Poor*. Minneapolis: Fortress, 2011.

———. *Jesus and the Spiral of Violence: Popular Jewish Resistance in Roman Palestine*. 1987. Reprint, Minneapolis: Fortress, 1993.

———. *Jesus in Context: Power, People, and Performance*. Minneapolis: Fortress, 2008.

———. "Josephus and the Bandits." *JSJ* 10 (1979) 37–63.

———. "'Like One of the Prophets of Old': Two Types of Popular Prophets at the Time of Jesus." *CBQ* 47 (1985) 435–63.

———. "Oral Communication, Oral Performance, and New Testament Interpretation". In *Method and Meaning: Essays on New Testament Interpretation in Honor of Harold W. Attridge*, edited by Andrew B. McGowan and Kent Harold Richards, 125–55. SBL Resources for Biblical Studies 67. Atlanta: Society of Biblical Literature, 2011. Reprinted in Horsley, *Text and Tradition in Performance and Writing*.

———, ed. *Paul and Empire: Religion and Power in Roman Imperial Society*, edited by Richard A. Horsley, 126–37. Harrisburg, PA: Trinity, 1997.

———. "Paul's Assembly in Corinth: An Alternative Society." In *Urban Religion in Corinth: Interdisciplinary Approaches*, edited by Daniel Schowalter and Steven J. Friesen, 371–95. Cambridge: Harvard University Press, 2005.

———. "Paul's Shift in Economic 'Location' in the Locations of the Roman Imperial Economy." In *Paul and Economics: A Handbook*, Thomas R. Blanton IV and Raymond Pickett, eds., 89–123. Minneapolis: Fortress, 2017.

———. ed. *A People's History of Christianity*, Vol 1: *Christian Origins*. Minneapolis: Fortress, 2005.

———. "The Pharisees and Jesus in Galilee and Q." In *When Judaism and Christianity Began: Essays in Memory of Anthony J. Saldarini*, edited by Alan J. Avery-Peck et al., 117–45. Journal for the Study of Judaism Supplements 85. Leiden: Brill, 2004.

———. "Popular Messianic Movements Around the Time of Jesus." *CBQ* 46 (1984) 471–93.

———. "Popular Prophetic Movements at the Time of Jesus, Their Principal Features and Social Origins." *JSNT* 26 (1986) 3–27.

———. "Power Vacuum and Power Struggle in 66–67 C.E." In *The First Jewish Revolt: Archaeology, History, and Ideology*, edited by Andrea M. Berlin and J. Andrew Overman, 87–109. London: Routledge, 2002.

———. *The Prophet Jesus and the Renewal of Israel: Moving beyond a Diversionary Debate*. Grand Rapids: Eerdmans, 2012.

———. *Revolt of the Scribes: Resistance and Apocalyptic Origins*. Minneapolis: Fortress, 2010.

———. "Rhetoric and Empire—and 1 Corinthians." In *Paul and Politics: Ekklesia-Israel-Imperium-Interpretation*, edited by Richard A. Horsley, 72–102. Harrisburg, PA: Trinity, 2000.

———. *Scribes, Visionaries, and the Politics of Second Temple Judea*. Louisville: Westminster John Knox Press, 2007.

———. *Sociology and the Jesus Movement*. New York: Crossroad, 1989.

———. "Submerged Biblical Histories and Imperial Biblical Studies." In *The Postcolonial Bible*, ed. R. S. Sugirtharajah, 152–73. Bible and Postcolonialism 1. Sheffield: Sheffield Academic, 1998.

———. *Text and Tradition in Performance and Writing*. BPCS 9. Eugene, OR: Cascade Books, 2013.

———. *Wisdom and Spiritual Transcendence in Corinth: Studies in First Corinthians*. Eugene, OR: Cascade Books, 2008.

———. "The Zealots, their Origins, Relationships, and Importance in the Jewish Revolt." *Novum Testamentum* 28 (1986) 159–92.

Horsley, Richard A., with Jonathan Draper. *Whoever Hears You Hears Me: Prophecy, Performance, and Tradition in Q*. Harrisburg, PA: Trinity, 1999.

Horsley, Richard A., Jonathan Draper, and John Miles Foley, eds. *Performing the Gospel: Orality, Memory, and Mark*. Minneapolis: Fortress, 2006.

Horsley, Richard A., with John S. Hanson. *Bandits, Prophets, and Messiahs: Popular Movements at the Time of Jesus*. 1985. Reprint, San Francisco: Harper & Row, 1987.

Horsley, Richard A., and Tom Thatcher. *John, Jesus, and the Renewal of Israel*. Grand Rapids: Eerdmans, 2013.

Horsley, Richard, and James Tracy. *Christmas Unwrapped: Consumerism, Christ, and Culture*. Harrisburg, PA: Trinity, 2001.

Jameson, Fredric. *The Political Unconscious: Narrative as a Socially Symbolic Act*. London: Methuen, 1981.

Joseph, Simon J. *Jesus and the Temple: The Crucifixion in Its Jewish Context*. Society for New Testament Studies Monograph Series 165. Cambridge: Cambridge University Press, 2016.

———. *Jesus, the Essenes, and Christian Origins: New Light on Ancient Texts and Communities*. Waco: Baylor University Press, 2018.

Kazen, Thomas. *Issues of Impurity in Early Judaism*. Coniectanea biblica: New Testament Series 45. Winona Lake, IN: Eisenbrauns, 2010.

———. *Jesus and Purity Halakah: Was Jesus Indifferent to Impurity?* Rev. ed. Coniectanea biblica: New Testament Series 38. Winona Lake, IN: Eisenbrauns, 2010.

Kelber, Werner H. *Imprints, Voiceprints, and Footprints of Memory: Collected Essays of Werner Kelber*. SBL Resources for Biblical Studies 74. Atlanta: Society of Biblical Literature, 2013.

Keener, Craig S. *Acts: An Exegetical Commentary*. 4 vols. Grand Rapids: Baker, 2012.

Kingsbury, Jack Dean. *Matthew as Story*. Philadelphia: Fortress, 1986.

Kirk, Alan. *Memory and the Jesus Tradition*. The Reception of Jesus in the First Three Centuries 2. London: Bloomsbury T. & T. Clark, 2018.

Kittredge, Cynthia Briggs. *Community and Authority: The Rhetoric of Obedience in the Pauline Tradition*. HTS 45. Harrisburg, PA: Trinity, 1998.

Klein, Naomi. *This Changes Everything: Capitalism vs. the Climate*. New York: Simon & Schuster, 2014.

Kloppenborg, John S. "Paul's Collection for Jerusalem and the Financial Practices in Greek Cities." In *Paul and Economics: A Handbook*, edited by Thomas R. Blanton IV and Raymond Pickett, 307–32. Minneapolis: Fortress, 2017.

Knight, Douglas A. *Law, Power, and Justice in Ancient Israel*. LAI. Louisville: Westminster John Knox, 2011.

Korten, David. *Agenda for a New Economy: From Phantom Wealth to Real Wealth*. San Francisco: Berrett-Koehler, 2009.

———. *When Corporations Rule the World*. 2nd ed. San Francisco: Berrett-Koehler, 2001.

Kovel, Joel. *The End of Nature: The End of Capitalism or the End of the World*. New York: Zed, 2007.

Kwok, Pui-lan. "Discovering the Bible in the Nonbiblical World." *Semeia* 47 (1989) 25–42. Reprint in *The Bible and Liberation: Political and Social Hermenteutics*, edited by Norman K. Gottwald and Richard A. Horsley, 17–30. Maryknoll, NY: Orbis, 1993.

Lenski, Gerhardt. *Power and Privilege: A Theory of Social Stratification*. 2nd ed. Chapel Hill: University of North Carolina Press, 1984.

Liu, Jinju. "Urban Poverty in the Roman Empire: Material Conditions." In *Paul and Economics: A Handbook*, edited by Thomas R. Blanton IV and Ray Pickett, 23–56. Minneapolis: Fortress, 2017.

Longenecker, Bruce W. "Exposing the Economic Middle: A Revised Economy Scale for the Study of Early Christianity." *JSNT* 31(2009) 243–78.

———. *Remember the Poor: Paul, Poverty, and the Greco-Roman World*. Grand Rapids: Eerdmans, 2010.

Luther, Martin. *Luther's Works*. Edited by Jaroslav Pelikan and Helmut T. Lehmann. 55 vols. Philadelphia: Fortress and St. Louis: Concordia, 1955–2020.

Mason, Steve. *A History of the Jewish War, A.D. 66–74*. New York: Cambridge University Press, 2016.

Marchal, Joseph A. "The Usefulness of an Onesimus: The Sexual Use of Slaves and Paul's Letter to Philemon." *JBL* 130 (2011) 749–70.

Mattern, Susan P. *Rome and the Enemy: Imperial Strategy in the Principate*. Berkeley: University of California Press, 1999.

Mayer, Emanuel. *The Ancient Middle Classes: Urban Life and Aesthetics in the Roman Empire, 100 BCE—250 CE*. Cambridge: Harvard University Press, 2012.

Meeks, Wayne A. *The First Urban Christians: The Social World of the Apostle Paul*. New Haven: Yale University Press, 1983.

Morley, Neville. "Economy and Economic Theory, Roman." In *The Oxford Encyclopedia of Ancient Greece and Rome*, edited by Michael Gagarin and Elaine Fantham, 3:12. Oxford: Oxford University Press, 2010.

Morris, Ian, and J. G. Manning, eds., *The Ancient Economy: Evidence and Models*. Social Science History. Stanford: Stanford University Press, 2005.

Murphy, Catherine M. *Wealth in the Dead Sea Scrolls and in the Qumran Community*. Studies on the Texts of the Desert of Judah 40. Leiden: Brill, 2002.

Myers, Ched. *Binding the Strong Man: A Political Reading of Mark's Story of Jesus*. Maryknoll, NY: Orbis, 1988.

Myles, Robert. *The Homeless Jesus in the Gospel of Matthew*. Social World of Biblical Antiquity Series 2/10. Sheffield: Sheffield Phoenix, 2014.

———. "Homelessness, Neoliberalism, and Jesus' 'Decision.'" In *Reading the Bible in an Age of Crisis: Political Exegesis for a New Day*, edited by Bruce Worthington, 217–44. Minneapolis: Fortress, 2015.

Nasrallah, Laura. "You Were Bought with a Price: Freedpersons and Things in 1 Corinthians." In *Corinth in Contrast: Studies in Inequality*, edited by Steven J. Friesen et al., 54–73. Novum Testamentum Supplements 155. Leiden: Brill, 2014.

Neusner, Jacob. *From Politics to Piety: The Emergence of Pharisaic Judaism*. 1979. Reprint, Eugene, OR: Wipf & Stock, 2003.

Niditch, Susan. *Oral World and Written Word: Ancient Israelite Literature*. LAI. Louisville: Westminster John Knox, 1996.

Nissenbaum, Stephen. *The Battle for Christmas: A Cultural History of America's Most Cherished Holiday*. New York: Knopf, 1996.

Oakes, Peter. *Empire, Economics, and the New Testament*. Grand Rapids: Eerdmans, 2020.

Osiek, Carolyn. *The Shepherd of Hermas: A Commentary*. Hermeneia. Fortress, 1999.

Parker, David C. *The Living Text of the Gospels*. Cambridge: Cambridge University Press, 1997.

Petersen, Norman. *Rediscovering Paul: Philemon and the Sociology of Paul's Narrative World*. 1985. Reprint, Eugene, OR: Wipf & Stock, 2008.

Phillips, Kevin. *Bad Money: Reckless Finance, Failed Politics, and the Global Crisis of American Capitalism*. New York: Viking, 2008.

Portier-Young, Anathea. *Apocalypse against Empire: Theologies of Resistance in Early Judaism*. Grand Rapids: Eerdmans, 2011.

Premnath, D. N. *The Eighth Century Prophets: A Social Analysis*. St. Louis: Chalice, 2003.

Price, S. R. F. *Rituals and Power: The Roman Imperial Cult in Asia Minor*. Cambridge: Cambridge University Press, 1984.

Rhoads, David, and Donald Michie. *Mark as Story: An Introduction to the Narrative of a Gospel*. Philadelphia: Fortress, 1982.

Roller, Duane W. *The Building Program of Herod the Great*. Berkeley: University of California Press, 1998.

Rossing, Barbara. *Rapture Exposed: The Message of Hope in the Book of Revelation*. New York: Basic Books, 2004.

Rostovtseff, Michael. *The Social and Economic History of the Hellenistic World*. 3 vols. Oxford: Oxford University Press, 1941.

Sachs, Jeffrey. *Common Wealth: Economics for a Crowded Planet*. New York: Penguin, 2008.

Saller, Richard. *Personal Patronage under the Early Empire*. Cambridge: Cambridge University Press, 1982.

Sanders, E. P. *Jesus and Judaism*. Philadelphia: Fortress, 1985.

Scheidel, Walter. "Real Wages in Early Economies: Evidence for Living Standards from 1800 BCE to 1300 CE." *Journal of the Economic and Social History of the Orient* 53 (2010) 425–62.

Scheidel, Walter, and Steven J. Friesen. "Distribution of Income in the Roman Empire." *Journal of Roman Studies* 99 (2009) 61–91.

Schwartz, Seth. *Imperialism and Jewish Society: 200 B.C.E. to 640 C.E.* Princeton: Princeton University Press, 2001.

Schweitzer, Albert. *Quest of the Historical Jesus.* Translated by W. Montgomery. London: Adam & Charles Black, 1911.

Scott, James C. *Domination and the Arts of Resistance: Hidden Transcripts.* New Haven: Yale University Press, 1990.

———. *The Moral Economy of the Peasant: Rebellion and Subsistence in Southeast Asia.* New Haven: Yale University Press, 1976.

———. "Protest and Profanation: Agrarian Revolt and the Little Tradition." *Theory and Society* 4/1 and 2 (1977) 1–38, 211–46.

———. *Weapons of the Weak: Everyday Forms of Peasant Resistance.* New Haven: Yale University Press, 1985.

Small, Jocelyn Penny. *Wax Tablets of the Mind: Cognitive Studies of Memory and Literacy in Classical Antiquity.* New York: Routledge, 1997.

Temin, Peter. *The Roman Market Economy.* Princeton: Princeton University Press, 2012.

Theissen, Gerd. *The Social Setting of Pauline Christianity: Essays on Corinth.* Edited and translated by John H. Schütz. Philadelphia: Fortress, 1982.

———. "Social Stratification in the Corinthian Community: A Contribution to the Sociology of Early Hellenistic Christianity." In *The Social Setting of Pauline Christianity: Essays on Corinth,* edited and translated by John H. Schütz, 69–119. Philadelphia: Fortress, 1982.

———. *Sociology of Early Palestinian Christianity.* Translated by John Bowden. Philadelphia: Fortress, 1978.

Udoh, Fabian E. *To Caesar What Is Caesar's: Tribute, Taxes, and Imperial Administration in Early Roman Palestine (63 BCE—79 CE).* BJS 343. Providence: Brown Judaic Studies, 2005.

Ulrich, Eugene. *The Dead Sea Scrolls and the Origins of the Bible.* Grand Rapids: Eerdmans, 1999.

Webb, Robert L. *John the Baptizer and Prophet: A Socio-historical Study.* JSNTSup 62. 1991. Reprint, Eugene, OR: Wipf & Stock, 2006.

West, Gerald O. "Doing Postcolonial Biblical Interpretation @home: Ten Years of (South) African Ambivalence." *Neotestamentica* 42.1 (2008) 147–64.

Winter, Sara C. "Paul's Letter to Philemon." *NTS* 33 (1987) 1–15.

Wire, Antoinette Clark. *The Case for Mark Composed in Performance.* BPCS 3. Eugene, OR: Cascade Books, 2011.

———. *The Corinthian Women Prophets: A Reconstruction through Paul's Rhetoric.* 1990. Reprinted, Eugene, OR: Wipf & Stock, 2003.

Worthington, Bruce. "Romans 13:1–7: With an Eye to Global Capital." In *Reading the Bible in An Age of Crisis: Political Exegesis for a New Day,* edited by Bruce Worthington, 245–64. Minneapolis: Fortress, 2015.

Wright, Benjamin G. III. "*'Ebd / doulos*: Terms and Social Status in the Meeting of Hebrew Biblical and Hellenistic Roman Culture." *Semeia* 83/84 (1998) 83–111.

Zanker, Paul. *The Power of Images in the Age of Augustus.* Ann Arbor: University of Michigan Press, 1988.

Žižek, Slavoj. *Violence: Six Sideways Reflections.* Big Ideas. London: Profile Books, 2008.

Subject Index

Acts (book of)
    as source, 112, 123–24
agrarian/agricultural economy, 46
    in Judea, Galilee, etc., 52–53
Agrippa (king)
    champion of Jerusalem/Herodian temple, 123
    extraction of goods from peasants to aid cities, 123
aiding the needy, 114–19
"all things in common" (sharing of goods), 114–19, 123
    economic alternative to Roman imperial order, 116
    in the covenant community at Qumran, 117–18
alternative communities, 132–41, 215–19
    in but not *of* the Empire, 132–41, 215–19
Apocalypse to John, 204–11
    not about End of the world, 204–5
apocalypticism, synthetic construct of, 48
associations (*collegia*), 108–9
authority (vs. power), 212

banks (finance capital), 160
    bailout of, 161
baptismal formula
    ending principal power-relations, 142
biblical studies, 1
    broadening of, 7–8
    diversification of, 165–66
    facilitating empire, 169–70
    product of bourgeois culture, 164
    under global capitalism, 16, 155, 164–65
"biblical" texts, 1–5, 173
    about all aspects of life, 2–5, 21, 155, 173,
    about collective action/movements, 2, 4–5, 171, 173
    about communities (not individuals), 216
    about economics/economic matters, 2–5
    about political–economic–religious action, 2–4, 171, 173
    about unfulfilled possibilities, 171, 173
    as religious, 5–6
    addressed a succession of imperial contexts, 166–67
    imagining alternatives to (new) imperial order, 171
    postcolonial interpretation of, 167
    resistance to domination, 17

Caesar (emperor)
    divine Lord and Savior, 106–7, 133
    elaborate built environment, 206
    elaborate honors to, 106–7, 135, 206–8
    inseparable from political economy, 107, 206–8

Caesar (emperor) *(continued)*
   presence of pervaded public space, 107
collection for the poor, 147–49
   opposite of centralizing Roman imperial economy, 149
Christianity (early), synthetic construct of, 8, 48
"come out or her, my people," 211
communications (media) in antiquity, 10–13
   oral, 10–13, 47
community cooperation, 217
Community Rule (Qumran), 57
   ceremony of covenant renewal in, 57
constraints on professional academics, 218–19
Corinth
   destroyed by Romans, 105
   Roman colony in, 105
Corinthians, 137–44
   Paul's declining economic support from, 140–41
   political-economic solidarity of, 140
   should conduct its own affairs separate from "the world," 138–39
covenant (Mosaic), 14, 56–57, 118, 175–78
   renewal/reenactment of, 14, 68–82
covenantal commandments/demands, 22–23, 72, 74–75, 78
   about avoiding political-economic-religious subjection, 23, 93, 176–77
   about social-economic interaction, 22–23, 176–77
covenantal community, 15, 78
covenant renewal dialogues (in Markan story), 76–80
covenant renewal episodes (in Lukan story), 80–81
covenant renewal speech (in Matthew and Luke), 72–76, 197
   addressing economic and social conflicts and disintegration, 72–76
covenantal cooperation and mutual aid, 16, 118
   Jesus' insistence on practice of, 34–36, 75–76, 93
covenantal (Mosaic) social-economic relations, 13–14

David
   as popularly acclaimed king, 181
Davidic monarchy, 180–82
   a contradiction of Mosaic covenant, 180
   apex of imperial power under Solomon, 181
   people's persistent resistance to, 182–82
Dead Sea Scrolls
   manuscripts of "biblical books" found among, 10
debt, 186–88
   means of generating wealth by impoverishing people, 185–86
Deuteronomic history, 180–84
deutero-Pauline letters, 149–50
disciples, 70
   recruited from fishing families/villages, 70

economic crash in 2008, 187
economic exploitation of the people, 62–63
economic injustice, 26–27, 28–30
   blessing of, 26–27
   Jesus condemnation of, 31–33
   reform of, 25–26
economic justice, 22–38
   insistence on, 23–25, 28–38
   practice of, 33–36
economic realities, 1–5, 100
   embedded in social-political structures and dynamics, 100
   see also political economy
economic right to a livelihood, 37, 77, 92–93
   collective responsibility to ensure, 37, 92–93
economic subsistence, 14

SUBJECT INDEX

economics, field of, 9
economic theory, 45, 99
Elijah, Elisha, 182–83
   people's resistance led by, 183
   Naboth's vineyard story, 183
empires
   ancient territorial, 156–57
   resistance against by people, 157
   escalated extraction by extortion, 174–75
ethne
   (other subject) peoples, not "Gentiles", 113
   renewal of Israel movement open to, 113–14
ethnic communities in Greek cities, 108
   of diaspora Judeans, 108
   resisting complete assimilation, 108

families/households, 52–53
   as basic units of production, 22
   Jesus' renewal of, 71, 77
   slave-holding kyriarchal, 142
food production, 175, 217
(civilizational) Forces/Powers (personified, divinized), 177–78
   determine/control peoples' lives/civilizations, 177–78
   in ancient Mesopotamia (Sky, Irrigation, Storm, etc), 178
   in Roman Empire (Caesar), 179
   in global capitalism (Capital)
   people "bow down and serve" (with production/labor/consumption), 177–79
"Fourth Philosophy," 64–65
freedpersons, 101, 106

Galileans
   required to live according to "the laws of the Judeans," 58
   peasant strikes, 30, 66, 195
   persistent resistance to rulers, 194–95
   uneducated common people, 115
Galilee, 58–59
   inhabitants called "Galileans" (by sources), 59
   taken over by Hasmonean high priests, 58–59
global capitalism, 155–64
   cannibalizes and exoticizes cultures, 70
   channels, manipulates desire, 159, 200
   controls every aspect of personal, social and political life, 156, 163, 200
   expands via debt, 159–61
   lacks authority, 213
   new form of empire, 155–64, 200
   development of, 158–62
   elaborately built environment, 209–10
   mystifying images, rituals, spectacles, 210
   privately owned by mega-corporations, 209
   replaced meaning with non-meaning, 163, 200
   sacred, 162
   sets conditions of biblical studies, 164–70
   systematically destroying the planet, 157, 209
   thrives on multiculturalism, 162
God-fearers/proselytes, 123, 126
"gods" (ancient)—*see* (divinized) civilizational Forces/Powers
Gospel stories (sustained narratives), 13, 41, 42–45, 68
   as sources, 13, 41, 42–45, 67
   fit the historical context, 43
   produced in and for ordinary people, 47
grain
   quantities extracted from Egypt, 100

Hasmonean high priests, 58
   expansion of rule, 58–59
   take-over of Galilee, 58–59
healings and exorcisms. 69, 73
Herod (Rome's client king), 60
high priests/priestly aristocracy (rulers of Judea), 61
   predatory on their people, 61
   (*see also* temple-state)

Hillel (*prosbul*), 63

the historical context of Jesus' mission
    development of, 51–67
homelessness (contemporary), 193
    projected onto Gospel stories, 193
the imperial Bible, 16, 168–69
    a charter for extermination of
        indigenous peoples, 169
    grand narrative of conquest of land/
        Canaanites, 169, 186
    underwriting Western imperialism,
        168
individualism, 6, 41–42, 49, 191–96
individual verses, focus on, 6–7
Israelite tradition, 49
    popular (oral), 11–12, 55–56, 196
ioudaismos (Judean ideology), 121
"itinerant radicalism," 192
    in reading of the Gospels, 192

Jerusalem community (of Jesus-
    loyalists), 112, 114–19, 202–3
    as base for expansion of movement,
        112
Jerusalem temple (-city)
    massively rebuilt by Herod, 120
    monumental symbol of Judean
        tradition, 120
Jesus
    confrontation with high priests, 44,
        86–91
    crucifixion/martyrdom as
        "breakthrough," 111–12
    generating a movement of renewal
        of Israel, 14–15, 45
    political-economic-religious project
        of, 14, 68–82, 94–95
    renewing/reenacting (Mosaic)
        covenant, 15, 71–80
    as (in role of) prophet (like Moses
        and Elijah), 14, 43–45
Jesus tradition rooted in Israelite
    popular tradition, 196
John the Baptist
    leader of covenant renewal
        movement, 65
Joshua (book of), 181
    narrative scheme of slaughtering
        Canaanites, 181
    stories of guerrilla warfare vs.
        Canaanite kings, 181
Judaism (early), synthetic construct of,
    8, 48
Judean diaspora communities, 15, 113
    allowed a degree of self-governance,
        120
    alternative communities in Roman
        imperial order, 113
    (economic) basis of movement's
        expansion, 113
Judeans (in Judea)
    referred to as "Judeans" (in sources),
        59
Judeans from/in diaspora
    ancestral laws "inscribed" in their
        memories, 119
    conflict between groups of in towns,
        123–24
    conflict with "Greeks" in cities, 123
    join the renewal of Israel movement
        in Jerusalem, 119–22
    in towns in Syria and Greece,
        122–25
    participate in sharing of goods/
        aiding the needy, 122
justice means aiding the poor, 148

love means aiding the poor, 148
Lukan story, 44

Markan story, 43–44
marriage, patriarchal
    relativized in communities of
        Christ-loyalists, 143
Matthean story, 44, 196–99
    portrays Jesus as prophet in renewal
        of Israel vs. rulers, 196

Nehemiah (Persian governor), 56
neo-liberal ideology, 190–91, 196
    ideology of global capitalism, 190
New Testament studies, 190–219
    congruent with neo-liberal
        ideology, 190

SUBJECT INDEX

Occupy Wall Street, 201-2
   crystalized opposition to global capitalism, 201
Onesimus, slave or brother, 146-47

parable of the tenants, 89-90

Paul (Saul)
   agenda of his mission, 15-16
   catalyzing assemblies, 15-16, 131, 133-41
   his counter-imperial gospel, 134
   his mission, 129-31, 132
   generating an alternative society in local assemblies 132, 133-41
   letters of, 13, 15, 131
   as sources, 13, 131-32
   rhetorical criticism of, 131-32
   opponent or advocate of slavery?, 141-42
   persecutor of the movement, 121
   previous interpretation of, 128-29
   urges slaves to claim freedom, 144-46
Pastoral letters, 149-50
Pauline legacy, 150-51
   use of common funds to aid poor and emancipate slaves, 150-51
peasants/people
   displaced, 100, 106, 133
   identity oppositional, 196
peasant strike (by Galileans), 66
Pharisees and scribes, 84-86
   Jesus' mockery and indictment of, 84-86
   traditions of the elders, 85
Philippi
   Roman colonization of, 105
Philippians, 136-37
   their coming "commonwealth" for the common good, 137
   "operate politically", 136
pistis (in Roman empire = loyalty), 114
political economy (structure and dynamics), 14
   conceptualizing, 14-15
   conflict in, 53, 66-67
   unstable, 53

popular messianic movements, 63-64
popular prophetic movements, 65
power (vs. authority), 212
   exercised by global capitalism, 212-13
print culture, 6-7
   assumptions of, 9-13
   challenged by new lines of research, 9-13
prophecy of temple destruction, 90-91
prophetic demonstration against temple, 88-89
prophetic parable against temple, 89-90
prophets (Israelite)
   condemnation of rulers and representatives, 87
Prophets ("biblical" books of), 179-86
   three layers of prophecies in, 183-84
   prophecies condemning wealthy rulers, etc., 185-86

religion
   as individual faith, 21
resistance to global capitalism, 199
   by alternative communities, 199
   by avoidance of debt (credit cards), 199
   by reduction of consumption, 199
   requires critical analysis of complex system, 199
renewal of Israel movement, 112
   advocating customs not lawful for Romans, 125
   actions contrary to decrees of Caesar, 125
   expanding in interstices of Roman order, 113
   in Jerusalem, 114-22
   opposed to Roman imperial order, 127
   spreads into towns in Syria, 122-24
   spreads to Greek cities, 125-27
revolts (by Judeans, Galileans), 60, 63-64
Roman Empire
   political-economic-religious structure and dynamics of, 15
   under God's condemnation, 214

Roman imperial conquest, 8
    brutality of, 104
    destruction of (classical) Corinth, 8, 105
    of Palestine, 59–61
Roman imperial order, 8
    alliance between imperial court and local wealthy, 105
    in Greek cities, 8, 105–7
    in Palestine, 8, 44, 68, 91, 93, 118, 155
    resistance to in the interstices, 108–10
the Roman state
    at center of Roman imperial political economy, 100–101
rule (kingdom) of God (direct), 14, 35, 43–44, 69–71, 74–75, 79–83, 122, 133, 187, 213
rulers
    extraction/exploitation of villagers, 46, 53, 62–63, 93
    Jesus' condemnation of, 88–92
    multiple layers of, 62–63

scribally produced texts (some later included in Hebrew Bible), 12, 51
    as sources, 12
scribes, scribal practice, 10–13, 47, 180
    devour widows' houses, 86
scribal circles, 47
    resistance by, 64–65
Second Samuel (book of), 181
    accounts of popular acclamation of David, 181
    revolt of Israel against David, 181
"Sermon on the Mount/Plain," 34–35
slaves, slavery, 101, 133
    central to the political economy of Roman Empire, 141
    Paul as advocate or opponent of?, 141–42, 144–47
    resistance/revolts by slaves, 109–10
    slaves in Corinthian assembly, 144
social stratification, 102–4, 193

sociology, structural–functional, 102, 191–92
    borrowed by biblical scholars, 102, 191–92
    downplays conflict, 102–4, 191–92
Solomon
    apex of imperial power, 181
    imposes forced labor, 182
the state, 212–13
    instrumental to global capitalism's power, 213
Stephen (martyr), 121–22
synagogues/*synagogai* (village assemblies in Galilee), 69
    Jesus' and disciples' mission focused in, 69
synagogues/*synagogai* of Judeans in Syrian towns, 114

temple-state, Jerusalem/Judean, 8, 51–52, 83
    under imperial regimes, 8, 53–54, 57
    as face of imperial rule, 83–84
    Jesus' confrontation of, 86–91
Thessalonians, 135–36
    aiding one another, 136
Theudas (popular prophet), 65
Torah ("biblical" books of), 173–79
    grand narrative scheme in, 174
trade
    in luxury goods for elite, 101, 184
tribute to Rome/Caesar, 59, 91–92
    Fourth Philosophy's campaign against, 59, 91
    Jesus declaration about, 91–92

village communities, 46, 52–53
    disintegrating from economic exploitation, 62
    focus of Jesus' and disciples' mission, 69–70
    semi-self-governing through assemblies, 194

writing/written (scribal) texts, 54–55
    (largely) confined to scribal circles, 47

www.ingramcontent.com/pod-product-compliance
Lightning Source LLC
Chambersburg PA
CBHW020407230426
43664CB00009B/1212